PRAISE FOR

CRACKBACK!

"Dr. Fitz Hill's *Crackback*, coauthored with acclaimed sports columnist Mark Purdy, is a compelling firsthand account of how African Americans were kept out of head coaching positions at the highest level of college football for decades. Hill has a great mind for football and did his doctoral dissertation on the experiences of African American coaches employed at predominately white colleges and universities and the barriers faced when attempting to advance from assistant to head coach. His is the most authentic voice available on the issue. *Crackback* is a must-read for anyone who cares about sport in America and for anyone who holds social justice as an important value."

—Richard Lapchick, Chair of DeVos Sport Business Management Program, Director, Institute for Diversity and Ethics in Sport

"This is about looking out for every African American kid in America who might be thinking about becoming a college coach. I think every college and NFL player ought to read this book—but I hope a lot more people do too."

—Doug Williams, Super Bowl XXII MVP and First African American Quarterback to Win a Super Bowl

"Dr. Fitz Hill has, as much as humanly possible, eliminated emotion and focused on the pure numbers that unequivocally highlight the bias in hiring of black coaches. "Crackback!" is an education that will allow us to make the necessary changes that will allow our children to be led by the best coaches regardless of color."

—Tyrone W̶ ̶ch at Stanford University, niversity of Washington

CRACKBACK!

Nick—

I pray that you feel the spirit of my heart while reading CRACKBACK! May GOD bless you for blessing others!

Fitz Hill

fitzhill@hotmail.com

CRACKBACK!

DR. FITZGERALD HILL
WITH MARK PURDY

TATE PUBLISHING
AND ENTERPRISES, LLC

Published by Tate Publishing & Enterprises, LLC
127 E. Trade Center Terrace | Mustang, Oklahoma 73064 USA
1.888.361.9473 | www.tatepublishing.com

Tate Publishing is committed to excellence in the publishing industry. The company reflects the philosophy established by the founders, based on Psalm 68:11,
"The Lord gave the word and great was the company of those who published it."

Published in the United States of America
ISBN: 978-1-61346-215-7
Sports & Recreation / Coaching / Football
12.02.03

ACKNOWLEDGMENTS

This book is dedicated to the person most responsible for instilling within me the necessary drive, determination, persistence, and the belief in God to tell the truth and write this book—my mother, the late Mary Stephen Hill, who died during the writing of this book. Work ethic combined with motivation to better myself and attempt to positively influence those around me was taught to me by Mom at a very early age. Today, my mother's teachings continue to affect the daily decisions I make for myself, my family, those that I work for and with, as well as the faculty, staff, and students I lead as the thirteenth president of Arkansas Baptist College.

Secondly, this book would not have been completed without the love and support of my wife, Cynthia. The collegiate coaching profession that I was a member of for over fifteen years can take a toll on a family, and without a committed wife and mother, a family can unravel in many ways. However, through the good and bad that come with life and the wins and losses that come with coaching, Cynthia remained steadfast with her unconditional love and support of me, personally and professionally. She was incredible filling the void I left as a father while my numerous coaching duties kept me away from our home. She has done an incredible job developing our children, Destiny, Faith, and Justice. Their names have been the themes of this book project.

Thirdly, I would like to publicly thank Dr. John Murry of the University of Arkansas, who served as the chair of my dissertation committee and worked so diligently with me to produce a piece of work that I will be proud of forever.

Fourth, the development of the book moved from conceptualization to realization in December 2004, when San Jose Mercury News sports columnist, Mark Purdy, agreed to help me take my doctoral dissertation, studies of black and white football coaches and my personal coaching experiences, to create the book you are getting ready to read. Mark's professional journalism skills and commitment to complete this project pro bono will indebt me to Mark for life. Mark and I went into the book project as professionals but have come out of the book writing process as cronies. I thank God for this genuine friendship that was developed during the project.

Finally, I thank God for blessing me to feel his spirit in the process of writing this book. This book provided some of the necessary therapy needed to remove emotional shackles that have kept me in bondage most of my adult life. Only God could do what he has done in my life, and I am so thankful for his newfound presence in my heart and hope that you feel my heart while reading this book.

TABLE OF CONTENTS

FOREWORD

BY DOUG WILLIAMS
Super Bowl XXII MVP
First African American Quarterback
to Win a Super Bowl

Sometimes you buy a shirt but for various reasons never wear it. That's the analogy I use if and when I am asked about black head coaches in college football and why it seems so hard for them to get hired.

What do I mean? Fans and the public buy the idea that the hiring and evaluating process for African American coaches in the college game should be the same as it is for white coaches. You won't find a soul in the universe who will disagree—at least publicly— with that statement. Everybody buys that shirt.

However, when it gets around to actually wearing the shirt… things get complicated. That's what this book is about. Because the evidence shows that even into the second decade of the twenty-first century, many African American coaches are not getting the fair treatment they have been promised. And in my opinion, Fitz Hill is the perfect guy to write about it.

I first met Fitz while being employed as scout for the National Football League, and he was an assistant coach for the Arkansas Razorbacks. I was excited for him when he was named the head football coach at San Jose State in 2000. At the time, I had the same job at Grambling State University in Louisiana. And as an African American in the college coaching profession, I was always interested when another man of my race succeeded in landing a job at the major college level.

Over the years, Fitz and I got to know each other much better. He called me up, and we had several conversations about Grambling coming out to play a game against San Jose State. We decided to make it happen and in 2003 played the game to a sellout crowd at Spartan Stadium.

Through the whole process, I learned about Fitz's enthusiasm and passion not just for football but for the issue of whether African American and other minority candidates are receiving equal opportunity in terms of being hired as college head coaches. He'd even written his doctoral dissertation about the topic.

Unfortunately, my Grambling team lost that game in San Jose. But I have great memories of that weekend. The game was billed as the "Literacy Classic," and we raised money and awareness for that cause. We also had a nice dinner to celebrate the game and brought our famous Grambling band to San Jose to perform.

A highlight for me, though, was participating in a panel discussion at the new Dr. Martin Luther King Library in downtown San Jose. We talked about African Americans' difficulty in finding head coaching jobs around college football and why it happens. Another panelist that day was the late Bill Walsh, the former 49er head coach. He had pushed the NFL to implement a program that sent African American college assistant coaches to the training camps of NFL teams so that those coaches could pick up knowledge, make contacts, and learn how to network with other coaches. Bill always thought that if people got a chance, they could show their talents—but not enough were getting a chance.

When it was my turn, I spoke about the challenges I faced at Grambling, an NCAA Division 1AA program (now known as the Football Championship Subdivision), which does not have the same resources as the "big guys." Grambling is also a member of the Southwestern Athletic Conference (SWAC), which is comprised of historically black colleges and universities. That means the head coaches are usually black. But even when successful, those coaches never seem to get a shot at coaching in Division I (now known as the Football Bowl Subdivision). I thought—and still think—that this isn't fair to those coaches. In that panel discussion, I laid down a challenge.

I proposed that the SWAC coaches switch jobs with coaches in the major conferences and see which group succeeded best. At the top major college programs, the coach can pull up to his assigned parking space in back of the athletic building, go inside, and just spend the day coaching football one hundred percent. At the SWAC schools, coaches aren't just coaches. They have to be both a mom and dad. They often are in charge of scheduling, the football budget, the players' academic counseling, the travel plans, and occasionally the laundry. At the bigger schools, there are assistants—and assistants to the assistants—who take care of those things.

I'd like to see head coaches from the Big Ten and Southeastern Conference try handling all that. I tell you what: if everybody switched jobs, I would put my money on the SWAC coaches doing better in the SEC than the SEC coaches would do in the SWAC.

All of this is why I was so happy when Fitz decided to write this book, bringing all of his research and experience to the table. The issue of why minority coaches have not been as successful in college football as they have in other sports is a complex one. But since football is America's favorite sport, it isn't an issue that should be swept under the table or ignored. It has affected a lot of people. Including me.

I had a great time playing pro football, first with the Tampa Bay Buccaneers and then winning a Super Bowl with my Washington Redskins teammates. I was proud to be the first winning African American quarterback in Super Bowl history. But in spite of my fondness for the NFL, even as I was playing in the league, I wanted very much to become a head football coach at the college level. I had been inspired by my former head coach at Grambling, the legendary Eddie Robinson. I saw what a great coach can do to influence the lives of young men.

To attain my goal, I did my best to put together a résumé that proved my worth as a coach. I began by coaching high school football in Louisiana, where I took a team to the state semifinals, then took a job as an assistant coach at the US Naval Academy. I accepted the head coaching job at Morehouse College, a historically black college that plays Division II football. And in 1998, I was lucky enough to follow Coach Robinson and take over the Grambling State program. I won three consecutive SWAC titles there and believe that I represented the school well. I hoped that a major college might call.

The University of Kentucky did after the 2002 season. I flew there and had what I thought was a great interview. I also met some university administrators and boosters. Mitch Barnhart, the athletic director, seemed very positive about my chances. But I never got an offer. Rich Brooks, the former coach at the University of Oregon, was hired instead. Barnhart was very honest in explaining the decision to me. I remember the word he used. He said that the "comfort" factor was an issue in terms of me fitting in at Kentucky.

It threw me for a loop. I figured I was qualified for the job and had proven myself at every stop of my coaching career. I'm not exactly sure what the Kentucky people meant about a "comfort" factor. When I think of "comfort" with people, I think about it as being able to visit someone at their home and have coffee, or drinking ice tea with them on the back patio. Was that what they meant?

You try not to be judgmental about this kind of stuff. But I later found out that Barnhart had been an athletic department intern at the University of Oregon when Coach Brooks was there. Barnhart had also worked at Oregon State. I can't blame Coach Brooks for using any of those connections to get the Kentucky job. But that's how it all works. And if African American coaches don't have those kinds of connections—because they continue to be denied opportunities to make those connections—others will surely be frustrated as I was. I don't want to say the good-old-boy network is still out there, but…okay, the good-old-boy network is still out there. Most of the decisions are made before anyone even shows up for an interview.

I figured that if Kentucky wasn't going to hire me after all I'd done to build my résumé, the chances of me becoming a college head coach anywhere were also not going to be that great. So I went back to the NFL in 2004 and worked as a personnel executive for the Tampa Bay Buccaneers. And when I look around, I see I am not alone. Many qualified African American coaches who could do amazing jobs at the college level now seem to gravitate to the NFL because they perceive that the opportunities in pro football are greater.

The NFL, of course, has the so-called "Rooney Rule" that requires every team with a coaching vacancy to interview at least one minority candidate. Some teams follow it better than others. As I said right at the start, sometimes you buy a shirt but never actually wear it. The intent of the rule is good, however. I don't know why college football doesn't do the same thing.

That question is discussed by Fitz in this book, too, along with so many other elements of the African American college coaching situation. I think it will be an eye-opener for a lot of people. I know that recently, more minority coaches have been hired at the FBS level. But check out where. The high-powered jobs haven't been given to the African American coaches. They usually end up at the schools with fewer resources and at programs that have struggled long before the coaches get there. My own journey has taken me back to Grambling for another term as head coach where we will continue to fight the good fight despite our own limited resources. So in my view, this book is just as timely as ever.

I realize that to the average fan, none of this may be a big deal. The average fan just wants to go to the games and have fun. But if you look at it in the big picture—the American sports picture—this is a very big deal. America is supposed to be the land of opportunity. At some schools, 70-75 percent of the football players are African

American kids because they have earned those spots on merit. But you see so few of them returning to be part of the coaching staff at their alma maters compared to their white teammates. And it's not by the player's choice. It's by the school's choice.

In fact, this whole thing isn't really about me and the other old folks in the profession. This is about looking out for every African American kid in America who might be thinking about becoming a college coach. I think every college and NFL player ought to read this book—but I hope a lot more people do too.

I guarantee you this: when you get to the last page, your eyes will be open a lot wider about this issue. And it's never a bad idea to be educated. Fitz knows what he's talking about. One day, he may educate enough people into doing the right thing. I know I'm rooting for him.

INTRODUCTION

Thanks for opening up these pages. This is a book about race and the effects of race on a significant element of American culture—college football.

I have discovered that the discussion of how skin color impacts opportunities can bring on an array of emotions in people. As I prepared this manuscript about how race restricts employment opportunities for black football coaches at predominantly white colleges and universities, several white people questioned if I should devote an entire book to this subject. I was told that I would be perceived as an angry black man if I tried to intelligently discuss the complex issues of race in college football. I listened and understood the ramifications of writing this book. But deep down in my soul, I couldn't rest and proceed through life without sharing the truth regarding the experiences of black football coaches who are employed at major college football programs.

I ask that before you judge or criticize me, please read the entire book from start to finish and do so with an open mind. I am no longer in the coaching profession and do not have a dog in this hunt. However, this manuscript is about my own experience, as well as those of other black and white coaches that I have studied for many years. I don't understand why I should refrain from telling the truth when both blacks and whites can learn from it. So here I go.

The truth is, race matters—even if we often wish that it didn't. Alternatively, some of us try to remain in denial and bury our thoughts about racial issues. So perhaps this is a grave that I shouldn't dig up. It is not my intention to offend anyone. Let me apologize in advance just in case I somehow do so. I pray that you understand my mission is simply to improve the current situation in college football—which in turn could possibly improve intercultural communications among ethnic groups in our country. Sports have always been on the leading edge of improving race relations in America. I don't think we should start retreating now.

Some people are simply ignorant when it comes to race. But at a certain point, I strongly believe that ignorance ceases to be the issue and people choose to deny the truth as they seek to control a situation. In my opinion, this is what is going on in college football. I want to help us move from ignorance and denial to truth. If you're not interested in the truth, this book won't help you. But this book is meant for more than sociology students. It's meant for fans of a great sport and fans of the great American dream.

Do you live for Saturday afternoons in the autumn? Do you like college football? Would you like it to be an even better game? Do you also care about our country truly being the land of equal opportunity? If you answered "yes" to any or all of those questions, you have come to the right place. Perhaps you picked up this book knowing that it addresses the issue of African American coaches in college football. But ultimately, it's also about improving a sport that teaches wonderful lessons to both its participants and its followers. Keep that in mind as you work your way through the chapters.

I began writing this book in the summer of 2005, not long after I resigned from my job as the head football coach at San Jose State, located in the heart of Silicon Valley in northern California. As a college graduate student in 1997, I had written my doctoral dissertation about an issue that had fascinated me since entering the coaching profession: why there were so few African American and minority head coaches in college football. Since then, progress has definitely been made. But it truly troubled me when, after seven African American coaches were hired before the 2010 football season, some observers were claiming that major college football had "solved" its black coaches "problem." Nothing could be further from the truth.

Take it from someone who has been on the front lines himself—and who still deals with this issue on a regular basis as a frequent guest lecturer at educational seminars on this topic: The barriers still do exist for black football coaches at the college level, and they are still frustrated. There remains so much room for improvement. And it is hurting college football more than the NCAA or university administrators realize.

It makes me chuckle a bit, because I've been fighting this same battle for so long. When I first proposed an examination of this topic as my college thesis, a few of my friends believed it to be a frivolous subject matter not worth pursuing on an academic basis. I believed just the opposite. College football is one of America's most popular sports. In many communities—and in some entire states—college football is the most popular discussion starter at office water coolers, family dinner tables, and playground gatherings. By definition, therefore, the color of the faces of the people in charge of this American institution is an important issue in American culture.

At the time of my dissertation, my studies revealed that only a tiny fraction of those faces were African American. This put college football far behind other areas of our society in terms of racial progress. To determine the reason, I spent more than twenty years compiling data and interviewing dozens of people. As subsequent football seasons rolled on, I kept updating my information. And I was continually dismayed.

Over these twenty-plus years, the National Football League seemed to be making progress in hiring more African American head coaches. But for a while, college football actually seemed to be moving backward. At the end of each season when head coaches were fired or stepped down, very few African American and minority candidates were interviewed for the job openings—and only a small fraction of those interviewees were being hired. The concepts and theories that I had developed while writing my dissertation were more on target than ever. Frequently, I was called upon to explain my ideas and offer my opinions regarding this social injustice by television shows such as ESPN Cold Pizza and Outside The Lines, HBO Real Sports with Bryant Gumbel, and ABC Nightline with Ted Koppel. I also did interviews on the topic with print organizations including *USA Today, Sports Illustrated,* the *Los Angeles Times, the Chronicle of Higher Education,* the *San Jose Mercury News,* the *Orlando Sentinel* and numerous other media publications and outlets.

My idea was to convert my dissertation into a book that I could give to people as a handy guide as they researched the issue themselves. I also thought that college football fans and college administrators needed a wake-up call on this situation and that my book would provide one. Of course, I also realized that I had to reformulate the issue in less scholastic terms. My dissertation's official title was: "Examining the Barriers Restricting Employment Opportunities Relative to the Perceptions of African American Football Coaches at NCAA Division 1A Colleges And Universities."

I know. *Ugh!* Who would possibly want to delve into something with such a clunky name?

My solution was to contact my eventual collaborator, *San Jose Mercury News* sports columnist Mark Purdy. I asked Mark, who is white and open-minded yet somewhat conservative—he calls himself a "militant moderate" politically—to help me. Our idea was to translate and expand the dissertation into language that the average fan could digest, contemplate, and maybe even argue about a little bit while enjoying a hamburger and beverage at a sports bar.

Why did I pick Mark? After deciding to leave San Jose State, I knew for certain that I wanted to write this book. After the press conference at which I announced my resignation, I asked Mark if we could get together and visit further over dinner. I know that sounds strange—a head football coach and a columnist going out for dinner. Mark had written some good and bad stuff about me. But I respected him and thought he was honest and fair. In fact, I asked him to participate in a panel discussion regarding the lack of employment opportunities for African American football coaches in August 2003.

But what really stuck out in my mind about Mark was something that had happened after our 43-3 drumming at Stanford in the 2004 season opener. Mark asked me a very interesting question, one that I wouldn't forget. As I walked out of the visitors' locker room that night, I was beaten down and dejected. A series of administrative foul-ups by our university had forced us coaches to field a group of players that had not even practiced in preparation for the game. Several Bay Area reporters hit me with questions about why we had executed so poorly. But after the reporters had finished cross-examining me, Mark asked me point blank: "When will I ever find out if you can coach?" He had covered the Spartan football program for several years. He knew my biggest hurdles were not the student-athletes on the opposing team.

As previously noted, Mark is white. I am black. Is that so important? Not to me. But there is a reason I wanted such a combination. For effectiveness, I felt I needed the perspective of both a white man and black man in this book. I didn't want it to be perceived as two black men with chips on their shoulders collaborating to whine and complain about this issue. I knew how that would be received by some in the college football audience—with rolled eyes. And how would that ever create needed dialogue? Although I hope many black people read this book, it is specifically intended to engage the fans of all colors who support major college football—and I especially hope it lands on the desks of those who make the hiring decisions at predominantly white colleges and universities.

My experiences have taught me that most white people do not want to be associated with discriminatory behavior and they rarely think of themselves as demonstrating such behavior. Consequently, when someone hints that racial bias could be a factor in a choice or statement being made by a white person, there is a tendency for that person to enter a denial mode or become very defensive. This often shuts out the possibility of analyzing any behavior that could be generated by a subconscious bias. It also explains why many white college administrators and boosters become part of the glass ceiling for black football coaches—but never recognize that as administrators and boosters, they are part of the problem and instead need to be part of the solution. Otherwise we'll never get anywhere. The intent of this book is to help those who never understood that they were part of the problem in the first place. If athletic departments don't believe that their hiring practices are flawed, then those practices are never changed.

Over the past five years as Mark and I have worked together, we've had deep conversations. Different backgrounds and experiences often result in a wide range of perspectives, which is a good thing. For this book to achieve maximum effect, I knew that I had to make Mark feel what *black* coaches feel, to understand our frustration. I wanted us to try and communicate their feelings through the written word in a way that has never been done. But I also wanted Mark to help me better understand the mind-set of white men; which he did very well. As you read these words, please remember this book is not about me or about Mark; it is about a hiring process that too often denies equality based on experience and qualification. If that process weren't flawed, there would be no need for this book. Rather than being complainers, Mark and I are on a problem-solving mission.

Although the book is written in my voice, I relied on Mark to help shape that voice. If you saw the Hollywood film *A Time to Kill* you get the idea. The movie is based on John Grisham's novel and stars Samuel L. Jackson in the role of Carl Lee Hailey, a black man on trial for murder. Hailey has killed two white men and accidentally wounded a police officer in a rage after the two white men brutally raped his young daughter.

In the script, the black community seeks an NAACP legal team to handle Hailey's defense. Jackson refuses the black community's offer, opting instead to be represented by Jake Brigance, a white attorney with a heart of gold, played by actor Matthew McConaughey. The Hailey character doesn't want a "Soul Train" show—a parade of black attorneys—taking the stage in a courtroom where a sentence of life or death will be decided by a jury consisting of ten white women and two white men. The wise Hailey figures that he needs a white man who can communicate to the white jurors.

Brigance sought to get deep inside of the psyche of the people deciding the fate of Hailey's life. He began touching their hearts when he told them to close their eyes and place themselves in a similar situation as Hailey. He asked them to do something that I doubt any of the white jurors in the southern town had ever done. He wanted them to change their glasses and see the world from a black man's view. He asked them to pretend they were of the black race during their deliberations and then decide what is just when applying the law for justice for the brutal and heinous crime that would emotionally handicap his innocent daughter forever. Brigance made Hailey's case in superb fashion and saved his life.

I haven't asked Mark Purdy to save anyone's life. But I hope he can be a Jake Brigance by helping me make the case for black coaches who desire employment opportunities at predominantly white colleges and universities—where on average, black student-athletes make up half the football rosters. Just as Hailey needed Brigance, I needed Mark to help take my knowledge and research and translate them into a high-impact narrative. Let me also ask you to attempt something similar, as did John Howard Griffin, the author and main character in the book *Black Like Me,* while reading this book.

Griffin was a middle-age white man living in Mansfield, Texas, in 1959 who became deeply committed to the cause of racial justice but was frustrated by his inability as a white man to understand the black experience. To get a view of being black in America, Griffin took a radical step and underwent medical treatment to change the color of his skin and temporarily became a black man. Griffin was shocked at the extent of the prejudice, oppression, and hardship that suddenly faced him because of skin color; nothing else within him had changed. Only after a few weeks of trick or treating as black man, Griffin discovered that he couldn't get any candy from white people, and he wrote about how he developed an attitude of defeat and hopelessness on his own face and within his self-esteem.

I know this is not 1959. But I can tell you with confidence that the code of injustice remains for black football coaches. And my hope is that you will allow yourself the opportunity to explore outside of your racial comfort zone while reading this book.

You'll have to be the jury and decide if Mark and I accomplish our goals. But in my mind, there is no question about whether the issue deserves healthy debate and intelligent discussion. During the writing process of this book, I was called to Washington DC for testimony before a congressional committee on this very issue. Myles Brand, the former NCAA president, stated numerous times before he passed away from pancreatic cancer in September 2009 that "we're not anywhere close to where we needed to be" in terms of his organization's member schools offering opportunities to minority football coaches. I believe Brand would still maintain this stance, even after the unprecedented flurry of minority hiring a few months after his death.

My research indicates that black coaches rarely get the opportunity to lead the best football programs—the ones with great traditions and the resources to consistently recruit the best players. There have been rare exceptions. But if you examine most of the coaching opportunities given African American coaches, you will see those opportunities occurred at non-BCS schools where programs must be built from the ground up, not maintained or sustained. Building a program or taking it from bust to boom almost always takes time—a luxury that black coaches are rarely granted, especially in comparison to their white counterparts.

I bring this up because I think it's no coincidence that in the five BCS bowl games following the 2010 season—the five biggest bowl games—none of the ten participating teams were coached by minorities. And of the seventy total bowl teams, five of the thirteen African American head coaches had their teams bowl eligible. However, only three actually coached in post-season play; Joker Phillips of Kentucky, Ruffin McNeill of East Carolina, and Charlie Strong of Louisville. Randy Shannon was dismissed from Miami at the conclusion of the regular season, although the Hurricanes were selected to play in the Sun Bowl. After working miracles at Miami (Ohio) and positioning his team to be selected to play in the GoDaddy.com Bowl, Mike Hayward accepted the head coaching position at Pittsburgh and assumed coaching duties there immediately. Unfortunately, he was fired before ever coaching a game due to being arrested for a domestic violence charge.

I suppose that you could have a big chicken-or-egg argument about all of this, debating cause or effect. Are certain college programs not getting to bowls because they have substandard black coaches? Or are the black coaches not getting to bowl games because they are at substandard programs? To me, it's no argument at all. The hiring process is simply not in place for minority coaches to get the best shots at the best jobs. And I firmly believe that if this process is not improved, the number of African American candidates being hired as head coaches will fluctuate wildly, much like the stock market has over the past ten years, rather than moving steadily ahead in a progressive fashion.

So how do we guarantee that such progress isn't halted? Read on. This is an issue-driven book with a purpose: true equality for coaches of all races who aspire to coach at any big-time football program in America. I hope we can get there, even if we may disagree on the most effective approach.

My biggest hope as I was writing this book, really, was that it might become irrelevant before I completed it—because colleges would have already matched the same progress in minority head coach hirings that the NFL has made. That would have been a great thing for black coaches and American sports. I could then have turned my attention to other concerns.

However, that hope was not realized. Between 2006 and 2008, the number of African American and minority hirings at Football Bowl Subdivision programs either stayed the same or moved backward. Then came the supposed "game-changing" movement following the 2009 season that I previously mentioned, when seven minority coaches were hired. At the conclusion of the 2010 season, five of the 21 vacancies were filled with African American coaches. Granted, that was a far better development than the hiring results after the 2008 football season, when none of the ten vacancies at BCS schools were filled by minority candidates. But by any objective measure, the National Football League (NFL) remains far ahead of the NCAA in terms of encouraging and promoting opportunities for African American head coaches.

I came up with the title for this book because I thought *Crackback* was a good analogy for the way African American and minority coaching candidates are treated by the college football establishment during the employment process. When those minority coaches desire to become college head coaches, they are still being subjected to the big tease. I talk to so many good men who believe they have put together a good résumé and are progressing on schedule to become a head coach. A few even begin to feel they are in line for a job opening and undergo what they believe is an earnest job interview and then...*wham*! Their dream is "crackbacked"! Sure, that also happens to many white coaches. But not in the same way. Not with the same underlying silent, vague, or whispered rationales that college administrators struggle to explain.

In football, a "crackback" block is one that an unsuspecting defensive player never sees coming, because the block comes from his blind side. "Crackback" blocks are either borderline illegal or *totally* illegal.

But they always accomplish their mission—they knock down a potentially effective football force. Dozens and dozens of African American coaches have attempted to build their careers the proper way, acquiring credentials that are either equal or superior to their white counterparts. But when applying for a head coaching vacancy, those African American coaches still can't even get an interview—or they may get one, only to be told they "aren't the right fit." This reality knocks the wind out of these coaches, just like a "crackback" block.

If you think this is an exaggeration, finish this book. Then see if you feel the same way. Whenever I bring up this topic, some people accuse me of reverse racism. In fact, I was asked by a highly respected white university professor who reviewed this manuscript if the fight was even still worth the battle. He perceived me to be somewhat angry and questioned if I was actually pushing for opportunities to be given unqualified minority candidates. Please allow me to clear up that perception.

I am not angry. I have never been more at peace about who I am and why God placed me on this earth. But I do want the people who follow me in the profession to get a fair shake.

No one is asking that colleges hire black coaching candidates just because they're African Americans. I'm only asking that black coaching candidates be interviewed as serious contenders for those jobs based on their qualifications. As things stand today at the majority of FBS programs, that doesn't happen. As I will outline in the pages ahead, that is a very shortsighted way to do business. If black candidates are indeed granted a serious and non-token interview, they can make a good or bad impression. They can win or lose the job, just like other candidates. But in this hiring "game," most of the qualified African American coaches don't even have the opportunity to earn a tie. Or even a moral victory.

While writing this book, I read an interesting item by ESPN. com's Big 10 blogger, Adam Rittenberg. He noted that, entering the 2009 season, Big 10 football programs had just two minority coordinators—and zero minority head coaches (Michigan's Rich Rodriguez, whose grandfather was born in Spain, did not identify himself as a minority). Rittenberg, in his online blog, suggested that the Big 10 should put the minority hiring issue on the "front burner."

The anonymous reader comments to Rittenberg's suggestion were typical: "Your article was written because black people think they need to be hired more simply because they're black." And this one: "Yes, let's fight racism by adding color as a qualification in order to get hired and throw out all other qualifications." And this one: "If you want it all equal, then we should cut back on blacks getting football scholarships to be more representative of the country's demographics."

Know what those comments told me? This book is more necessary than ever. So let's get started. I sincerely appreciate your decision to let me in the door to try to make a solid first impression. That's not a chance many black coaching candidates receive.

CHAPTER ONE
THE CRACKBACK EFFECT

Halftime. I was talking to my team. Shouting at times…and I was loving every second of it. For a coach, there is no smell better than that of a football locker room at halftime, with sweat and adrenaline and grass stains combining to form an exhilarating aroma. Every face stares in your direction, hanging on your every word. It is a cliché, I suppose, but the bonding and unity among team members and coaches is intrinsically understood. At those moments, when everyone is working together for the same purpose, no one thinks about skin color or politics or girlfriends or what's for dinner that night. We want to play hard and win together. It's beautiful.

In 2002, I was in my second season at San Jose State. We'd made remarkable progress. In an attempt to record the program's second winning season since 1992, our football team was in the hunt for our first bowl invitation in twelve years. This, after writers had picked us to finish last in our conference. And now here we were in the last game of the regular season, leading Fresno State by three points, only two quarters away from a real Cinderella finish. I was so proud of our young men. This was why I had always wanted to be a head coach.

So I began my halftime speech.

I told our players that they would need the greatest effort of their football lives in the last thirty minutes of the game. But I also cautioned them. The first half had been hard hitting. Every play had been hand-to-hand combat, which wasn't surprising, since Fresno State is San Jose State's traditional rival. With trash talking and shoving going on after the whistle, I was worried that if the trend continued, one of our players might be flagged for a penalty at a crucial moment.

"What we can't have happen," I said, "is a push or retaliation! Don't be selfish and take away fifteen yards from us just because you want to show someone how tough you are! We don't need that. Don't be counterproductive to our mission." Raising my voice, I added, "It doesn't take a man to push back. It takes a man to walk away from that stuff! You aren't tougher because you pushed somebody! Just keep it coming; keep it coming! *That's how you play!*"

We ran out the door and hit the field for the second half. After falling behind, we stormed back and were poised to win in the final minute. In a perfect world, our star receiver would have caught a pass on the day's last play and outrun every Fresno State player to the end zone. But it wasn't a perfect world. Our player dropped the ball with a wide-open field ahead of him. We lost the game, 19-16, finishing our season with a 6-7 record. We didn't get the bowl invitation. Yet because of our team's accomplishments, the *Sporting News* selected us as the Western Athletic Conference's turnaround program of the year; I received a slight raise and a new four-year contract as well as being invited to coach in the 2004 Hula Bowl with some of football's finest coaches. But just two years later, I resigned after being asked to do so by San Jose State's president. I am no quitter. But the lack of institutional support and four years of frustrating losses had taken a physical and emotional toll on me and my family.

Since then, I've churned those four years over and over through my brain. In retrospect, I think that the Fresno State loss perfectly exemplified my career at San Jose State. Just as our team had done, I worked very hard but didn't quite get it done. And to this day, I keep thinking about that halftime speech—because now I wonder if I had it wrong about pushing back.

Let me explain. For four seasons, I was head football coach at a NCAA Division 1A school, the top tier of the college game now known as the Football Bowl Subdivision. I am also an African American. The combination of those two things made me way too unique, because I had become a member of a far-too-exclusive club. African Americans have made progress in so many areas of sport and society. But as college football head coaches, we are rarer than an undefeated season.

How rare?

According to the NCAA record book, during the 143 years that college football has existed (through the 2011 season), there have been 269 unbeaten, untied teams at the Football Bowl Subdivision (FBS) level. On average, one or two teams do it per season. In those same 143 years, there have been just 47 times when those major colleges have hired African American head football coaches. And after being hired, those 47 individuals have coached a combined total of 148 seasons. By my rudimentary calculations – although some math professor would probably come up with the exact formula – that means it is roughly five-and-a-half times more likely that a fan of major college football has seen an undefeated, untied team than a fan has seen an African American college coach introduced at a press conference. That's how rare minority hirings are.

You probably think that more African Americans would be hired if they were qualified, right? Wrong. They are qualified; however, there is no set criteria for an objective evaluation in hiring head football coaches. As a result, institutions tend to hire people they are comfortable with—and will always say they have hired the best people for the job. But in most cases, they haven't even looked outside their circle of "usual suspects" to know that for sure.

I think about the ridiculous odds against black head coaches getting the top coaching jobs every time I hear a speech by Ward Connerly, director of the American Civil Rights Coalition. I have no reason to question his sincerity. Connerly is an African American who opposes affirmative action for minorities. For the record, I, too, oppose affirmative action for the unqualified regardless of race or gender. But I wonder if Connerly might rethink his position when confronted by this fact: As recently as the 2010 football season, in the history of our country, the same number of African Americans had served the United States as secretary of state as had worked as a head football coach in the Southeastern Conference – two.

That's right. Condoleezza Rice and General Colin Powell were trusted to negotiate with the world's top leaders beginning with Powell's term as secretary of state in 2001, which was three years before any SEC athletic program trusted an African American to coach football players in what is usually considered to be the country's top conference. By the time Rice succeeded Powell in 2004, Sylvester Croom had been hired at Mississippi State—but it didn't exactly start a flood of diverse hiring practices. When Croom resigned in 2008 after his fifth season at Mississippi State, there were still zero minority head coaches at the other SEC schools. Joker Phillips did become Kentucky's head coach two years later, and Vanderbilt hired James Franklin for the 2011 season.

Croom's 21-38 won-loss record was reason for his termination by Mississippi State. By college football standards, that's the usual standard operating procedure. My issue, though, is not with terminations. It's about the limited opportunities for African American coaches to ever get a chance to be terminated. The SEC is not on island in this category. For example, in the history of the Atlantic Coast Conference, just two African American coaches have led football programs. As the Big 10 kicked off the 2011 football season, not one of the conference's teams was led by an African American head coach.

Bottom line: I guess it's fortunate that General Powell and Secretary Rice had a goal of emulating Henry Kissinger instead of Bear Bryant. I often question whether I should advise young African American coaches to think about a career switch and aspire to the secretary of state job—or maybe, now, to the presidency itself—because the odds of their becoming a college head coach at the FBS level have not been encouraging.

You don't think so? You want the brutal facts? Between 1982 and 2008, there were 477 head coaching vacancies at FBS schools. Black coaches were selected to fill just 26 of those openings. And as the 2011 season began, only 16 of the 120, or 13% of the Football Bowl Subdivision coaching jobs were filled by African Americans.

I am a sensible man. I don't like to cause trouble for trouble's sake. In my early years as a college assistant coach, during late-night bull sessions with other assistants when I was the only black guy in the room, I would actually sit there and pretend to laugh at racist jokes aimed at African Americans. I did not want to be branded a troublemaker or a whiner—and more pragmatically, I didn't want to commit career suicide. As I've moved up through the coaching ranks, I have prided myself on being a diplomat on this issue.

But is it possible that I've been too diplomatic? Maybe so.

As I once cautioned my team to avoid, I don't want to draw a penalty flag for a personal foul. But after events of the past several years, I am thinking that I need to shove and push back a little bit.

Sure, some of this is personal. It really hit home during one practice at San Jose State, where I allowed my then four-year-old son, Justice, to tag along with me. I was very grateful to have the opportunity to serve the school as its head football coach. However, history had taught me that others had helped pave my way. Were it not for Dr. Martin Luther King, Mrs. Rosa Parks, and other civil rights leaders, I may not have been blessed with the chance to work at San Jose State. I am so grateful that Dr. King and Mrs. Parks pushed back. For their actions they were flagged, penalized, and jailed for trying to right a wrong. If they had not pushed back, I am not certain our country would have done the right thing simply because it was the right thing to do. The lack of minority hirings by FBS college football programs is the best evidence.

If my son decides to become a college football coach and work his way up through the ranks, I want him to earn a head coaching job based on his qualifications and the content of his character, not denied an opportunity based on his skin color. After all, this was the dream of Dr. King. In the arena of collegiate football coaches, this dream has yet to come true. Employment bias along the color line is hard to define and even more difficult to prove; however, the facts speak to the problem, because today there are African American coaches who are qualified and have impeccable character, yet when these jobs become available, these men become invisible.

For that reason, I have to push back. College football is supposed to exemplify the good things about our country, one in which I strongly believe.

I have to push back and not walk away, because if we concede that college football is an important part of our American culture, then we must admit that the lack of employment opportunities for African American head coaches is damaging that culture, every person who plays college football, every person who teaches the game, and every person who loves the game as a fan. No matter what color those people are.

I have to push back and not walk away, because if my son, Justice, is one day good enough to play college football at a FBS institution, he should have as many options as possible to play for a coach who happens to resemble his dad.

I have to push back and not walk away, because I have always believed that the best way to confront ignorance is to smack it in the face with hard data. So I have spent my entire academic life gathering facts and trying to present them in a reasonable manner.

African American males currently make up nearly fifty percent of all football athletic scholarships awarded at FBS schools. Those scholarships are awarded on merit. Why, then, are African American coaches at the same level so few and far between?

For the moment, I will set aside my own experiences at San Jose State, which I will address in a later chapter. At least I was fortunate enough to have my turn as a college head coach. Many other African Americans did not, have not, and will not—unless there is a profound change in how universities do business. To me, that's a problem. If we don't have the best people coaching college football, we not only do not have the best college football possible, we also don't have the best colleges possible. The students at those schools are being cheated. So is the entire university community.

Here's what I mean: Imagine if Vince Lombardi had been a black man in the 1950s. Given the country's racial atmosphere at that time, he would never have been given the opportunity to coach the Green Bay Packers. And if that had been the case, how many players, fans, and Americans in general would have been denied the chance to be taught and inspired by one of the greatest coaches ever?

Of course, you could say that Lombardi was incomparable. You could say that no man of any race could equal him. No argument there. But there have been coaches nearly as good—coaches who have been, say, three-fourths of a Lombardi in terms of knowledge, leadership, and toughness. And I have to believe that in the 1950s, at least one African American coach was in that category. But in the 1950s, there's no way that our theoretical three-fourths Lombardi would have been hired as a head coach by any pro franchise or college program, except at the historically black schools.

And today? Today, our theoretical three-fourths Lombardi would probably have an excellent chance to be hired—in the National Football League. To its credit, the NFL no longer seems to think that an African American man in charge on the sidelines is such a horrible sight. As of January 2011, seven of the thirty-two head coaches in the NFL were black. That's roughly 22 percent of the available positions.

Now, ponder this: To match that same percentage in major college football, we would need to see twenty-six African American head coaches on the sidelines. And that's eleven more than we currently have—even after the supposedly impressive "new wave" of seven minority head coach hirings at FBS schools before the 2010 football season and the four black coaches hired after the completion of the 2010 season.

In my view, that last statement is depressingly stunning. Please understand one thing: I am not in favor of quotas. To a certain extent, I even hate using numbers when talking about this crisis. But when those numbers have been—and still are—so clearly out of whack, how can the numbers possibly be ignored? Civil rights legislation was passed just for this reason. But there is obviously a huge disconnect in the college football employment setting. In fact, I have concluded that the situation is denial of the worst kind—and a form of employment segregation.

Keep in mind that behind each of those numbers that represent a coach hired or not hired, there is a story.

In 2002, a coach named Ron Brown was employed as an assistant football coach at the University of Nebraska. He had worked there for more than a decade. Brown possessed an impressive résumé with impeccable credentials. And, yes, he was also an African American. When his alma mater, Brown University of the Ivy League, began searching for a new football coach, Ron Brown was contacted and asked to interview for the job. During the interview, Brown was informed that there were individuals who had reservations about hiring a black football coach.

Here's how Brown was quoted in the *Dallas Morning News*:

The athletic director told me, "Some alums are not happy because you're African American." They said, "We don't want to play that experiment here." It really bothers me. I played there. You get all the pats on the back when you're playing. All of sudden, there's a drawn line.

Later, Brown personally confirmed this story to me. And remember, this happened to him at an Ivy League school! We tend to think of our universities as bastions of diversity, enlightenment, and open-minded thinking. But in terms of head football coaches, who often become the faces of those schools, the very same universities are less diverse than your average law office, police department, accounting firm—or even your average United States Supreme Court. How can this be?

First, however, we must admit that we have a problem and confront the cruel truth about why it exists. In our country, most people think of racial discrimination in terms of overt and purposeful bigotry. If someone uses a racial insult in public, you hear it. If a restaurant gives a man and his wife bad service because of the couple's race, you see it. If someone is denied housing because of his or her race, you can often document it. That sort of racism is a big bug you can stalk, track down, swat, and eventually eradicate.

But institutional racism is a far sneakier insect. It is an insect that bites silently. Sometimes you don't feel the bite until it starts to swell up much later. Employment discrimination in the college football hiring process is more subtle and covert. It is a matter of nonverbal messages and small inequities that add up over time. It is often more of a passive racism than an active racism. But it is racism just the same.

If you think that I am on a witch hunt, relax, because I'm not. I believe that most white athletic administrators and coaches are honorable men and women. I have had the opportunity to work beside many of them. I believe most of them do not intentionally attempt to treat African American coaches any differently than they treat white coaches. But as honorable and as good hearted as these athletic directors, administrators and coaches may be, their subconscious bias and behavior is often a crackback block that denies equality in the profession. Many can't see that current hiring practices and trends are flawed.

I do not intend for this to sound like an insult. But here is the absolute truth: These well-meaning white collegiate administrators are often blinded by their blissful ignorance. Their pride and ego enable them to actually believe that they are hiring the most qualified head coaching candidates and that skin color is no factor in their decisions. The opposite is true. Race has always been an issue in the United States.

My employment experiences reveal that trying to get white administrators to understand their subconscious bias is frequently like trying to get a fish to discover water, which is impossible to happen unless you take the fish out of the water. Many white men do not understand that they have been born with a certain degree of privilege based on skin color—basically because people often equate white skin with superiority. That situation lingers and is difficult for many people to totally shake even when equality is legally mandated. If we are all created equal, how is it that since 1982, black collegiate football coaches have been hired for just 47 of the 546 head coaching vacancies?

I've heard a good analogy used for stuff like this: If you put a frog in a frying pan and gradually turn up the heat, the frog won't jump out, because his amphibian nature will adapt to the temperature. I think that's what has happened to these administrators. I would bet that many of them didn't even realize that minority opportunities in college football coaching actually regressed between 1997 and 2007. I would bet many of them don't realize today how far behind the NCAA is on this issue compared to the NFL.

Black coaches should go to school on the story of Title IX and how it was eventually enforced by the federal government to give women equal opportunity to play college sports. But to make sure it was implemented without delay, the heat was cranked up instantly in federal courts. If a university was not in compliance, the government sued the university. And if the university did not toe the line, there were financial consequences—namely, the withholding of federal money.

It is unfortunate that many white college administrators don't see how they are building glass ceilings—and walls and fences—because of an ingrained collective mindset. This mindset usually involves a fear that alumni and financial supporters of the football program will not embrace an African American head coach. My studies on this subject have led me to believe this mind-set exists because when white administrators and influential boosters picture their ideal head coach, they almost never picture a black man.

This "white only" mind-set no longer predominates college basketball. Many men of color have succeeded in that profession—Tubby Smith, Nolan Richardson, John Thompson, and John Chaney, just to name just a few. These days, no one thinks twice when an African American man is hired to coach a Division I basketball team. The presence of these men on the sidelines, coaching their teams to conference championships and the Final Four, has made it easier for athletic directors to envision other African Americans as the ideal hiring for their schools.

College football is different. White athletic and academic administrators have routinely gone on the record supporting equal opportunities for African American football coaches. But what they have truly been thinking is something else entirely. You doubt this? I would refer you to a quote from Notre Dame's former athletic director Kevin White, who is now the athletic director at Duke. But as you may recall, in 2001, when White was searching for a head football coach for the Irish, he wound up hiring George O'Leary—who was forced to resign less than a week after he took the job because he had lied on his résumé.

How could this have happened? Notre Dame clearly should have done a better background check on O'Leary. But it seems university administrators had been swept away by his charm and image. White even admitted as much.

"George kind of appeared to us all like something out of central casting," White told reporters later when trying to explain how Notre Dame had made such a mistake.

There you have it. When university administrators were casting the role of head coach in South Bend, they first envisioned a middle-aged white guy who talked a good game and fit the right "image" for Notre Dame—and White admitted it! If there is a more telling remark about the current state of affairs in college football, I can't think of one.

Now, do I believe Kevin White is a racist? Of course not. The next person he hired at Notre Dame, after O'Leary's awkward exit, was Tyrone Willingham, an African American. But do I believe that White's remark shows how benignly insidious the prejudice against minority head coaches can be? Absolutely.

I want to give many white administrators credit for trying to overcome this stereotyping. But here's the irony: These administrators—either in good conscience or because university superiors force it upon them—frequently create "guidelines" or "processes" to try and give minority coaches a "fair" chance for jobs. Yet these very "guidelines" and "processes" often create more racial hostility and frustration among coaches themselves.

How do I know this? I've asked the coaches.

Over the past two decades, I have conducted numerous studies on this topic. I have asked both black and white coaches across America to fill out surveys and offer their opinions about the situation. I promised them anonymity if they responded. Many did.

Let's examine six of those replies—three from African American coaches and three from white coaches—and see what they tell us.

- An African American assistant coach: "Unfortunately, in this profession, employment is generally based on who you know. White athletic directors know other white athletic directors. White head coaches know other white head coaches and so on, down the line. So when a job opportunity arises, a person will call who he knows."

- A white assistant coach: "Until minorities get off the 'victim' parade, they will always hold themselves back. Capable, decent, hard-working people achieve and accomplish, and they are duly recognized. 'Victims' have an aroma about them that makes others grow weary of their eternal griping. First, the minorities said to unlock the doors. They were unlocked, as they should have been. Second, the minorities said to open the doors. They were opened. Now, they say, 'Carry me through the door.' Where does it stop? A legitimate survey might surprise you in regard to who's getting the best shot at jobs in this profession."

- An African American assistant: "White administrators fill the football team with African American athletes, who most of the white administrators fear, so they hire a couple of us to make sure the natives don't get restless. They rarely put us in positions of any significance... The thing that really chaps me is when the administrators say they don't know any qualified African American candidates. If they would take the time to open their eyes, they might find some in their own program."

- A white assistant: "It seems you are inferring that black coaches are discriminated against in hiring practices. It is my opinion that the opposite is occurring. White coaches are finding it more and more difficult to find jobs. I know that certain jobs are targeted specifically for black coaches, and white coaches are not even considered for those positions."

- An African American assistant: "There seems to be a mentality that two black coaches on a staff are basically enough.

If you have two, then you're okay. I've been at my school going on four years, and we've had no more than two coaches of color during that time. There also is a perception among white assistants that we have it made because of our color. What they don't realize is that we are competing for those two spots out of nine available assistant jobs, while they are competing for the other seven."

- A white assistant: "Many good, young white coaches are losing out and getting out of coaching because of race hiring. I am fifty-three years old and worked in high school, small college, and eighteen years at the 1A level. During that time, I have lost jobs to African American coaches who have been 'handed' jobs despite lesser qualifications. If we force incompetent people into leadership roles, it will eventually lead to a destruction of interest in the sport."

Notice a common theme? Not one of these guys, black or white, believes he is receiving a fair shake. The African American assistants are convinced they won't ever advance to top coaching positions because of the white establishment. The white assistants are convinced that African Americans get preferential treatment when applying for jobs.

Both groups cannot be correct, of course. So what's the deal? The data suggests that black coaches' perceptions are factually linked to the coaching opportunities that they have or have not received. The data also suggests that white coaches who historically have filled a majority of those coaching vacancies claim that opportunities are being stripped from them to hire what they perceive to be *unqualified* black coaches.

Here's a great example: I asked all those who took the survey if they agreed with the following premise: *An African American coach's intellectual understanding of football strategy is often questioned by white colleagues, because the African American coaches do not receive the same respect as their white peers.*

Seventy-eight percent of African Americans assistant coaches agreed with that statement. Twelve percent of white coaches did.

People say that African American coaches are "griping" and "constantly complaining" about the lack of opportunities, but white men whine just as much! My research also indicates that some black coaches fervently believe there is rancor and competition between black coaches themselves, because so few employment opportunities exist. It's hard enough under ideal circumstances for coaches to work together in the intensely competitive world of top-tier college football. When these often unresolved race-related resentments are bubbling beneath the surface...well, next time you wonder why your favorite team's coaching staff didn't seem to be on the same page during a certain game, the cause might be something more subtle and deep than miscommunication over play calling.

Despite all this, collegiate leaders don't do much to show they care. They have apparently lost interest in any sort of self-analysis about the issue. I hear many administrators say that their current hiring practices do not discriminate on the basis of race. Several years ago, Roy Kramer, who was then commissioner of the powerful Southeastern Conference, said almost those exact words—and he has never retracted them. He went on the record with his contention that SEC institutions are hiring equally across the board and that there were no racial overtones in the hiring process. Yet at that point, there had never been a black head coach in his conference! Was this just coincidence? Bad luck?

Obviously, major college administrators do not communicate very well with the football coaching staffs at their schools. If that were the case, those administrators would uncover the same discontent that I discovered.

Earlier in this chapter, remember how I cited the paltry number of minority head coach hirings in major college football since

1982? You would think that, with increased awareness of this issue in the twenty-first century, college administrators would want to open the door as widely as possible to as many diverse applicants as possible. Instead, at several schools, administrators have adopted a closed-door "tag team" hiring process: before a head coach even quits, his successor is already anointed in advance. With just one exception—at Kentucky, when Joker Phillips was named the "coach in waiting" for when Rich Brooks eventually retired in 2009—this has eliminated the chance for any minority candidate to even be interviewed. Heck, it has eliminated the chance for a coach of any race to be interviewed for those jobs. That's also not right.

I am certain of this much: The presidents of America's universities—and the schools' boards of trustees—have work to do. If they are trying to "fix" the racial inequities in football coaching by telling athletic directors and head coaches to hire minorities for a certain number of positions, this "fix" appears to create more problems than it is solves.

We must do something about this situation. And we can. But we need people of all colors to buy into the solutions. In a football game, there are certain occasions when a coach will take a penalty flag for a deliberate purpose or cause. In this case, by doing so I will probably anger some folks—just as my players would have angered me if they had been flagged for a personal foul that would have backed my team up.

Here is what my sideline experience has taught me: while the second retaliation is usually the one that gets penalized, the majority of push backs were provoked by initial acts of aggression. In this book, I am pushing back in response to acts of gross injustice from the "referees" who work in the administration offices of American universities. These are people who are supposed to be promoting equal opportunity. It's currently not happening.

CHAPTER TWO

FROM ARKADELPHIA
TO REALITY

Before we get down to the real nitty-gritty, I thought it might be useful for you to know how I developed such a passion for the issue of racial equality among college coaches. I always thought my hometown of Arkadelphia, Arkansas, was an ideal place for a kid to grow up and live. It turns out I was right. The chamber of commerce there cites a *Money* magazine story that proclaimed the town to be one of America's "50 Fabulous Places to Raise a Family." I wish all of you could visit Arkadelphia, a city of some ten thousand people about seventy miles southwest of Little Rock. You would better understand why, as an adult, it was such a shock for me to belatedly discover that most communities in America are not like Arkadelphia in terms of building a support system for a young man trying to find his way in life.

That doesn't mean the place was perfect. I was born in 1964. That means I grew up just after forced integration was mandated in the South. I think it is safe to assume some people in town didn't think this was progress. Race and class differences in many parts of America are as common as ice cream and apple pie. As a child in the South, then and today, you learn your place as a black person in America. And if you decide to recalibrate yourself as an independent critical thinker on these issues, you must be aware of the risks. This is especially the case if you (A) want the approval or validation of white people and (B) don't desire to hear negative voices in the black community who say that your comments make it difficult for them to handle the questions asked by their white bosses or friends who might hear those comments. I know. It happened to me.

But not as a preschooler, of course. Arkadelphia's population is roughly 70 percent white and 30 percent African American, so my family and I were definitely in the minority. But I can honestly say that growing up there, I found no impenetrable barriers to hold me back. Except for a few stupid name-calling incidents, the only troubling racist episode of my own youth occurred in 1977 when I was 13, during my first season of Babe Ruth baseball.

That summer, the coach of a team called Glynn's Truck Stop refused to draft black players. Just for that reason, I remember wanting so badly to beat him and his team, even though one of my closest white friends was one of his players. Fortunately, my bitterness didn't carry over into my relationships with most people in town. I can't speak for all young black youth who were raised in Arkadelphia. But my personal experience does help explain why I was so frustrated when I realized that the barriers that were largely absent in Arkadelphia did exist in the college coaching world. I would soon discover that there were a lot more Glynn's Truck Stop coaches out there than I realized.

Much of Arkadelphia's ambiance radiates from the two universities: one public—Henderson State University—and one private—Ouachita Baptist University. Located across the street from each other on the northeast side of town, they have a combined enrollment of about fifty-three hundred. If you include faculty members, administrators, and other support personnel, then probably one of every two Arkadelphians has some affiliation with the two schools.

Growing up in a college town has many advantages, mostly in terms of education, cultural opportunities, and athletic events that I loved to attend. The elementary and secondary schools are forced to certain standards of academic achievement and excellence, because many of the children's parents work for the universities. They demand and foster an elevated scholastic environment. My mother had a secretarial job at Peake High, the all-black public school in town. When integration arrived, Peake as I knew it would change forever, because the African American students were sent to Arkadelphia High. My mom followed, working in the administrative offices.

It wasn't an entirely peaceful time. In the early '70s, I remember the day a racial disturbance occurred at Mom's school. I was in the first or second grade, in a building just fifty yards west of Arkadelphia High. I vividly recall seeing a long line of black students headed west on Pine Street. While observing this through a chain-link fence, I spotted one of the black students in my neighborhood, who angrily ordered me to punch a white friend who happened to be standing beside me. This was all very confusing.

Since kindergarten, I had lived in an integrated educational environment, playing during recess with other little white boys and girls. My dad was a Baptist church deacon. My mother was a church leader at the Methodist congregation and had a Sunday ritual of inviting college students over for supper following the services (partially as a lure for them to attend church the next week). My dad had several jobs, including one as production manager at the local soda pop bottling plant. I started helping out there when I was twelve.

Looking back, we certainly weren't rich, but we definitely weren't living in poverty. We had a two-bedroom house, so my brothers and I shared the second bedroom. Three boys, one closet, one bathroom. We made it work. We had a big backyard, and everybody came over to play games with us—football, baseball, basketball, whatever. Competing in sports was like breathing to me. I played football and basketball and ran track at Arkadelphia High. And I made an effort to be accepted and liked by everybody. Although the school was mostly white, that did not have a negative effect on me. After holding numerous student offices from seventh grade onward, I was elected student body president my senior year. I did, however, learn the dynamics of race by listening to my brothers, my parents, and my relatives discussing their own experiences.

I had black friends who developed crushes on white girls. But I understood the negative consequences that would come from going public with such a relationship. I am positive that if I had allowed a friendship with any white girl to knowingly blossom into a deeper relationship, I probably would not have been elected to any school office. I guess I would call that racial politics. Others might suggest that it was Southern social mores.

Being a good athlete and honor roll student gave me privileges at Arkadelphia High. And being a good person was no option. My mother supervised that category every day as the high school's registrar. I knew that if I had to visit the principal's office, I would have to see my mother first. The success of our football program and my ability to make spectacular catches on Friday nights definitely made it easy for me to transcend racial environments with ease. I graduated in 1982 and headed off to play football at Northeast Louisiana University (now the University of Louisiana at Monroe) with a full scholarship. And that's where reality first smacked me in the face.

As a high school athlete in Arkansas, I had been somewhat sheltered. Our football team at Arkadelphia High was a southern version of the Texas high school program described in the book *Friday Night Lights*. Over three seasons, we won thirty-two of thirty-six games, including a state championship and two district titles. That success caused the townspeople to look at my teammates and me in a very supportive way.

Across the Arkansas-Louisiana border, things were different. At the Northeast Louisiana campus in Monroe, I played for an all-white coaching staff that, to be honest, had difficulty understanding the cultural issues facing many black athletes. In 1982, this was a national problem. In retrospect, I attribute that to the lack of diversity among coaching staffs at predominately white colleges and universities.

Of course, during that era, racial division appeared to be part of the culture in northern Louisiana. I would understand what I was dealing with several years later when David Duke, former Grand Wizard of the Ku Klux Klan, almost won the state's gubernatorial race. I was amazed that a blatant racist could receive nearly fifty percent of the vote. On my recruiting trip to Monroe in January 1982, a black athlete told me that the white alums and boosters would take care of me as long as I didn't "mess with their white women." I also recall white store clerks giving me a wary eye when I went out shopping. That hadn't happened in Arkadelphia. I had never stolen anything in my life. I didn't like being perceived as a thief.

One Sunday afternoon in 1982, during my first preseason football training camp at Northeast Louisiana, some black teammates were talking and laughing in the locker room about a racial incident that had occurred earlier in the day. A white assistant coach had invited his entire group of student-athletes—white and black players—to his church for a worship service. Unfortunately, for reasons I never fully understood, the one black player who took the coach up on his offer was not allowed to enter the church. According to the black player, an usher standing at the door asked him if he was looking for someone. And before the player could respond, the usher quickly replied: "There is no one here by that name." The student-athlete left without trouble, and it was never brought to the attention of the white coach. Nobody wanted to make racial waves.

I am glad that I didn't take up that coach on his invite. My mother had done her homework and found a church I could attend while enrolled at Northeast Louisiana—a black church that welcomed me unconditionally.

I withdrew from Northeast Louisiana in September of 1983 because of my father's health and personal problems. He had been diagnosed with stomach cancer in the spring of 1980, although he had previously visited our family physician in Arkadelphia several times and was simply prescribed medication for severe indigestion. It is no secret that many black men are infrequent visitors to doctors. Yet I wondered if he would have received better treatment had he been white. Would they have sent him for x-rays or tests on the first visit? Or did they just ignore evidence that would eventually cost him his life? Before my college experiences in Louisiana, I would not have asked that question. But I was asking it now.

I guess what I'm really talking about is the black experience that Arthur Ashe, the late tennis champion, referred to during his battle with AIDS. When asked if the disease was the heaviest burden he had to bear, his response shocked many white people. "No," Ashe said, "being black is the greatest burden I've had to bear. Race has always been my biggest burden. Having to live as a minority in America. Even now it continues to feel like an extra weight tied around me."

The longer I have lived, the more I have come to understand the profundity of Ashe's words. And they kept hitting home during my dad's illness. I'm not sure he ever got the proper care. After my dad's first stomach operation for cancer, the surgeon told my family the operation went well but that daddy would probably never work again. However, the doctor that represented the Social Security disability benefits division looked at my father and saw a healthy black man. This doctor rejected the surgeon's prognosis, gave my daddy a clean bill of health, terminated his disability benefits and told him to resume employment. Daddy took a job as a janitor. He had no choice. We were on a fixed income. Once the disability checks stopped rolling in, my father sucked it up for his family and basically worked himself to death. The cancer eventually resurfaced, this time in a more aggressive form. I withdrew from Northeast Louisiana and returned home to Arkadelphia to spend the final eight weeks of my daddy's life with him. He died in November of 1983. Watching life ebb out of his once-strong body was very painful.

One night, my mother called me to the restroom to assist her with my father. He looked at me but didn't recognize me as I tried to help him stand. I kept asking, "Daddy, you okay?" He didn't respond. He was delirious. I told my mother to call the ambulance.

I reached down to pick him up, and I will never forget that feeling of bones in my arms as I cradled him like a baby. He weighed barely seventy-five pounds. The paramedics arrived shortly thereafter and took him to the hospital. He passed away the next morning.

Soon after my father's death, I contacted college coaches about resuming my football playing career. Not surprisingly, I also began to think more deeply about my purpose in life. The death of a loved one does that to you—but in my case, even more so. As we prepared to lay Daddy to rest in what we called the "country" graveyard just outside town, I observed something that I had never noticed as a kid when I mowed that same field with my uncle and cousins to earn spending money. In the middle of the cemetery property, a chain-link fence divided the white people's graves from the black people's graves. How come I'd never seen that fence? Why was it even there? Were people in my town convinced that their dead bodies needed to be separated? Did they also think that heaven or hell was segregated?

After burying my daddy, I would never approach life the same way. I realized that over the years, as I grew up in my idyllic little town with so many friends of all colors, I might have been lulled into a fantasy world. I was blissfully ignorant of the racial divide that still pollutes the minds of so many people long after Rosa Parks and Dr. Martin Luther King had supposedly awakened America. I made up my mind to show people that no fence of any kind would ever keep me from my dreams.

First, though, I had to think of my mom. Shortly after my dad's death, she suffered a stroke that left her helpless. After she had spent nine months in the hospital and a residential care facility, I brought her home and took over managing and operating the household. To pay bills, I managed an Arkadelphia shoe repair shop. Two prominent white men, a bank president named Ed Snider and a businessman named Peter Rudolph, helped me launch a small business—a coin laundry. I took out several thousand dollars in student loans to support myself through undergraduate and graduate school. Meanwhile, Coach Buddy Bob Benson, the football coach at Ouachita Baptist, came through on that scholarship he had offered me four years earlier. To further augment my income, I joined the Army ROTC at Ouachita, which paid an extra $100 per month.

If you are wondering how I juggled all that without being totally exhausted, the answer is: I didn't. My aunt, June Callaway from Berkeley, California, came to visit my mom and saw how I was running myself into the ground. Very generously, she offered to take in mom as a permanent houseguest. At first I was hesitant about the separation. But I knew it was for the best. I could concentrate on school and football, earn a degree, make my mother proud (which was very important to me), then get a really good-paying job and take care of her every need.

Snider and his bank loaned me $3,000 so my mom and I could fly to California. I had developed a very close relationship with the Snider family over the years. Ed Snider was also president of the Little League in Arkadelphia, and his son, Steve, grew to be one of my best friends. The fact that the Snider family was white and I was black made no difference to them or me. The Sniders not only supported me emotionally but also financially to help me through a very turbulent time. My family members were also there to offer emotional assistance. But without the Sniders' financial aid, I am not sure what I would have done. Still, I knew the best way to get where I wanted was by putting my nose to the grindstone at Ouachita. So that's what I did. I moved into a dorm room and got down to business.

During the Christmas holiday season of 1984, I drove from Arkadelphia to Berkeley to visit Mom. I took along a gift from Betty Snider, Ed's wife, who was always giving me inspirational material. This time, she had purchased a cassette called "You Can Be A Winner," an audiotape motivational program by Grant Teaff, the Baylor University head football coach. I didn't think about putting it in the tape deck until, while driving through Arizona, I could no longer get any radio reception. I popped the cassette into the deck and began listening.

Coach Teaff talked about how the most influential people in almost every American community were the football coaches—more than bankers or lawyers or anybody else. It made me think about my own high school coach, John Outlaw. In his first season at Arkadelphia High, he united our community by pulling together a fragmented group of boys from all races and economic backgrounds to win the Arkansas Class AAA state football championship. By the time I was done listening to Coach Teaff's tape, I was convinced. Coaching football was the way God would use me.

And so, during my junior season at Ouachita Baptist in 1985, I contacted head coaches across the country to see if they might have an opening for a graduate assistant position in the fall of 1988. That was three years away, but it was when I expected to have my diploma and begin my coaching life. I probably sent out thirty letters to Division I schools and received around twenty replies. The nicest response was from Terry Donahue, the UCLA head coach. His letter was full of so much encouragement I went to Los Angeles to see him—uninvited—in the spring of 1986. I waited around his office all day until he had fifteen minutes to visit. He told me to stay in touch and keep him abreast of my progress.

Unfortunately, it didn't work out for me at UCLA. My plans were delayed because of my ROTC commitment. Also, as an all-conference player at Ouachita, I also had dreams of an NFL career and was invited to a one-day tryout by the New England Patriots. They didn't sign me, so my path was clear. When I was offered a position as a graduate assistant coach at Northwestern State in Louisiana, a Division 1AA program (now FCS) with a good reputation, I jumped at the chance. I knew I would learn a lot, because I was familiar with two coaches on the staff. One had been my high school defensive coordinator, and the other had been my position coach during the year I spent playing at Northeast Louisiana.

There were four graduate assistants on the Northwestern State staff in 1988. Two were black and two were white. Earl Buckingham was the other black graduate assistant. We both moved into the athletic dormitory, received a tuition scholarship to graduate school, and a stipend of $1,000 per month. And yes, I did receive an education. Quickly, I grasped the stratified racial dynamics of college coaching staffs.

For student-athletes on the football field, opportunities were increasing. But in terms of the coaching staff…well, there were very few black assistant coaches, usually token hires, at predominately white colleges and universities. By hiring just one black assistant, many head coaches at Division 1A institutions thought they were being aggressive in diversifying their staffs. I remember reading a 1992 story in the *Dallas Morning News* by Ivan Maisel. The headline was: *"Black Coaches Sidelined."* Maisel methodically exposed the lack of employment opportunities for minority coaches. R.C. Slocum, the head coach at Texas A&M, disagreed with the premise and offered Maisel this quote: "There is no one coaching that has any more opportunity than a young black coach. I can give you example after example."

I was truly shocked at Coach Slocum's perspective on the issue. I remember thinking that he should be drug tested. The situation was even worse at Division 1AA schools such as Northwestern State. The head coach, Sam Goodwin, was an awesome man whom I still deeply respect. But at the time, he employed no full-time black assistant coaches. I assume that he was trying to compensate for his full-time staff's lack of diversity by employing two black grad assistants. But I never discussed the situation with him. Like other young black coaches of that era, I didn't want to get a reputation as someone who made race a big issue.

During my playing years at Ouachita, I'm not sure why it did not bother me as much that we didn't have a full-time black coach on the staff. I never had a problem with any of the assistants. I think the staff knew I was battling a lot of personal off-the-field issues related to my family. We did have a black student assistant who was working to complete his degree. Behind his back, a lot of the black players made fun of him for the way he behaved around the white coaches.

But after studying this issue for so many years, I now understand. The black student assistant was simply working within the system, as many black men do, to survive in a world so often dominated by white men. If it meant eating cheese (also known as "skinning and grinning") by laughing at things that weren't funny, then as a black coach, you did so. If it meant shutting up and ignoring your seething anger when you knew that something wasn't right, you did that too. You realized that you were replaceable and another black coach would swoop in to take your job and happily play the role of a token.

It didn't take very long for Earl and me to realize that one of our main responsibilities at Northwestern State was to manage the African American student-athletes on the team. Earl understood this better than I did. He had served as a graduate assistant at the University of Arkansas, his alma mater, and he tried to educate me on the racial dynamics of the profession. But I was arrogant. I didn't think Earl's stories, descriptive as they were, applied to me. Arkadelphia had taught me that I could transcend race. I knew what I expected. I thought that I would be the first black head coach to win a Division 1A national football championship.

Earl and I had a great relationship with all of the players at Northwestern State, especially the black student-athletes. We loved those kids, and they reciprocated the love. They were happy to have someone who would tell them the truth and hold them accountable for their actions both on and off the field. We had very few problems, because they knew we cared.

Let me give you some examples.

In August of 1988 during preseason and two-a-day drills, a black player more or less challenged the authority of a Northwestern

State assistant coach, who then recommended in a staff meeting that the player be kicked off the team for insubordination. Earl and I objected. We thought the coach didn't understand the cultural issues that caused the young man to react the way he did. This particular player was from New Orleans. It is safe to assume that the young man had played at a predominately black high school where nearly all of his coaches were African American. Now, here he was in the rural town of Natchitoches, three hours away from home, where the social dynamics were totally different. The student-athlete had few if any genuine relationships with the coaching staff off the football field. The young man might never have been asked to work this hard before in his entire life. He was perspiring and risking injury while being yelled at by a white coach that the black player didn't perceive cared about him as a person. He was tired and confused and responded in a negative manner.

In that situation, if the white coach has no established relationship with the black student-athlete, the player can easily believe he is being treated as a faceless object, not as a human being. And when the white coach begins screaming at the black player, the black player more often than not will be offended—and see the screaming not as a coaching tactic but as a disrespectful challenge.

In the above case at Northwestern State, both Earl and I knew that this player was not a bad person. We argued successfully on his behalf. Had we not been there, I believe the young man would have been removed from the roster. He went on to have a great season and was drafted by National Football League, where he played several years and had a successful career.

On another occasion, a black player sustained a serious injury. His entire family showed up to meet with Coach Goodwin because they were concerned. Goodwin asked me to join him in the meeting. I thought he wanted me in the room to provide information about the player's progress. However, Goodwin simply wanted me to sit there and make the family feel more comfortable. When I

realized immediately that there was a cultural communication bar-
rier between Goodwin and the family members, I tried to put them
at ease. Coach Goodwin and I were sensitive to their feelings. The
family wanted to know that their son was going to be all right. I felt
that I made them feel that way. I guess it was a "black thing"—a
cultural understanding between a young southern black boy from
Arkansas and a southern black family from Louisiana. It's hard to
explain, but simply through eye contact, I believe I connected with
the family. Afterwards, everyone was pleased, including Goodwin.
I remember feeling that I had added some value to my net worth
on the staff by being able to communicate the concern of our white
head coach to the black player's family.

At that juncture of my career, I was feeling pretty good about
myself. I was learning some of the X and 0 strategies of football,
but not as much as I was learning about building relationships and
managing student-athletes, especially African American players.

But it wasn't just the African American players. Growing up in
Arkadelphia and attending Ouachita Baptist prepared me well for
situations related to race, particularly as a member of an underrep-
resented minority. At Ouachita, I was often one of the few African
Americans in any given class. This helped me greatly later in my
life as I learned to navigate the white culture with ease. I worked
very hard at mastering the best way to communicate effectively with
white administrators and faculty members. In turn, the white faculty and staff guided me through the ropes without demeaning me.
But they were demanding of me in the classroom. They worked on
my writing and communication skills. One of my white professors,
Dr. William Downs, was the first teacher to address my ebonics way
of speaking—an African American vernacular English—that I had
learned growing up in Arkadelphia. Dr. Downs wanted me to work
on being more articulate. At first I was puzzled. I thought I had it
all going for me. I was a good student but needed to improve my

communication skills. So I took a voice and diction course as well as other classes to work on my speech and enunciation.

These experiences taught me that if you think someone of another race cares about you—as the faculty and staff at Ouachita did in helping me deal with my family issues—then you won't be offended by constructive criticism. Between my time at Ouachita and Northwestern State and later at the University of Arkansas, I suppose my life experiences earned me an honorary doctorate degree in living as a minority among the majority. Social scientists refer to this as becoming "bicultural"—being able to adapt with ease from one culture to another. However, I was determined to remain genuine to myself and in the process learned this to be difficult if you are overly concerned about being accepted or validated by white people.

Of course, nobody had to teach me how to be black. I was born that way and have never wanted to be anything else. Living as a black man in America, I witnessed that being white comes with a lot of unspoken privileges. If you are white, you are more often considered qualified until you prove you can't do the job. If you are a minority, particularly an African American male, you have to prove that the stereotypes do not apply to you. That is why learning about football strategy and technique was so important to me. I didn't want to be branded just as a recruiter. I was determined to learn the intricacies of football—especially the passing game, because I loved it so much. Black football coaches are often not challenged to learn the strategies of the game.

Which leads me to another story.

One of my close African American friends was once employed as an assistant coach at Clemson University. This particular coach was an excellent recruiter and was assigned to recruit student-athletes from the state of Georgia, a great talent pool of student-athletes. This particular coach always found himself in a fierce recruiting war with the University of Georgia Bulldogs. One year, a student-athlete signed a national letter of intent to accept a scholarship at

Clemson rather than Georgia. The student-athlete happened to be African American. Following that recruiting battle, Ray Goff, the head coach at Georgia, had a vacancy on his staff. Goff attempted to hire my friend from Clemson to fill that vacancy.

According to my colleague, he had built a great relationship with the family of that African American athlete, who eventually signed with Clemson. The family simply felt more comfortable with him than with the Georgia coach who was recruiting the young man. My guess is that the student-athlete and his family told Coach Goff how much they liked the assistant coach from Clemson. Coach Goff wanted badly to hire my friend—so badly that Goff told him that he wouldn't even have to coach very much, just focus on recruiting.

My point: Coach Goff wasn't focused primarily on developing the black assistant's skills as a coach. Goff just wanted this black coach on the Georgia staff because he had proven to be effective at signing black talent. Job security for the majority of black assistant coaches at major schools is tied to their recruiting ability—or more specifically, their recruiting ability in terms of signing up African American talent. In later research, I would discover that 82 percent of African American coaches perceived that they were hired at colleges and universities primarily for the recruiting and monitoring of African American student-athletes.

A white coach once told me a story about a black coach who was employed by a very prominent Big Eight football program in the 1980s. The white coach said that the token black hire on their staff was rarely involved in preparing strategic game planning each week. The black coach's main responsibility was to recruit, act as a father figure, and supervise the black student-athletes, all of which he did very well. On game days, he wore a headset—but it was disconnected. He was only playing the role of an assistant coach and was not allowed input into mid-game adjustments. The white coach told me that they referred to the black coach as "dead-set" in tribute to the dead earphones.

One night while doing research for a class during my own college days at Northwestern State, I came across a magazine article written by Dr. Richard Lapchick, a sports sociologist who at the time was employed at Northeastern University in Massachusetts. The article discussed the dearth of African American football coaches at the college and pro levels—and how the few coaches who actually were hired tended to be pigeonholed in positions where their intellects were neither sought nor valued. Most of the country's Division I programs, Lapchick wrote, had an informal quota system with just one or two black coaches on each staff.

I thought, "Man, that's what I'm dealing with right now." I remember talking with Earl about it. Before coming to Natchitoches, he had played football at the University of Arkansas and served as a grad assistant there. Earl said that during his time at the school, the staff had never included more than one full-time black coach, which I confirmed through my research.

Earl, a former student-athlete at Arkansas, also shared stories of the lone black assistant coach who was on the Razorbacks' staff at that time. Many of the black players, he said, were not fond of the coach, because they discovered that he could not be trusted. He was perceived to be all about himself. He was perceived as an "affirmative action baby" but didn't recognize his blessings and his responsibility to lift up others who resembled him. A few names given to black people like this are "Uncle Tom," "Sellout," or "Oreo."

Earl and I were now both experiencing a familiar situation at Northwestern State—just as I had as a player at Northeast Louisiana and Ouachita Baptist. When I thought back to my high school experience, I realized that it, too, was consistent with Dr. Lapchick's research. Coach Willie Tate was the only black man on my high school's football coaching staff. But there was one difference: Coach Tate was not a token. He was the offensive line coach who had real responsibilities. Both black and white kids loved him. I would later discover how rare he was. My research revealed that black offensive line coaches employed at predominantly white high schools and colleges are few and far between.

At my first American Football Coaches Association convention, held in January of 1989 at Nashville, Earl introduced me to Larry Brinson. At the time, he was the only black coach on the staff of Arkansas Razorback head coach Ken Hatfield. Later that spring, Hatfield hired another black assistant coach, Richard Wilson, and, for the first time in the history of the program, there were two full-time black coaches. Additionally, Brinson recommended to Coach Hatfield that I should be hired as a graduate assistant. Coach Hatfield offered me the position. I knew it was the move to make. Arkansas was a major school in a major conference and had just won the 1988 Southwest Conference football championship. Plus, I would also be moving back to my home state that I loved dearly.

Unbeknownst to me, the new job would also propel my education in the racial dynamics of college football to new levels, at warp speed. Brinson and Wilson were truly mentors to me. I loved being around them. They were an awesome support system for a young, eager coach. But their mentoring was just part of the learning process for me in Fayetteville. As an athlete, I had always found equality on the field based on talent. As a soldier, I had seen how the military tried to eliminate racial barriers. But in my chosen profession of coaching football, too much was still not equal. And at Arkansas, my first true look at a top-tier major college football program, my eyes would be opened even wider.

CHAPTER THREE
SCOREBOARD WATCHING

Even though I grew up in Arkansas, I only attended one Razorback football game as a youngster. My uncle and dad took me to the game when I was in junior high. I remember feeling so special, because we were going to watch the Hogs. It wasn't a common thing at my house. My dad's boss gave him the tickets. Looming above us when we arrived, Little Rock's War Memorial Stadium seemed to be the biggest thing in the world.

What an experience! The tailgating, the huge crowd, the rows and rows of seats, the marching band forming the big *A* at the fifty yard line, the noise, the whole package. I had watched some Arkansas games on television, but to actually be there in person was both a thrill and a defining experience. Every big college football fan knows what I mean.

It also explains why, in 1989, I found Head Coach Ken Hatfield's invitation to become a graduate assistant coach to be irresistible. Just as University of Arkansas fans are famous for their "hog-calling" cheer, I felt that I was being called to Fayetteville because I had something to offer the biggest school in my home state.

From Northwestern State University, a Division 1AA where I'd been working, I was moving up to big-time football—the top tier of college football for a team that was consistently ranked in the country's top 20. I knew that the jump from one level to the other was a huge one. The budget, the resources, and the possibilities were so much greater at Arkansas—I totally understood that.

What I could not have understood, however, was that the next twelve years of my career would provide a perfect vantage point for me to continue my study of the dynamics of minority coaches and college football. It was an interest that began to blossom a few months before I moved to Fayetteville.

In January of 1989, I attended the American Football Coaches Association convention in Nashville. Even as a twenty-four-year-old neophyte, I knew the convention was where you went to get a job—or find a better one. Earl had given it to me straight—that the AFCA conference sessions could be helpful and important. But the real action was in the hotel lobby. That's where everyone gathered to make contacts and exchange gossip. It's kind of a "walking want-ads" summit. Everyone there hopes to buttonhole a head coach about a job or at least get on the radar for future employment opportunities.

If the head coach isn't accessible, the offensive or defensive coordinator will do. That's why head coaches are often swarmed by eager young coaches looking for jobs. For that reason, a lot of head coaches and coordinators avoid the hotel lobby. And the eager young assistants trying to break into the profession or get a better coaching job are never found anywhere else.

I can still remember that 1989 convention as if it were yesterday. Splitting the gas charges, Earl and I rode up to Nashville together in my 1982 black Toyota Supra. Since Northwestern State didn't provide any expense money, Earl and I ended up sleeping on the floor in Coach Brinson's hotel room at the Opryland Hotel. Rather than eating filet mignon with the big guys, we were scraping by on the discount buffet.

Swept up in all the excitement, we spent a lot of time in the hotel's immense lobby. That's where I began learning how both black and white coaches "cheesed" their way up the coaches' ladder. I would soon discover that black coaches who perfected the art of "cheesing" were more likely to get jobs at predominantly white colleges and universities.

During that convention, I recall standing in the lobby with some other African American assistants from around the country when David Lee, who had just been named head coach at Texas-El Paso, strolled past us. I mentioned to my friends that I might want to speak with Lee about working for him. Lee was white, which was the case with virtually every Division I head coach in January of 1989. But he had been the quarterback coach at the University of Arkansas. That meant Lee and I both had Arkansas ties.

One of my new lobby buddies interrupted my wishful thinking about Lee, saying, "Don't bother talking to him. He's already hired his one black coach."

"Is there some law that says he can't hire two?" I asked.

"You haven't been around long, have you, brother?" my lobby buddy retorted. He then explained that the hiring of one black assistant coach on each staff was "situation normal" at the college level, i.e., unofficial "policy."

Sadly, I discovered that my lobby buddy was right. I also quickly learned that many people are reluctant to address the situation head-on with open minds, because it made them uncomfortable. To this day, the issue only surfaces as a discussion topic during what I call the "hurricane hiring season" in late November and early December. That's when coaches are hired and fired at a dizzying pace, usually without an identifiable process for qualified candidates of any race. Universities and athletic directors often keep the process quick, restricted, and secret. After a flurry of attention given to the lack of minority hiring, the process fades at the end of the "hurricane season."

As I moved into my graduate assistant job at Arkansas, I began to keep an informal tab on minority hiring in my profession. This would later develop into a formal study and my doctoral dissertation. People say I am obsessed with charts and graphs. They're right. But it's only because the charts I assembled during my years of doctoral research were so amazing. If there is strength in numbers, what does it say when the number of black head coaches and coordinators remains so miniscule? Are those raw facts meaningless?

The answer: It depends on whom you ask. Some people don't think those raw facts are as important as I do. Many don't see the point of keeping such detailed records on the progress of minority coaches. Some disdain the practice as "scoreboard watching" and say it's wrong to put too much emphasis on the numbers. I have heard people say that when it comes to hiring a head coach or a coordinator, each hire is an individual situation with unique circumstances. Here's what I don't think those people realize: Each of those numbers is indeed a unique case. But collectively, they are very significant.

Let's say you do want to go the individual route, though. That's no problem, because each individual number in my charts and graphs also represents a real person with a story. And each of those stories, if examined closely, provides a clue about why the numbers are what they are.

My own story is an excellent example. In 1989, my first summer of preseason practice with the Razorbacks, I served as the graduate assistant for Jack Crowe, the offensive coordinator and quarterback coach. We worked well together, and I absorbed a lot of knowledge from him. He told me that when the season began I would be with him in the upstairs coaching booth, giving him any help he needed as the game progressed. Because I knew that would be a terrific learning experience, I was really looking forward to it.

The sidelines at a college football game can be a very exciting place but can also be very hectic. Upstairs in the press box, where Crowe called the plays, it was a more clinical environment. One of the best in the business, Crowe had been a successful play-caller at Clemson, where his teams won the ACC title each of his three years as offensive coordinator and quarterback coach. I knew that I would soak up some serious Xs-and-Os knowledge by spending those games at his side.

Then, *poof!* Just like that, my balloon was punctured. John Bland, a former Arkansas quarterback whose eligibility had expired, came on board as a student assistant working with the offensive staff. I liked Bland. He was a cool guy, and we got along great. I figured that, just like me, Bland was there to help us win and gain as much football knowledge as possible. So imagine my surprise when one day in a staff meeting, Crowe suddenly announced that he would be joined by Bland—not me—in the coaches' booth during games. No mention of me or of what I had been promised. No explanation of what my new or different role might be. With my stomach churning, I didn't say a word. But I was dejected and stunned.

For the next several days, I stewed. At night, I tossed and turned. As the only black graduate assistant, I naturally wondered if my race had anything to do with Crowe's decision. This is what doesn't register with many white people: If you are black, race is usually the first thing you think about when a decision such as Crowe's affects your life. That's especially true if the person making the decision doesn't take the time to provide a good reason—or any reason—for the choice. I had been given an empty vessel to fill up with my own possible explanations. I didn't know Crowe very well, but I knew the history of discrimination and remembered the stories the lobby coaches had told me at the coaches' convention. Those thoughts filled my empty vessel.

After several of those sleepless nights, with the season fast approaching, I confronted Crowe. Before I spoke to him, I thought very carefully about what I wanted to say. I rehearsed it in my mind. After working up the courage to ask him about the situation, I went to his office one morning before our staff meetings and reminded him of my original coaches' booth assignment. I asked him if I'd done something wrong, something that made him think that I should not be up there with him on Saturdays. I told Crowe that I felt as if he had demoted me before our team had played a single game of the 1989 season.

Crowe listened carefully. I don't think he had realized that his choice—which was not a big deal to him—had affected me so profoundly. After complimenting me on being very professional in the way I had addressed the issue, he acknowledged that I was indeed a graduate assistant coach and therefore one rung up the ladder from Bland, who was a student assistant. Based on our conversation, Crowe said he would return me to my original post in the coaches' booth with him, and Bland would be on the sidelines during games.

The incident taught me something that probably applies to all coaches, but I think it especially matters when you're a coach of color. Minority coaches are too often stereotyped as being less capable and less willing to rock the boat, because the last thing they want is to be perceived as having chips on their shoulders.

The lesson I took away from my meeting with Crowe was this: You need to speak up and be counted, or you will allow yourself to be marginalized. Over the years, however, I learned to be strategic in picking battles related to race. I learned not to waste my time trying to change the racial attitudes of people who were ignorant. Because Crowe was very intelligent, I'm glad I decided to confront him. It was a liberating experience. From that point forward, I believe Crowe's respect for me increased, and we developed an excellent working relationship. African American coaches need mentors such as Jack Crowe.

The rest of that season was a dream for the Arkansas program. We won the Southwest Conference championship and played Tennessee in the Cotton Bowl. I tried to be the best possible graduate assistant for Crowe, doing whatever he asked. I ran off copies of game plans for him, brewed his coffee, picked up his laundry, did computer analyses of our opponents, and helped prepare the defensive scout team that worked against our offense.

In our staff meetings, though, I did notice an interesting dynamic. That season, we had two full-time black assistants at Arkansas. Brinson, whose floor I had used as a bed at the AFCA convention, was the running backs' coach. Richard Wilson was the receivers' coach. These guys looked after me as if I were their little brother. Just like Crowe, they were role models for me. I thought it was great that Coach Hatfield was progressive enough to employ two minority coaches at a time when most Division I programs had only one—and some had none.

Yet even though Brinson and Wilson were coaching the players who would be scoring most of our team's points, my perception was that the two African American voices in the meeting room were not consulted much when it came to strategy and planning. I made a mental note of this. At the time I didn't feel comfortable discussing this with anyone. But my antennae were up. And when my old boss at Northwestern State University called to offer me a job as his quarterbacks' and wide receivers' coach after the 1989 season, I accepted and vowed that I would be more forceful in offering my input when it came to game plans.

A funny thing happened in the summer of 1990, though, after I took the Northwestern State job. I ran into Crowe at a coaching clinic in West Texas, and he called me up to his hotel room. He had been elevated to Arkansas' head coaching job after Hatfield made an unexpected move to Clemson. In the hotel room, he told me that a volunteer assistant coach had left Arkansas and offered me an opportunity: I could replace the volunteer assistant coach and earn a salary of $11,000 per year, plus room and board. The catch was, I would have to move into the Arkansas athletic dormitory, where I would live in a two-bedroom apartment and serve as a counselor as well as a coach.

I immediately accepted. I was making nearly $30,000 annually at Northwestern State, but I knew that Arkansas would be a better launching pad for the career I sought. I packed up and rolled back into Fayetteville with a U-Haul and my wife, Cynthia. She was excited to be moving back to our home state. We had been married only eighteen months, but she was already used to the crazy twists and turns of coaching life. As a graduate assistant at Northwestern State, she kept me company on the post-midnight, three-hour drives across Louisiana to exchange game films with our next opponent. Cynthia was always there for me, looking beautiful and willing to do whatever was necessary for us to squeeze in some personal time during the most hectic months of the year.

What she didn't see coming—and I didn't either—was a call to duty from Uncle Sam. When I made my ROTC commitment back at Ouachita Baptist, it required that I spend eight years on reserve duty. Soon after moving back to Fayetteville, just before the 1990 season, I woke up one morning to find that Saddam Hussein had invaded Kuwait. In less than six weeks, I was on a plane with my US Army Reserve unit to Daharan, Saudi Arabia. As a first lieutenant transportation officer, I coordinated trucks and the delivery of rations and supplies at a desert base south of the Kuwait border. I'm proud of the fact that I was awarded a Bronze Star for the many sleepless nights I spent keeping the troops supplied and the trucks moving during Desert Storm—which was good practice for the work routine I would have to follow as a coach.

Luckily, after seven months I returned intact to Cynthia and Fayetteville, where, on my first night back, Coach Crowe and his staff took us out to dinner and presented us a certificate for a weekend getaway at a beautiful Northern Arkansas resort. Then it was back to the dorm. When I had been in Saudi Arabia, bunking down in a tent, I would hear sirens for incoming missile alerts and realize how fragile life really was. During sandstorms, I would retreat to my quarters to shield my mouth and eyes from the coarse blowing muck. I vowed that if I returned safely to Arkansas, I would try to take advantage of the opportunity to improve myself in every area. Within weeks of returning, I applied to the Arkansas graduate school and was accepted into the doctoral program.

From the start, there was no question about what my doctoral dissertation topic would be. At Northwestern State, I had written my master's degree research project about employment opportunities for black and white college football coaches, and the perceptions those coaches held about those opportunities. My doctoral dissertation was going to be an extension of that subject, except that I wanted to concentrate more on the African American college football coaching experience. Why? As I looked around, I discovered to my surprise that no one had documented the experiences of black football coaches in an academic way—especially at the level of assistant coaches and coordinators, where the next head coaches are often found.

My decision to do that dissertation changed my life. It would lead to, literally, a new horizon of learning for me and my eventual status as an "expert" in the field. Knowing the topic would be controversial, I didn't publicize what I was researching or discuss it with my boss.

My research would show that in college football, many minority coaches with brilliant football minds were not getting the chances their qualifications merited. College administrators seemed to have certain perceptions about African American coaches and their abilities. Sometimes those perceptions were a benign lack of awareness, the same sort of thing I had gone through with Jack Crowe when I was a graduate assistant. Sometimes it involved a tendency to hire one minority coach and declare that the affirmative action "problem" was solved. And sometimes, the roadblocks were even more subtle than that.

When I came back to Arkansas as a full-time coach in 1992 after Jack Crowe had been named head coach, for example, I noticed that when he was addressing issues involving race, he would speak directly and exclusively to Ken Rucker, the oldest African American assistant on the staff. Rucker was a mentor of mine. I respected him greatly. But it bothered me that Crowe didn't seem to care about my perspective too. I felt comfortable talking with Crowe about this because of our close relationship. I knew he wouldn't be offended if

I brought it up. So during my performance review later that summer, I pointed out that just because Rucker and I were both African American, it didn't mean we always had the same thoughts and ideas about everything.

Since I was twenty-eight years old, I was closer in age to the student-athletes and had been living in the dormitory with them. Given my more youthful outlook, I thought my observations would also be helpful to Crowe and would provide a different viewpoint than Rucker's. It didn't mean Crowe had to agree with either one of us. I merely thought he should hear both of us, the same way that he would listen to more than one white coach on various discussion topics.

Again, Crowe was very receptive and thanked me for bringing it to his attention. Born in Alabama, he had coached at Auburn and Clemson. As was common at that time, the staffs on which he worked often employed just one African American coach. My guess is that Crowe, as with many of his white peers, was not used to hearing multiple viewpoints from minority coaches. Now recognizing the need to be more sensitive, from that point forward he made sure to seek out my opinion when a racial issue—or any issue on which he needed input—arose.

One of the roots of the problem, as I would learn through my research, was that few African Americans had the same sort of comfortable relationships with their white colleagues. Plenty of young black coaches were convinced they were as invisible, as I'd felt when Crowe had reversed his promise to me about being in the coaching booth with him. I must admit, I don't know if those black football coaches attempted to diplomatically address their employment issues or concerns with their white superiors as I tried to do. But I do know that many black coaches felt the same frustration I had.

I developed my dissertation methodology by adapting the techniques of corporate research regarding opportunities for African Americans. I formulated a questionnaire to send to every African American football coach at the Division I level. There was no easy place, no directory or phone book, to find them all. I asked Rick Schaeffer, the Arkansas sports information director, to order football media guides for all 108 Division I schools. I told him I wanted to check out how other schools were publicizing and marketing their football teams to prospective recruits, which was true. But I also knew that in those media guides, there would be pictures of every assistant coach. So I went through each guide, checking out the faces and writing down the names and addresses of every minority coach in each book. During the 1995 football season, I sent out 219 surveys—the entire population of African American football coaches. Remarkably, 175 of them were returned. That's roughly 80 percent, an exceptional response for such a survey. Clearly, these guys wanted their voices heard.

The survey was very detailed. I asked respondents for their personal résumés in a way that I could conduct an objective analysis. I wanted to see if their experience and background fit some sort of profile, and if so, what that profile was. For instance, I discovered that the largest percentage of the coaches were age thirty-five to thirty-nine, that 71 percent of them were married, that nearly 37 percent had a master's degree, and that 83 percent had attended a public college or university. I also discovered that 93 percent had played football at predominately white institutions and only 6 percent had played at historically black colleges.

The other percentages were also interesting. I discovered that 67 percent had played at the Division I level and nearly 70 percent had received athletic honors—all-conference, all-American, or something similar. Beyond that, 52 percent of the African American coaches had signed a professional football contract with the NFL or Canadian Football League, and 30 percent had been on a pro football roster. And not surprisingly, 71 percent of the African American coaches had worked as graduate assistants at Division I schools.

In the other part of the survey, I asked the respondents fifty-seven questions. I wanted their perceptions of the work environment and their feelings about employment opportunities. Most of these questions were adapted from similar studies in the corporate sector. In addition, while developing the survey, I was able to utilize my coaching experiences as they related to race. I incorporated some of the anecdotes I'd heard at the coaches' convention and worked up questions to see if those anecdotes were isolated or part of a pattern. I wanted to quantify the perception of employment barriers. Did those perceptions differ by age? By coaching position? By region of the country?

When the answers came back, there were few surprises. A lot of people had gone through the same experiences I had—or, in the case of older coaches, had endured even more years of uncomfortable treatment. When I assembled the data, my conclusions were not difficult to reach.

- Black football coaches had not shared the same opportunities as black student-athletes, who in 1995 were receiving 51 percent of all football scholarships at Division I universities. Because of the pressure to win, these scholarships were clearly issued on merit, based on athletic ability. Few, if any, of these scholarships were awarded based on the color of the students' skin.

- When athletic ability and skill are the most important factors in football success, African Americans tend to find many doors of opportunity open for them. Not so with African American coaches. In my survey, most of them said they felt those doors were still shut. Why? The survey respondents thought stereotypes still existed about African American coaches, and the evaluation process for hiring them was purely subjective. In other words, you couldn't run a forty-yard dash to prove you were a great coach. You had to convince a school committee or school president on an individual and subjective basis. The test isn't true or false. It becomes an essay. And who decides what is right or wrong in essays? It's the teacher. In the case of football coaches, it's the athletic directors, head coaches, boosters, and often the university president.

- My survey also indicated that African American coaches had been stratified into non-central coaching positions—in other words, the African Americans weren't getting many jobs as offensive or defensive coordinators or as assistant head coaches or even as offensive line coaches, regarded as strategy-intensive positions that need to be manned by a critical thinker.

  Because there were so few African American coaches in those non-central positions, they were seldom considered for head coaching jobs. In the profession, serving as a coordinator is usually a prerequisite to becoming a head coach. A person who is "stuck" in lesser coaching responsibilities may develop a stigma of not possessing the qualities that are necessary to lead a football program.

- African American coaches believed that many white athletic administrators became overly defensive when confronted with equal opportunity issues. Administrators were quick to defend their decisions and claimed they hired the best coaches, regardless of color. Of course, this didn't explain why all those years when Eddie Robinson was winning championships as head coach at Grambling State and sending dozens of players to the NFL, no major school offered him a job.

- African American coaches thought that traits such as "competence" and "leadership" were not qualities that white administrators frequently associated with black coaches.

- The black coaches reported feelings similar to those expressed in a study conducted by the Center for Creative Leadership, a North Carolina training institute for corporate managers. The CCL found in a survey that for black professionals in majority white organizations, success was linked far more to building and maintaining relationships than it was for white professionals.

  One black professional noted that his success was related directly to an ability to put his white colleagues at ease in the workplace. In my survey, 86 percent of the respondents agreed, saying that to obtain employment in the profession, it was necessary to make their potential white employer feel comfortable. This sounds obvious, doesn't it? But shouldn't football acumen have something to do with it as well? I am sure to some extent it does. But my studies revealed there is a difference between what's expected for black coaches and white coaches. This leads to both black and white coaches being pigeonholed in their coaching assignments.

- By an overwhelming margin, African American football coaches also believed their success with white employers was based more on the coaches' perceived ability to recruit black student-athletes from inner-city neighborhoods rather than the ability to "coach." The black coaches also perceived they were responsible for serving as father figures to many of the black student-athletes.

- Like other middle-class African Americans employed in predominantly white organizations, black football coaches thought they were routinely viewed by white colleagues as examples of equal opportunity in the workplace. However, both African Americans in the corporate world and African Americans in the coaching world identified similar employment-related barriers—which led them to believe they were not truly accepted as equals by many of their white colleagues.

- Black football coaches felt that because of racial stereotyping, they were compelled to work constantly to overcome negative perceptions that they were not capable of leading or managing a major college program—no matter what their coaching accomplishments or achievements had been in the past.

- By a significant majority, 90 percent of African American coaches believed that a "diversity plan to increase the number of black coaches is necessary." They strongly felt that most athletic directors and college administrators hired head football coaches without even considering minority candidates.

It took me a year to collect the data and another year to write the dissertation, all of this while coaching full-time. But I never grew tired of the project, because I knew that the dissertation's conclusions had everything to do with how I could take care of my family in the future. The most fascinating thing about the process was that as I was chronicling the perceptions of African American football coaches from around the nation, I continued to wake up every day in Fayetteville and feel as if I were a lab experiment myself.

It was an eventful time to be an assistant coach for the Arkansas Razorbacks. We had won one Southeastern Conference western division championship in 1995, and then the following two years there were numerous staff changes, including head coach Danny Ford. My status as one of the few African American assistant coaches in school history made the time even more eventful. By my count, I was the fifth African American hired as a full-time Razorbacks assistant coach. I felt honored. But God's inspired vision within my spirit would not allow me to become complacent.

As an assistant secondary coach, I had become a full-time member of the Razorbacks' staff in 1992. But after the season opener—a stunning upset loss to The Citadel—Coach Crowe was fired. Crowe walked into our staff meeting at 1 p.m. the next day and told us he had been dismissed. Bill Gray, the associate athletic director, then herded us into the coaches' locker room and told us we couldn't go anywhere. They didn't want us to contact anyone until after Crowe's firing had been officially announced. At that moment, sitting in that small, windowless room after the rug had been pulled out from under us, I knew for sure I would finish my doctorate. What a crazy business. I wanted to make sure I had other options if I needed them.

Later that afternoon, after we coaches were "released" from our lockup, defensive coordinator Joe Kines was promoted to the head coaching job for the rest of the season. I certainly had no problem with that decision, because I had enjoyed working with Kines on the defensive side of the ball. But to give him help with the offense, the school hired Danny Ford, the former head coach at Clemson. Winning a national championship there in 1981, he had also developed a reputation as a backslapper with a single-minded approach to the game. He had played football for Paul "Bear" Bryant and had received a big break at age thirty when Clemson named him the Tigers' head coach. He compiled a 96-29-4 record there and won three Atlantic Coast Conference championships. But his program was put on NCAA probation at one point and in 1990, Ford resigned after falling out of favor with the Clemson administration. After arriving at Arkansas, he quickly made his presence felt. He had a dominating personality.

Frank Broyles is a living legend in Arkansas. He was the Razorbacks' head football coach from 1958-1976 and won a national championship in 1964, after which he could do no wrong in the eyes of most state residents. He also served as Arkansas' athletics director from 1973-2007. The school's athletic department building is named after him. Broyles did—and does—have a great business mind as well. He perceived that he needed a coach with a winning reputation to help the Razorbacks restore their winning tradition and sell some tickets. Consequently, Broyles made a decision to name Ford the permanent head coach, after the conclusion of the 1992 season.

Reassigned to the position of defensive coordinator, Kines apparently received a "crackback" block from Ford, who claimed that he only became interested in the job when it was apparent that Kines wouldn't get it. Kines was very close to being named the permanent head coach after we upset Tennessee in week six of the 1992 season. The Vols were undefeated at the time, and we played a great game. But after SMU beat us at home and we stumbled to a 3-8 finish, Broyles decided that Kines could not continue as head coach. I guess when Coach Broyles decided that he couldn't sell tickets with Kines leading the program, he called Ford in his office and asked him if he would be interested in replacing Kines. In January of 1993, Ford was hired as Arkansas's new head coach.

Although I learned a lot and grew in many positive ways while working for Coach Ford, the next five years were a living hell. I can remember crying after one meeting with him. Here I was, a grown man who had fought for our country in Desert Shield and Storm, and I felt more tension walking into Coach Ford's office than I did while in the desert when the Scud missiles alert sirens were sounded. I am confident that things didn't turn out the way Coach Broyles had envisioned by turning the program over to Coach Ford, who was particularly insensitive when it came to racial matters.

Ford frequently referred to the black guys as "boys" and didn't understand why they would be offended. He would tell racially tinged jokes in front of me. When I mentioned that I wanted to attend the BCA (Black Coaches Association) meeting in Atlanta, Ford didn't even know what the BCA was.

"The BCA…what kind of church meeting is that?" he asked.

Is it any wonder that, by the start of our 1993 season, I was the lone black assistant football coach at Arkansas? Ken Rucker, the only other African American coach, had left for Baylor University. My singular status was painfully obvious—especially to the black players, black recruits and their families, and black fans, but Ford didn't seem to care. Fixated on results, not people skills, he told me after the 1992 season that if I could sign up two great high school defensive linemen that he coveted as recruits, I would receive a salary bonus. I signed both.

I'm still waiting for the bonus.

Still, we finished with a 5-5-1 record in 1993, a noticeable improvement over the previous year. But in a postseason meeting with Ford, I mustered up enough courage to tell him we needed a more diverse staff. Some of the African American kids on the team and some high school recruits perceived me as a "token." I brought to his attention a recent recruiting experience I'd had at Kimball High School in south Dallas, where I was trying to sign Delon Washington, the top-ranked running back in the state of Texas, who had offers from nearly every school in the country. I thought we might have an inside track on him, because my sister-in-law, a University of Arkansas graduate, worked at Kimball High.

During my recruiting visit to the high school, however, Delon told me that he had been advised by his coach not to consider schools that only employed one black coach, because that meant the black coach was probably just a "token." I was shocked, but I understood. Student-athletes in urban America are almost always coached by black coaches. Many of them are concerned that their players, if they attend a predominantly white university, will find the adjustment to be jarring and difficult. One way to ease that difficulty is to have African American coaches who can help guide the black athletes through the adjustment. In Washington's case, this was just his head coach's way of looking out for his player's best interests.

I shared this story with Ford as an example of why our staff's diversity was so critical to our recruiting efforts. I also mentioned our rural location and explained why diversity was very important for a university in Northwest Arkansas, especially when it came to recruiting black athletes from urban communities. Schools with whom we were competing for players—Georgia Tech, USC, Miami, and others—were located in larger and more diverse communities, which made it easier for them to recruit minority athletes. Initially, however, Ford wasn't buying it.

Trying to think of other relatively isolated schools that had successful football programs, he asked, "Why can't we recruit like Nebraska? They don't have many black coaches, do they? How many black coaches do they have?"

Naturally, because of my research, I knew the answer off the top of my head.

"Three," I replied. "Nebraska has three African American assistant coaches."

"Really?" asked Ford, seemingly surprised.

Within a few months, he had hired David Mitchell, an African American from Syracuse, as our running backs' coach. I had recruited and basically pleaded with David to take the job and was so happy when he did. I thought he could help us improve our recruiting, teach our runners great technique, and strengthen our program. With David on the Arkansas staff, a new and different dynamic arose. David and I hung out together, but it was more a cultural affinity than a racial one. We attended the same church and listened to a lot of the same music. He also shared many coaching stories with me. David knew a lot about being the only minority on a coaching staff, because he'd been in the same situation at Arkansas State. A seasoned veteran of the college football wars, he had a great knowledge of the running game. David, like me, knew the art of "cheesing" very well.

Once when I was visiting David in his office, a white athletic administrator looked in and asked: "What are you guys plotting to do?"

Because of the racial climate fostered by Coach Ford, I had grown defensive, and I instantly replied without thinking. "We're plotting the same thing you plot when you go into one of the white coach's offices," I said, subtly pointing out how white coaches often "clustered" in each others' offices but were never perceived to be plotting anything. The administrator "cheesed" and forced a laugh. So did I. The guy was attempting to be funny, I realized. But I also knew that the root of the joke had racial implications. Coach Ford had made me very sensitive to his insensitivity.

For example, in one staff meeting, we were talking about our athletic department's health care plan. It wasn't top tier. One coach remarked that he'd had better benefits at a previous stop. I mentioned how it could be a tough situation for me, because I had three people who needed the plan.

"You have three dependents?" one coach asked.

"No, I mean myself, my wife, and daughter," I said.

"Yeah, he's like all the black guys," Ford chimed in. "He's got babies all over the place."

I hate to say it, but I bit my tongue. Still a young coach, I didn't want to lose my job. I also hate to admit that I did the same thing on another occasion when Ford and the rest of our Arkansas staff traveled on a private plane to Pine Bluff, about two hundred miles southeast of Fayetteville. The occasion was a fish fry with the Razorback Booster Club. At the event, I ran into my old pal, Earl Buckingham, who was coaching at Arkansas-Pine Bluff, our sister university. Its coaching staff had been invited to attend the event. Earl and I spent a lot of time together at the party, laughing and talking about old times. As you can imagine, because I was delighted to see Earl and the other black football coaches on his team's staff, I was able to turn off my "cheese" machine.

Coach Ford, meanwhile, was also enjoying himself. He was drinking beer, slapping boosters on the back and being his usual caustic self. But he must have noticed how I spent the evening. As we climbed back in the car to return to the airport, in front of all the other coaches he looked at me, chuckled and said, "Fitz, when you get around black people, you just don't know how to act."

Am I saying that racism is this overt on every college coaching staff? Absolutely not. But the racism that so frequently lurks beneath the surface isn't necessarily less harmful than the type Ford routinely displayed.

I really didn't know what he meant. I was never a schmoozer at those functions, no matter the racial background of the crowd. I had never consumed an ounce of alcohol at a booster event and was very sensitive about being perceived as a professional for possible future employment opportunities. In Ford, I saw just the opposite. I saw a man whose true feelings surfaced after drinking several beers. Still, I held my tongue once more. I'm a forgiving guy. But over and over the same remarks kept popping up. Ford even asked me to turn down an invitation to participate in the NFL's minority coaching program that included a trip to the Tampa Bay Buccaneers training camp. Instead, Ford thought I should be out glad-handing high school coaches at local clinics, something I was already doing plenty of.

Finally, following the 1994 season in which we won just four games, I knew that I could no longer work for Coach Ford. I walked into his office and told him I was planning to resign. I boldly but respectfully explained to him that I didn't enjoy being around him and I wasn't going to continue suffering through his concept of racial "humor."

Had it not been for Joe Kines, who was still on the Arkansas staff after being replaced as head coach by Ford, I would have resigned in the summer of 1993. This is one reason why I credit Kines for having the most impact on my coaching career. He kept me from walking out on Arkansas. "I am not going to let you quit," Kines said. "You have too much to offer these young men."

More importantly, Kines understood my pain as it related to Ford. Every time Ford made those racial jokes in my presence, Kines told me he would cringe inside. I think Kines knew that Ford was killing me emotionally. That's why Kines did all he could to pick me up on a daily basis. I was really a dead man walking. I hated going to work and felt like a $50,000-per-year slave.

To Ford's credit, after I walked into his office and calmly told him of my intention to leave, he finally seemed to listen. He apologized for his previous remarks, and said he would make an effort to be less caustic and racially insensitive. In the end, I did decide to stay—not so much because of Ford's promises, but because so many of the student-athletes said I was one of the main reasons they had come to Arkansas. I couldn't think of leaving them. Because it would have been deceiving them, I couldn't have lived with that. Also, I was just starting the dissertation process, the final step in gaining my doctoral degree. Therefore, even though I had a good job offer to become the assistant head coach at the US Naval Academy in the spring of 1995, I didn't make the move. Although I had accepted the position, I couldn't go through with it. I truly loved so many people at Arkansas. I was—and still remain—a Razorback loyalist.

After completing the dissertation in the spring of 1997, I defended it and obtained my doctorate in May of that year. Eager to get reactions after it was published, I remember telling people, "Nobody has ever done this kind of research about African American coaches or college football. It's cutting edge."

As an educator and a coach, I assumed that a lot of people would want to examine the dissertation and use it as a tool. Katie Hill, who was then serving as senior associate athletics director at Arkansas, embraced my study. Thinking it would help promote employment opportunities for coaches of color, she attended my dissertation defense and was always supportive of my career. But I also remember

Katie telling me that it is easier to change an organization from the inside than from the outside. In other words, I shouldn't become too strident in my criticism of the college athletic establishment.

My intent wasn't—and isn't—to be critical of anyone. I merely wanted people to see my facts and figures. I sent my study to the NCAA and heard very little back from the organization. I made speeches to various groups about the topic. I pointed out that football is such a huge part of the college culture—and that at any given school, the largest gathering of students is usually at a football game. So this wasn't just a sports issue. It was also a societal issue.

In the fall of 1997, I asked the *NCAA News* if I could write an article for the publication to report my study results. The editors gave me the thumbs up, and my piece appeared in the publication that winter and received some good reaction. Whenever I spoke about the issue, people were interested and polite. Nobody contested my information, but no one took any action to fix the problem. At the same time, the NFL was developing its policy about the hiring process to make sure minority candidates would be considered for every open head coaching position.

The overall lack of response to my efforts, however, was disappointing. Maybe I was naïve to think that the NCAA or the college presidents of America would see the figures in my dissertation and, at the very least, commission a study of their own to verify and expand upon my data. I thought the organization might seriously examine the representation of minority coaches at all levels of the college game. Of course, I certainly thought that by 2011, college football would have a systematic approach to ensure there would be a diverse interview pool for coaching vacancies. Why hasn't the NCAA created a standardized system of qualifications and experience for potential head coaches, to provide clear-cut objectives about what athletic directors were seeking? These are the questions for which I'm still searching for answers today.

How wrong could I have been? To this day, very few if any of those objectives or qualification standards have been defined. There are seminars to discuss the issue. The Black Coaches Association wields some influence when there's an opening. The NCAA also stages an annual seminar for promising young black coaches, to which I was frequently invited to speak. The NCAA spends a lot of money on these educational programs for black coaches.

But there is no organized program to prevent an athletic director at a large public university from hiring a new head coach just a few hours—or minutes—after the old one resigns or is fired, without the job "search" opening being offered to anyone else. This public university, because it is supported by taxpayer dollars from all races, might well have a very detailed hiring process for other high-profile positions on campus. Usually that process will involve interviewing a diverse field of candidates, but the same school's athletic department is allowed to ignore the policy completely.

If you were an eager young assistant coach who happened to be an African American or another minority, how would that set of circumstances make you feel? This is the question I ask when people say I'm making too big a deal of college football's race-based hiring practices: If that eager young assistant coach were your brother, and he deserved the opportunity to be a head football coach or offensive or defensive coordinator, would you want him to not get the job because his skin was the "wrong" color if he had all of the other qualifications? If it were your son, would you want his race to be the reason he wasn't given an equal shot at the position, although he was more qualified than many of the white candidates?

The mission of my dissertation was to study if minority coaches were getting a fair shake and to objectively examine evidence related to the situation. I soon grasped the reality that the dissertation was only the start of an even bigger project, just the opening kickoff. I also realized that year by year I needed to keep an eye on the coaching scoreboard in college football. So beginning in the spring of 1992, that's what I have been doing. And while progress has definitely been made, it's not much compared to other areas of our society—or even to other areas of football.

Might I ever stop counting those numbers because doing so will no longer be necessary? Might we ever get to the point where a white head coach can say he's found seven qualified coaches who happen to be black, then hire all of them as assistants without worrying about what boosters will say? I'd truly like to think so. In fact, I believe we can and will. But not in the immediate future, unless the college football establishment starts working faster and harder to make it happen. University presidents and athletic administrators may not have read my dissertation. I sure hope they read this book.

CHAPTER FOUR

THE PIONEERS AND COMMUNITY ROLE MODELS

I know some people believe I'm probably making too big of a deal about today's coaching inequities in college football. But I cannot apologize for telling the truth—and feel that it is necessary to do so. Why? Because I know there are still people in America who have the same mind-set as the late Al Campanis.

Campanis was the general manager of the Los Angeles Dodgers baseball team in 1987 when he agreed to an interview with Ted Koppel on his *Nightline* show. The occasion was the fortieth anniversary of Jackie Robinson's first major league game. Koppel, however, began asking Campanis why, at the time, there were so few black baseball managers and zero general managers. Campanis replied that African Americans "may not have some of the necessities to be, let's say, a field manager, or, perhaps, a general manager."

Within weeks of the interview, Campanis was fired. The following year, in another interview, he tried to clarify that he was referring to the lack of African Americans with experience in these areas, rather than their innate abilities.

God bless his soul, but Campanis was still wrong. What lack of "experience" did he mean? When the Negro Leagues folded in the late 1940s, the men who managed those teams did not mysteriously vanish into thin air. They were more than available to manage in the major leagues. They certainly had the experience and "the necessities." But no major league team wanted to give those gentlemen a job simply because they were not born white.

The Campanis episode gives a good example of the principle I often cite about how race dictates space—and how opportunity can dictate outcome. Leroy "Satchel" Paige is the best illustration. Paige was a Negro League pitching phenomenon whose exploits seemed mystical until they were actually witnessed. Joe DiMaggio and Paige had the opportunity to square off on a Sunday afternoon in January of 1936 at the Oaks Ball Park in Emeryville, California.

Paige was performing as part of a barnstorming tour with a group of other black players and arrived for his first Bay Area appearance with a seventeen-game winning streak. On the tour, he had outpitched such major league stars as Dizzy Dean and Schoolboy Rowe. Paige had also struck out the likes of Lou Gehrig, Charlie Gehringer, Hack Wilson, and Pepper Martin, all future Hall of Famers.

In Paige's biography, *Don't Look Back,* written by Mark Ribowsky in 2000, the 1936 duel in Emeryville was highlighted. DiMaggio was twenty-one years old and coming off an MVP season with the minor league San Francisco Seals in which he had led the Pacific Coast League with a .398 batting average.

"DiMaggio was there grinning to beat all," Paige was quoted as saying in the Ribowsky book. "I didn't hear all that he said, but I did hear him saying something like, 'Now I know I can make it with the Yankees, I finally got a hit off Ol' Satch.'" DiMaggio later called Paige the greatest pitcher he ever faced. Paige must have been special; it was reported that a Yankees scout at the game reportedly sent a telegram back to the home office that said: "DiMaggio everything we'd hoped he'd be: Hit Satch one for four."

Following the matchup, a *San Francisco Chronicle* reporter wrote, "If Satchel Paige had white skin, he would be worth $100,000 to any big league club that could afford to lay out the money." In comparison, Babe Ruth never made more than $80,000 for a season, and DiMaggio signed his rookie contract for just $8,500 a few weeks after the Bay Area exhibition.

Eddie Murphy, a writer for the *Oakland Tribune*, suggested it was perhaps time for baseball's color line to be erased. Eleven years later, Jackie Robinson finally received the opportunity to do what Satchel Paige should have been able to do more than a decade earlier. Skin color was the only reason that Paige did not receive an opportunity to pitch in the major leagues in his prime. And the same roadblock was there for African American pioneers in the collegiate coaching profession.

Yet even today, the Campanis-like argument that I often hear goes something like this: "Hiring more black head coaches in college football would be great, but you have to give it more time because there aren't enough qualified candidates." Incorrect. There are plenty of qualified candidates today. And there always have been. Just study the history books. Anyone who does that with an objective eye can quickly put to rest the myth about the shortage of experienced talent in the coaching pipeline. In fact, when you look at the big picture, the biggest disgrace in college football is not what's happening today.

It is true that many good minority candidates fail to even get interviews for head coaching jobs at schools in the Football Bowl Subdivision (the former Division 1A). That's not good. But at least a few of them do go through the interviewing process. And some of those coaches do get FBS head coaching jobs.

But what about the minority coaches of five or six decades ago? Until 1979, no African Americans were offered a chance to lead what was then called a Division 1A program. Zero. None. College football should forever be ashamed of that dismal fact. Believe me, before 1979, there were many African American and minority coaches who could have won conference championships at the FBS level, but they never even got to try. It is especially ironic that today, the Football Writers Association of America honors its college coach of the year with the Eddie Robinson Trophy. If there had been such an honor back in his day, Robinson never would have been able to win the award himself. No Division 1A school would have hired him.

Keep in mind that college football at historically black institutions has been played since 1892. And during all of those years, sports historians agree, there is no question about which man was the best coach at those schools. Robinson worked at Grambling for fifty-six years (1941-1997). He had forty-five winning seasons and either won or shared seventeen championships in the Southwestern Athletic Conference. Eight times, his teams were declared the mythical "black college football champions." Robinson did most of this while working with a tight budget and far fewer resources than the big-time schools. In the early years of his Grambling tenure, Robinson also had to coach men's and women's basketball and ran the physical education department.

Granted, many of the men coaching against him were in the same boat. But in games against his peers, Robinson dominated. While rolling up his 408 victories, he coached more than three hundred future professional players. Those three hundred-plus men did not spontaneously learn the skills necessary to play the game at such a high level. Robinson was teaching them those skills at Grambling.

"Nobody has done or ever will do what he has done for the game," Penn State coach Joe Paterno once said of Robinson.

I'll grant you this: If Robinson had been hired by a Division I school halfway through his tenure at Grambling, it's not likely he would have won 408 games—especially if he were coaching at a school with lesser resources. But he would have won games. A *lot* of games. And if he had been allowed to coach at Alabama or Ohio State or Oklahoma, I am convinced he would have won national championships. I don't even think that's arguable.

And Robinson was not the only minority coach from forty or fifty years ago who was capable enough to lead a big-time school. In fact, I have my own opinion about which man could have been the first great African American major college coach. His name was Fritz Pollard.

Pollard was an Ivy Leaguer. He attended Brown University in 1915 and became an All-American running back, leading his team to the 1916 Rose Bowl game. Brown lost to Washington State that day, but Pollard will always be remembered as the first African American to play in the Rose Bowl. After dropping out of school to serve in the US Army during World War I, Pollard wound up tutoring and coaching a student army training corps football team at Lincoln University, a small Pennsylvania school. In 1919, Pollard joined the American Professional Football Association, forerunner of today's National Football League. And that's where his story gets really interesting.

After playing one season for the Akron Indians at $200 per game, Pollard was briefly jobless when the Indians folded. But very quickly, Pollard signed up with the squad that replaced the Indians, the Akron Pros. He served as both a running back and "co-coach" for the Pros. Basically, Pollard called all the plays, because head coaches in those days were forced to sit on the bench and not move. Sending in plays from the sidelines was a totally foreign concept that wouldn't come to football for decades. Pollard later claimed that he and the Pros' quarterback, another former Brown player, installed the wide-open offense that resulted in the Akron Pros posting an undefeated season and winning the league title.

Pollard left the Pros in 1923 and went on to play with four other early NFL teams, using his coaching skills at some of those stops too. But the league gradually stopped signing African Americans as part of a "gentleman's agreement" to put only white players on the field. Pollard responded by organizing his own team comprised entirely of black players. The team was sometimes known as the Brown Bombers and other times as the Blackhawks. They played "home" games in New York and Chicago but also barnstormed to play exhibition games against NFL all-star teams with all-white rosters.

While records are sketchy, the Pollard teams won most of those exhibition games. His relatives, in fact, say that Pollard went 19-0 against the NFL stars. At his induction into the Pro Football Hall of Fame in 2005—the College Football Hall had welcomed Pollard in 1954—one of his grandsons spoke lovingly of his grandfather's innovations as a head coach. According to Steven Towns, Pollard was known for his unique formations and trick plays. In those barnstorming games, designed to entertain the big crowds who showed up, the Brown Bombers really let loose.

"As a matter of fact," Towns said, "my grandfather had to tone down his offense so that opponents would keep playing the Brown Bombers, because they were running up the scores."

As the NFL prospered, however, it grew harder and harder for Pollard to turn a profit with his team. So he left football and began a successful business career. He owned coal companies, operated a movie studio, published a weekly paper in New York, and received credit for founding the nation's first African American investment company.

It stands to reason, that a man as bright as Pollard would have made a great college football coaching candidate. He passed away in 1986, and as far as anyone knows, was never interviewed about that topic. But another of his grandsons, Fritz Pollard III, said in a 2004 interview with the *Boston Globe* that his grandpa would almost surely have loved to test his coaching prowess at Brown, his alma mater.

"He loved Brown," said Fritz Pollard III, who also attended the school. "When he came up to Rhode Island to receive an award in the state's Hall of Fame, he took me to Brown. I was about eleven then."

Of course, Brown University never hired Pollard. The school never even interviewed him for its head coaching job. Not that the school should be singled out. Dozens of other big-time football universities never gave Pollard an opportunity. And he's not the only African American coach that those schools could have hired.

Those schools could have hired Jake Gaither, who won six mythical black college championships at Florida A&M during his tenure. Gaither finished his coaching career with a .844 winning percentage before stepping down in 1969 after a thirty-six-year career at the school. One of his biggest fans was former Ohio State Coach Woody Hayes, who called Gaither an offensive genius for his use of the "split-line T" formation.

Those same schools could have hired:

- Earl Banks, who from 1960 to 1973 never had a losing season at Morgan State, a historically black institution. Banks said he patterned his teams after Vince Lombardi's Green Bay Packers, focusing on "fundamentals and tough football."

- "Big John" Merritt of Tennessee State, who never had a losing record in twenty- two seasons at the school beginning in 1952. He owned a graduate degree from the University of Kentucky. The main street running through Tennessee State's campus is named after him.

- Arnett "Ace" Mumford of Southern University, who won eleven Southwestern Athletic Conference championships and had an undefeated streak of forty-five games from 1947-1950. His former players say that some of Mumford's offensive innovations in the 1940s later showed up in the NFL and college football programs ten years later.

- Bill Willis, who after an All-American career as an Ohio State offensive tackle in 1942-1944, received no offers to play in the NFL—which during that time had an unwritten rule against signing black players. Willis instead took a job as head coach at Kentucky State University, another histori-cally black school. When Willis eventually realized that major college coaching jobs were never going to be open for him, he accepted Paul Brown's invitation to play for the Cleveland Browns of the new All-American Conference. Willis went on to become a Pro Football Hall of Fame tackle.

Yes, the major colleges could have hired any of these men as head coaches. But they didn't. I could give you eight or ten others who were nearly as qualified as the half dozen that I've mentioned. I could also talk about the other pioneer African American coaches who paved the way at smaller predominately white schools, such as Don Hudson, who became the first black coach at a predominately white school in 1971, tiny Macalester College in Minnesota—fol-lowed shortly by Ron Stratten at Portland State in 1972 and Cass Jackson at Oberlin College in 1973. I just trust that I have convinced you that if college administrators had really been looking for good minority coaching candidates in those days, the candidates were there—long before Wichita State made the bold move of hiring Willie Jefferies in 1979 and making him the first African American head coach at the Division 1A level.

Of course, if you've been a skeptic about this, you probably still are. You might say we will never know for sure if Gaither or Banks or Merritt would have succeeded at a Division 1A school. And you would be right. It's impossible to be one hundred percent accurate about any speculative statement such as that one.

However, I do know that the following statement is 100 percent correct: These men were denied the chance to prove you wrong. And again, this was solely due to their skin color. Robinson and Pollard, as both coaches and human beings, deserved a crack at challenging their white peers. I believe they would have accepted the challenge with relish and done just fine for themselves.

Did Eddie Robinson or Fritz Pollard lack "the necessities"? I doubt that very seriously. The only thing they lacked was the opportunity. My goodness, think of what we missed. Wouldn't it have been a terrific thrill to see Eddie Robinson coaching against Woody Hayes or John McKay? Better still, what about Fritz Pollard standing across the sidelines from Knute Rockne? What amazing matchups those would have been.

"There's no question in my mind that Coach Robinson could have won at Notre Dame or Ohio State or one of those schools," said Willie Brown, the Pro Football Hall of Fame cornerback who played for Robinson at Grambling in the early '60s. "One of the best things Eddie did with all the talent coming in at Grambling was assess a player's skills and figure out his best position. I know he could have done that at a bigger place. That would have been something to see."

But wait a minute. Why are we just talking about the past? Why should we assume that we aren't missing some great matchups today? What if Tony Dungy had been hired as a college head coach at his alma mater, Minnesota, instead of becoming a head coach in the NFL? We could have seen some great annual Big 10 battles between Dungy and Paterno at Penn State, or Dungy and Jim Tressel at Ohio State. What if Mike Tomlin, the Pittsburgh Steelers' coach, had instead been offered a job at a FBS school—he never was—and had accepted a position at, say, Georgia Tech? He would be having some amazing yearly matchups against Frank Beamer at Virginia Tech. But the record shows that Tomlin, who would go on to coach the 2008 Pittsburgh Steelers to a Super Bowl Championship and return the team there in 2011, could not get a sniff from the major college football programs when he was available and eager to lead any of them. The president of the Black Coaches Association (BCA), Floyd Keith, told me personally that between 2003 and 2006, he called many college athletic directors recommending Tomlin as a great head coach candidate. But those recommendations fell on deaf ears.

The common wisdom is that Tomlin was a prime beneficiary of the "Rooney Rule," which requires teams to interview at least one minority candidate for every head coach opening. This rule, pushed by Pittsburgh owner Dan Rooney, was created in 2003 to promote more employment access at the head coaching level for men of color. The rule was expanded in 2009 to cover general manager vacancies as well. Thus far, college football has resisted the creation of its own Rooney Rule. But I wish the NCAA or BCS would reconsider. The Rooney Rule has benefited both black coaches and the NFL by promoting diversity and equal opportunity.

Perhaps you saw the film *Remember the Titans*, in which Denzel Washington played the role of a high school coach. The movie was based on a true story in Virginia and related the tale of an African American coach, Herman Boone, who found ways to overcome institutional racism during a time of forced integration. He created success for an entire community, black and white alike, in ways other than on the scoreboard. Every time I watch that movie, I think about how other coaches as skilled as Boone might have been able to influence other communities positively. And I think about the athletes at the FBS or Division 1A level—black athletes and white athletes—who back in the day were denied the gift of being coached by Robinson or Pollard or so many others.

Those coaches were available to make a difference back then. History teaches us that they are available today if more colleges would just give them a chance.

CHAPTER FIVE

THE LONELY THIRTY-EIGHT

Intercollegiate football was first played in 1869. And while early records are sketchy, it's safe to assume that over the years, well over two thousand men have served as head coaches at institutions playing major college football. However, through the 2011 season, only thirty-eight African Americans were perceived to have the necessary qualifications that resulted in them being hired to lead those programs at predominantly white colleges and universities.

The Lonely Thirty-Eight, I call them.

It's not because thirty-eight is such a tiny group—although it is, compared to the thousands of white men who have led major college programs. It's because at some point all of them have felt they had to carry the burden of African American coaches everywhere, all by themselves. I know. I've been there.

As a coach, you think about these things when deep in the evening you are alone in your office watching videotape or wondering how to motivate a team for a big game.

"If I lose this game and then I lose my job," you ask yourself, "will another black guy ever get a chance at this school...or any other?"

I know. It sounds illogical. But given the relatively small number of black men who've been in the position, plus the stress of the job, I understand how it happens. My research has taught me that unlike their white peers, African American coaches are often evaluated collectively. That realization weighed on me before every game I coached.

We can learn so much by studying history. That's because history is not about speculation. It is not about theorizing why minorities were hired or not hired, or how they might have performed if they had been hired. The Lonely Thirty-Eight were not passed over. They were actually hired. Then they succeeded or failed. Wins are wins. Losses are losses. I thought it would be helpful to examine each of the thirty-eight in a case-by-case fashion.

My plan, then, is to list the entire roster of those lonely coaches in chronological order and tell their stories. I believe it will put the history of African American coaches in perspective. I should note that five of the thirty-eight men have been head coaches at more than one BCS school. In each entry, I will cover all of those coaches' stops. I also thought it might be useful to rank each of the jobs on degree of difficulty using a scale of one to ten—with ten being the most difficult. USC or Florida, for example, would be a one on the scale as places where resources are top notch and it should be easier to succeed. On the opposite end, Buffalo or Temple would be a ten. And believe me, there are more tens than ones on this list.

Let's start at the beginning:

(1) WILLIE JEFFERIES, Wichita State 1979-82

Fate could have picked many men to serve as the first African American major college coach. But it tapped the shoulder of Jefferies, a civil engineering graduate from South Carolina State, a historically black university. Soon after receiving his diploma in 1961, Jefferies began his coaching life in the small South Carolina town of Granard, where he won three state championships at the local high school and compiled a 65-7-2 record in the process.

Jefferies was then hired as an assistant coach at North Carolina A&T before joining the University of Pittsburgh staff under Johnny Majors in 1972. The next season, he became head coach at his alma mater and was immediately effective, taking a South Carolina State team that had finished 1-9 the season before his arrival and turning it into a 7-3-1 team.

Undoubtedly that's why the people at Wichita State gave Jefferies a call after the 1978 season. Years later, it's still hard for me to believe that a predominantly white college sought the services of Coach Jefferies. I've frequently wondered why Eddie Robinson didn't get that call first, given the success he enjoyed at Grambling State University throughout the 1950s and 1960s.

In 1979, the Wichita State Shockers was a struggling football member of the Missouri Valley Conference, not one of the high-profile leagues. Perhaps that is the reason Jefferies's hiring did not receive much hype. It should have been a monumental event, much like Jackie Robinson's entry into major league baseball. Sixty years after Fritz Pollard became the first African American to coach in the NFL, Wichita State people made Jefferies the first black coach in major college history.

Jeffries didn't have an easy tenure there, as his teams fought to compete on the outer fringes of Division I. But this would mirror many occasions in the future when a program with limited success would be one of the rare programs that offered a head coaching job to an African American candidate. Under Jefferies, the Shockers won twenty-one games and lost thirty-two. But in the 1982 season, Jefferies had an 8-3 record and defeated Kansas of the Big Eight Conference. Things went downhill after that. First, there were alleged recruiting violations under Jefferies's watch. Then in 1987, Wichita State dropped football. Jefferies eventually returned to South Carolina State, where he finished his coaching career very successfully. In his two combined stints there, he won 179 games and six Mid-Eastern Athletic Conference championships.

Jefferies was inducted in the American Football Coaches Association Divisional College Football Hall of Class of 2010. He was also honored by his South Carolina hometown, which named its high school gymnasium in his honor.

Degree of Difficulty: 9
Grade: B

(2) DENNIS GREEN,
Northwestern 1981-85,
Stanford 1989-91

With its football program in the middle of a horrific losing streak—and as the Big Ten's only private school—Northwestern University could afford to take a chance on a young African American coach in 1981. And that's exactly what happened. Dennis Green was only thirty-two years old when he was hired. He had a modest résumé as an assistant coach at the University of Dayton, Iowa, and Stanford but possessed energy and an upbeat attitude.

It took Green a while, but he made his mark at Northwestern. In his second season, he ended the Wildcats' thirty-four-game losing streak with a victory over Northern Illinois that caused the students to rip down the goalposts and throw them in nearby Lake Michigan. Green's team won only three games that season, but he was still named Big 10 coach of the year by impressed voters. Three seasons later, convinced that the Northwestern administration was not playing for keeps, Green resigned with a won-loss record of 10-45 and took a job as running backs' coach for the San Francisco 49ers under Bill Walsh. Green had previously worked for Walsh at Stanford.

In 1989, Green returned to Stanford as the man in charge, making him the first African American to hold head coaching jobs at two different universities. In his three seasons there, Green went 16-18. His best team advanced to the 1991 Aloha Bowl. He then returned to the NFL as head coach of the Minnesota Vikings and had a modestly successful career as a pro head coach. As the 2010 season began, Green was serving as head coach and general manager for the Sacramento Mountain Lions of the United Football League.

I think it should be noted how relationships play a pivotal role for black coaches to be hired at better institutions when they have a losing record. For instance, there is a very low probability that Green would have been selected as the head coach at Stanford after going 10-45 at Northwestern without the endorsement of Bill Walsh.

Degree of Difficulty (Northwestern): 10
Grade: B+

Degree of Difficulty (Stanford): 5
Grade: B-

(3) CLEVE BRYANT,
Ohio University 1985-89

By all rights, Cleve Bryant's tenure at Ohio University should have gone better. The school was his alma mater, and he had quarterbacked the 1968 Bobcats team to the Tangerine Bowl in Orlando. He had then served apprenticeships as a successful assistant coach at the University of North Carolina and with the NFL's New England Patriots. In 1985 when Ohio called him home, Bryant eagerly accepted.

However, he inherited a mediocre program and could never gather any momentum to make a turnaround. After a winless season in 1987, Bryant rallied the Bobcats to a 4-5-1 record the following year but could never do any better. He was dismissed the following season and left Ohio U with an overall 9-44-2 record. I wonder if Bryant now wishes he had a passed on such a job. After his unsuccessful debut as a head coach, he never received another chance to lead a team. He was relegated to assistant coaching jobs at several schools until he accepted a position as associate athletics director of football operations at the University of Texas. That's where he works today.

Degree of Difficulty: 10
Grade: D

(4) WAYNE NUNNELY,
University of Nevada Las Vegas 1986-89

This was another case of a university hoping that an alumnus could elevate a football program's won-loss record. Nunnely was a UNLV graduate who plowed ground as an assistant coach at Cal State Fullerton and University of the Pacific before being named head coach of the Running Rebels at age thirty-four in 1986.

Nunnely could not move UNLV forward, however. He never won more than four games in a season and was "promoted" to an administrative position at the school in 1990 after compiling a 19-25 record in four seasons. But in 1988, Nunnely and Bryant became the first African American head coaches in NCAA Division 1A history to coach against one another, in a game UNLV, and Nunnely won, 26-18.

During the 2010 football season, Nunnely was working as an assistant coach for the San Diego Chargers.

Degree of Difficulty: 7
Grade: C

(5) FRANCIS PEAY,
Northwestern 1986-91

When Dennis Green left Northwestern for the NFL in the spring of 1986, the school appointed one of his top assistants, Francis Peay, as interim head coach. The Wildcats responded well to the move. They finished the 1986 season with a record of 4-7 — the most victories for a Northwestern team since 1973. However, Peay did not campaign to be named permanent head coach.

The school made him an offer anyway, and Peay signed a five-year contract. Even though Peay never improved on his initial season, the school honored that contract. Peay, a former NFL player with an imposing six-foot-five frame, could simply not get his team over the hump. His contract was not renewed after the 1991 season, and he left Northwestern with a 13-51-2 record. Peay, who never coached again, is retired in Illinois.

Through the 2010 football season, Northwestern was the only school to have successive African American head coaches. This is significant because it provides another example of my principle about race-defining space. White administrators never think twice about replacing unsuccessful white coaches with another white coach; it is standard operating procedure. But when a black coach has been terminated in Division 1A football, it has been as rare as snow in Miami for that black coach to be replaced by another black coach. Remember, Green was not terminated. He left Northwestern for what he perceived to be a brighter opportunity in the NFL—and he was right.

It's now been two decades since Northwestern became the first Division 1A program to hire back-to-back African American head coaches. At the conclusion of the 2010 season, Miami (Ohio) became the second institution to hire back-to-back African American head football coaches. This is progress at a turtle pace but it is indeed progress.

Degree of Diffiulty: 10
Grade: C

(6) WILLIE BROWN,
Long Beach State 1991

I suppose you could find worse ways to be named a head football coach than the way it happened to Willie Brown. But none come to mind. He was an assistant coach on the Long Beach State staff on New Year's Eve in 1990 when the head coach, George Allen, died of a pneumonia-induced heart attack.

Upon Allen's death, school officials asked Brown to take over, and he could hardly say no. A Pro Football Hall of Fame member, Brown appeared to have natural leadership ability. But he had so many things going against him at Long Beach State. The school was just trying to hang onto its program—but not trying very hard. After Brown finished the 1991 season with a 2-8-2 record, Long Beach State dropped football. Brown went on to a very successful career as an assistant coach with the Oakland Raiders, the team for which he had played in the NFL.

Degree of Difficulty: 9
Grade: C-

(7) JAMES CALDWELL,
Wake Forest 1993-2000

Caldwell was an assistant coach under Green at Northwestern and then moved on to Colorado, Louisville, and Penn State before he was hired by Wake Forest. At the time, the Demon Deacons were perennial losers in the Atlantic Coast Conference. Caldwell also had his struggles at Wake Forest. But in 1999, he led the school to its first winning season in seven years—and defeated Arizona State in the Aloha Bowl. Unfortunately, he couldn't sustain the success. He was forced out after the very next season, leaving with a 26-63 overall record.

In spite of Wake Forest's losing ways, however, Caldwell established a reputation as a scholar of the passing game. Four times under his tutelage, the Demon Deacons ranked among the nation's top 25 teams in passing offense. After leaving the school, he was quickly hired by the NFL's Tampa Bay franchise as its quarterbacks' coach. A year later, Caldwell was then hired away for the same job by Indianapolis Colts' head coach, Tony Dungy. Subsequently, Dungy promoted Caldwell to assistant head coach, the job he held when the Colts won the Super Bowl after the 2006 season. Caldwell became head coach of the team in 2009 when Tony Dungy resigned.

In spite of Caldwell's college record, he was interviewed for the Dallas Cowboys vacancy in 2007 after Bill Parcells resigned. It was an example of how, for an African American with Caldwell's résumé, the probability of getting a head coaching job in the NFL is greater than the probability of ever resurfacing as head coach in the collegiate ranks. Between the time he left Wake Forest and the time he was named the Colts' head coach, why didn't another college program recognize the promise Caldwell held and give him another shot at coaching FBS football? If he was good enough to coach the Indianapolis Colts to the Super Bowl in 2010 in his first year as a NFL head coach, why wasn't Caldwell good enough to lead a program at another BCS school? The frustrating part for me is, sometimes I think I'm the only one asking these questions.

Degree of Difficulty: 7
Grade: D+

(8) RON COOPER,
Eastern Michigan 1993-94,
Louisville 1995-97

As Dennis Green learned, in the coaching profession it always helps to have an important supporter on your side. Cooper was fortunate enough to have Lou Holtz. After serving as an assistant coach at several schools, Cooper in 1991 landed a job on Holtz's staff at Notre Dame. Both of them helped take the Fighting Irish to Sugar Bowl and Cotton Bowl victories. Holtz then recommended Cooper for the vacancy at Eastern Michigan, which had just finished a 1-10 season. That's correct—yet another woeful, struggling school was turning to another eager young black coach for redemption. I know that white coaches take bad jobs too. But the difference is that black coaches rarely receive the opportunities to serve in better jobs if they perform badly in a challenging opportunity.

Although Cooper was only thirty-one years old when Eastern Michigan called him, he jumped at the chance. After going 4-7 his first season, his team improved to 5-6 in 1994 and won five of its last six games. This gained him some regional attention and persuaded the University of Louisville to pursue and hire him for its head coaching vacancy. Cooper managed to go 7-4 in his first season with the Cardinals but won only six games in the following two years. Being the first black head coach at a predominantly white institution can present a new set of social dynamics along racial lines that athletic departments are often uncomfortable dealing with. With a new forty-thousand-seat stadium set to open, the school administration thought it needed to make a move that would be popular with fans, so Cooper was fired. He moved on to become head coach at Alabama A&M, a Division 1AA program, then eventually landed at South Carolina working for Lou Holtz. These are the sorts of connections that are common in coaching. It's called "the network." And it's great that African American coaches now have access to "the network." Entering the 2011 season, Cooper was employed as an assistant at Louisiana State University.

Degree of Difficulty (Eastern Michigan): 10
Grade: B+

Degree of Difficulty (Louisville): 6
Grade: C-

(9) RON DICKERSON,
Temple 1992-97

Ron Dickerson played defensive back on the undefeated 1972 Miami Dolphins team before working as a college assistant for such successful coaches as Jackie Sherrill and Joe Paterno. He would soon learn that none of these experiences prepared him for what he would face at Temple University.

An urban, public school of thirty-four thousand students in Philadelphia, Temple reminds me a bit of San Jose State, where I coached. It possessed decent football tradition and had produced winning teams. But somewhere along the way, the program lost direction. Dickerson was hired in 1992 to get things focused and revive a winning spirit. Even though he tried hard, he failed because adequate support systems were not in place. Even with the support of famous alumni such as Bill Cosby, who had endorsed Dickerson's hiring, the task was too much.

In retrospect, Dickerson now realizes he was a bit naïve. In a first-person piece he later wrote for a website sponsored by the US Sports Academy, Dickerson lamented the fact that his former bosses, Sherrill and Paterno, did not sufficiently warn him of the hurdles he would face at Temple.

Dickerson resigned following the 1997 season. His overall record in five years at Temple was 8-47. For the 2009 season, he was employed as an assistant coach at Lambuth University, an NAIA program in Tennessee. He became Lambuth's head coach in 2010.

Meanwhile, after Dickerson left Temple, the school left the Big East Conference and dropped down a notch to the Mid-American Conference, a second-tier league in the Football Bowl Subdivision. Almost immediately after this move, Temple experienced great success, including a bowl trip. To me, this indicates that the problems faced by Dickerson and the head coaches that preceded him had more to do with their resource gap in budget, facilities, and so forth. Temple's resources weren't sufficient to compete in the Big East Conference but were more than adequate for the Mid-American Conference.

In the Big East, the Owls were fighting with sticks while their opponents were using guns. Unfortunately for Dickerson, fans don't like to hear about resource issues—wins and losses are always seen as leadership issues.

Degree of Difficulty: 10
Grade: D

(10) MATT SIMON,
University of North Texas 1994-97

The University of North Texas, a large public school located thirty-five miles from Dallas, is another of those institutions that dances around the fringe of Division I football as a member of the Sun Belt Conference. The program is most renowned as the alma mater of "Mean" Joe Greene, the Pittsburgh Steelers defensive lineman, but it does not match the profile or the budget of its statewide brethren such as Texas A&M, Texas Tech or the University of Texas.

In 1994, when Matt Simon was hired, North Texas was still in the process of making the jump to Division 1A and the Big West Conference from its previous status as a 1AA school in the Southland Conference. Simon had established a reputation as an effective offensive assistant coach at New Mexico and Washington. He did not disappoint the people who had hired him at North Texas. His first team there finished with a 7-4 record and won the conference title. Simon was named Southland Conference Coach of the Year.

Things soon grew much tougher. North Texas was a very good Division 1AA job but a horrible Division 1A job. After moving up to the more difficult level, Simon won only two games in 1995, then went 5-6 in 1996 and was released after a 4-7 season in 1997. Like so many other talented African American coaches, Simon subsequently abandoned the college ranks and found success in the NFL, first as running backs' coach of the Baltimore Ravens and then in the same job with the San Diego Chargers. During the 2009 football season, Simon decided to return to his hometown in northeastern Ohio and took a job as head football coach at Gilmour Academy, a high school in a Cleveland suburb.

Degree of Difficulty: 9
Grade: B

(11) BOB SIMMONS,
Oklahoma State 1995-2000

Simmons grew up in Alabama as the son of a sharecropper during the racially charged 1960s. He starred in football at Bowling Green State University in Ohio and after earning his degree worked as an assistant coach under a man who would become his mentor, Don Nehlen. When Nehlen was hired as West Virginia's head coach in 1979, Simmons followed. He later would reveal that one night, his family woke up and found a cross blazing in the front yard of their Morgantown home. Simmons's son, the only black child at his elementary school, was also taunted with racial slurs.

After eight years at West Virginia without a promotion, Simmons left for the University of Colorado. That's when I first became aware of him, because I was working as an assistant at Arkansas at the time. Bill McCartney, the Colorado head coach, made a concerted effort to hire minorities on his staff. This gave the Colorado program a recruiting advantage over the programs that still employed the traditional one or two black assistant coaches, especially when it came to wooing African American high school players and their families. It sent those players a message that Colorado was open-minded about hiring minorities who deserved the chance. It also disproved the notion, espoused by many at the time, that there were simply not enough quality African American coaches to fill staff positions. These were good men and good coaches. They proved it in 1991 when they helped coach Colorado to a national championship.

Those guys knew how to get it done on the high school recruiting trail too. I was visiting with an athlete at Carter High School in Dallas one afternoon in hopes of getting a prospective student-athlete to sign a letter of intent with Arkansas. A car pulled up, and four African American coaches from Colorado piled out of the vehicle. If I recall correctly, Simmons was one of them.

Before the 1994 season, McCartney promoted Simmons to the position of assistant head coach. So when McCartney resigned after the last game of that season, Simmons had every reason to think he would be named the next Colorado head coach. McCartney personally recommended him to the administration. But the school hired Rick Neuheisel, a young white coach with less experience.

I'm not criticizing Neuheisel as a person. At both Colorado and Washington, his next stops, I think he brought a refreshing style to the profession. But it is disheartening for African American coaches when they help build a program and bust their tails in every way possible, only to see the university hire a coach with a thinner résumé and zero head coaching experience. The Colorado administration explained its decision by saying Simmons wasn't the "right fit."

Though disappointed by Colorado's decision, Simmons refused to complain. Instead, after hearing that Oklahoma State was also looking for a head coach, Simmons was asked to interview for the job and was hired. But at that time the Oklahoma State program was hardly on par with Colorado's. Over the previous four years, the Cowboys had won only seven games against Division I competition. Who knows how successful Simmons might have been if he had been handed the reins to a big-time winning team instead of a scuffling loser?

On balance, he did a good job at Oklahoma State. After taking two seasons to install his system and eliminate the losing attitude, Simmons and his 1997 team really took off, winning the first six games of the season on the way to an 8-4 record, a top twenty-five ranking and an Alamo Bowl appearance—the Cowboys' first postseason bowl trip since 1988. Simmons was named Big 12 Coach of the Year.

At the conclusion of the 2000 season, Simmons resigned under heavy pressure, claiming it was for health reasons. He concluded his time at Oklahoma State with a 29-37-1 overall record.

A year later, Tyrone Willingham hired Simmons as an assistant at Notre Dame. He followed Willingham to Washington in 2005. Simmons worked as the tight ends coach and special teams coordinator until he was released following the 2007 season. In January of 2010, Simmons was hired as special teams coordinator and assistant head coach at Portland State. However, on August 8, 2010, it was reported in *The Oregonian* that Simmons had departed the staff. The story offered no further information.

To me, Simmons's story provides the perfect illustration of how the African American coaching experience in college football is so different from the experience of white coaches. After Simmons did all the right things to earn a head-coaching opportunity that didn't materialize at Colorado, he observed a man who possessed no head coaching experience hired to take over the program that Simmons had played a major role in building. Have similar things happened to white coaches? I am quite sure they have. But not nearly as often. The employment statistics are like game film. They don't lie. As I have mentioned, college football rosters are usually manned by more than 50 percent African American players – and most college coaches are former college players. Now, obviously not every former college player, black or white, becomes a coach. But I think it's roughly in the same percentage for both races.

Let's be conservative, though. Let's postulate that black coaching candidates comprise not 50 percent, but just 25 percent of the potential employment pool. Yet since the 1982 through the 2011 season, 498 of the 545 head coaching vacancies – or 91.4 percent of the openings – have been filled by white men. What that means: The

25 percent of the employment pool comprised of African American and minority candidates is filling just 8.6 percent of the job openings. The other 75 percent in the job pool, comprised of white candidates, is being hired for more than 90 percent of the jobs. Of the two groups, which one has the most right to wonder if the odds are unfairly stacked against it?

Degree of Difficulty: 6
Grade: B

(12) TY WILLINGHAM, Stanford 1995-2001, Notre Dame 2002-04, Washington 2005-08

Without question, Tyrone Willingham is the most successful African American Division I Football Bowl Subdivision head coach in history. Even after being dismissed from his last job at the University of Washington, his seventy-six career victories in major college football gave him twice as many as any other previous black head coach.

Also without a doubt, Willingham is the most controversial African American college coach in history—but not because of anything he said or anything outrageous that he did. Willingham might be the least outrageous coach I know. He is quiet, intense, and thoughtful. He was coaching at Stanford when I was at nearby San Jose State, so we visited from time to time. That's why it was fascinating for me to watch what unfolded when he moved on to Notre Dame, where he was eventually dismissed.

After playing quarterback at Michigan State, Willingham worked for several universities as an assistant coach before he joined Dennis Green's staff with the NFL's Minnesota Vikings. In 1995, Stanford hired Willingham as head coach after Bill Walsh resigned with the program in very decent shape. During Willingham's seven years with the Cardinal, he went 44-36-1, including four winning seasons. In 1999, he took Stanford to the Rose Bowl for the first time since 1971. In 2002, Notre Dame interviewed him for its head coaching job but hired George O'Leary instead. Five days later, O'Leary resigned after it was revealed he had lied on his résumé. Notre Dame called back Willingham and made him an offer. He accepted.

Willingham knew exactly how significant his hiring was. Notre Dame is one of college football's iconic brand names. Virtually every game the Fighting Irish play is on national television. The image of an African American coach on the sidelines at Notre Dame sent a powerful message—not just to college football fans across the nation, but to his own campus community. Willingham was the first African American to be hired as a Notre Dame head coach in any sport. His first season with the Fighting Irish unfolded like a dream. A 10-3 record took his team to the Gator Bowl. He was named Coach of the Year by ESPN and the Maxwell Football Club. He also became the first Notre Dame coach to win ten games in his first season at the school.

But the dream collapsed a year later. The Fighting Irish finished 5-7 in 2003 and were shut out twice. The following season was not much better, with a 6-5 record, which included a twenty-five-point loss to Purdue and a thirty-one-point loss to the University of Southern California. Two days after that game, Notre Dame terminated Willingham's employment with two years remaining on his contract and paid him to leave.

The dismissal of Willingham in spite of his 21-15 overall winning record at the school set off torrents of controversy. Previous Notre Dame coaches with less than stellar seasons, including Gerry Faust (18-15-1) and Bob Davie (21-16), had been allowed to serve out their entire contract terms. Even Notre Dame's outgoing president criticized the firing. The athletic director implied that it had not been his decision either. Fingers pointed at the board of trustees and the big money donors.

Willingham was quickly snapped up by the University of Washington, where he struggled to win games for different reasons. Nevertheless, Willingham's tenure at Notre Dame will always dominate his biography. He has been remarkably quiet on the topic. The day of his firing, he met with the media and handled himself with dignity, as I expected he would do.

"To say I am disappointed, I think that very much misses the mark," Willingham said, admitting his hurt. "But at the same time, I understand that I didn't meet the expectations or standards that I set for myself in this program, and when you don't meet your own expectations, you won't meet the expectations of others. My goals have always been to inspire people to be the best they could be, on and off the field. I believe that I have been true to that in my time here at Notre Dame and appreciative of the opportunity…I don't get into what's fair and what's not fair."

After arriving at Washington, Willingham declined to comment when a reporter asked him to reflect on his Notre Dame experience.

"I won't touch that," he said. "I don't talk about it. It's a great place. A wonderful place. I did not do all I wanted to do."

Here's my take: Notre Dame's leaders are not racist in the overt sense. Or maybe even in the non-overt sense. But any rational person would wonder if they allowed race to play a part in their decision making regarding Willingham. Look at the evidence. White coaches with identical or worse winning percentages at the school—Faust, Davie, Joe Kuharich (17-23 in four seasons)—were allowed to finish out their contracts. Notre Dame was always proud of that fact, saying it made the school different from universities that put winning above integrity. But when it came to Willingham, the rules changed.

Here's the analogy I would use: A landlord puts an advertisement in the paper seeking to rent out an apartment for $500 a month. But when a black couple shows up to look at the place, the landlord apologizes and says that after doing some extra calculations, he has decided he must charge $1000 per month for the rental. The black couple walks away discouraged and doesn't take the place. But the next day when a white couple shows up to rent the apartment, the landlord says the $500 rent still applies. Now, you could choose to believe that the landlord was simply indecisive and subject to changing his mind on a whim. But the more logical conclusion is that the landlord had a different standard for black couples than white couples.

I think that's what happened at Notre Dame. You could choose to believe that school officials, impulsively, woke up one morning and suddenly decided to abandon their previous standards of allowing the head football coach to complete his contract with the institution. A more logical conclusion is that those standards changed for a reason. Willingham did not make some of the school's landlords—those trustees and big donors—as comfortable or confident as a white coach did. At the very least, it's indisputable that they didn't cut Willingham as much slack as the white coaches who preceded him.

Was it employment bias based on skin color? I wasn't in the room with the decision makers that pulled the plug on Willingham. But you be the referee. Examine the facts and make the call. I know that my coaching and life experience have shaped my perceptions and opinions. But I believe this is another classic example of how race matters. Willingham was blindsided by a crackback block from an institution that did not live up to the principles that it had proudly maintained for the coaches that preceded him and followed him. Charlie Weis was hired to replace Willingham. Weis posted a 22-15 won-loss record in his first three seasons. That's one more game than Willingham won in his three seasons.

For Notre Dame administrators, Willingham's 21-15 record was unacceptable, and they did not allow him to complete his five-year contract. And yet for Weis, a 22-15 record was good enough to keep Weis on the job. I chuckled when remembering that Willingham was fired a few days after the 2004 season and didn't get a chance to coach the Irish in the Insight Bowl. If he had, maybe they would have won the game and Willingham would have earned that precious twenty-second victory and received another two years as head coach, just as Weis did.

At least Willingham had a chance to rebound from his Notre Dame experience by being hired at the University of Washington before the 2005 season. After an ugly 2-9 record in his first season, Willingham had the Huskies out to a 4-1 start in 2006, including an upset of previously undefeated UCLA. But then quarterback Isaiah Stanback injured his foot in the sixth game, and the team never recovered, losing six of its last seven to finish 5-7. In 2007, Willingham avoided getting fired after a 4-9 record against an extremely tough schedule. Websites called for Willingham to get out of town—or worse—and ESPN reported that a Washington alum pledged $200,000 to the school if it would fire Willingham and his athletic director.

Admirably, the administration stood by both men. Nothing could protect Willingham, though, when the 2008 season also went south after quarterback Jake Locker was hurt. The Huskies finished 0-11, their first winless season in 119 years of football. *Ouch!* Willingham had to go. My only thought is that perhaps Washington football players had different priorities than Stanford or Notre Dame football players, inside and outside the classroom. And maybe Willingham never adapted to that mind-set. Whatever the reasons, he didn't get it done. It's too bad. Willingham is still an excellent coach and one I admire greatly.

Degree of Difficulty (Stanford): 5
Grade: A

Degree of Difficulty (Notre Dame): 3
Grade: B

Degree of Difficulty (Washington): 3
Grade: D-

(13) JOHN BLAKE,
Oklahoma 1996-98

Given that John Blake was a former player and coach at Oklahoma with tremendous loyalty to the school, it's a shame that his three seasons as head coach there weren't more successful. His hiring was one of the rare times an African American coach has been given the opportunity to take over a top-tier football program. While coaching at San Jose State, I had the opportunity to visit with Blake about his experiences at Oklahoma. Depending on whom you talk to, Blake was either in over his head trying to run a Division 1A football program or was not given enough authority to make the decisions involving his coaching staff. After visiting with Blake, I know he believed the latter was the case. He basically felt that someone in the school administration was always looking over his shoulder, questioning his every decision.

Blake was only thirty-four years old when Oklahoma hired him as head coach in 1996. He had played on the defensive line for Barry Switzer at the school and then worked as an assistant coach there before the Dallas Cowboys hired Blake as defensive line coach. The Cowboys won two Super Bowls while Blake was there. He seemed the perfect guy to step in and guide the Sooners after Howard Schnellenberger abruptly left after one season.

Switzer also endorsed Blake heavily for the job, which clinched the deal. But early on, problems were apparent. Blake was an excellent position coach and a terrific recruiter. He made a great impression on kids and their parents, especially in the African American community. But after his first couple of teams didn't produce winning records, many alumni and fans questioned if he was prepared for the organizational challenges of operating a major college football program. His first team had a 3-8 record, which was Oklahoma's worst season since 1895. Blake followed up with a 4-8 team and a

5-6 team, the first time in seventy-eight years that Oklahoma had experienced three consecutive losing seasons.

Even in Blake's worst seasons, no one ever questioned his ability to assess talent and recruit it. His successor at Oklahoma, Bob Stoops, was the beneficiary. He won the 2000 national championship with thirteen starters who were recruited by Blake. Since leaving Oklahoma, Blake has been an assistant coach at Mississippi State, Nebraska, and North Carolina. He abruptly resigned from North Carolina in early September of 2010 amidst an ongoing NCAA investigation into possible improper contacts with agents.

Degree of Difficulty: 1
Grade: D-

(14) TONY SAMUEL,
New Mexico State 1997-2003

During his seven seasons at New Mexico State, Tony Samuel did one of the most underrated good coaching jobs in America. The school is located in the city of Las Cruces, the second largest city in New Mexico—with a population of just eighty thousand residents. In 2005, New Mexico State joined the Western Athletic Conference, the same league that I competed in at San Jose State.

Samuel grew up in New Jersey and was a member of Coach Tom Osborne's first recruiting class at Nebraska. He then worked as an assistant coach at Western Michigan and Stanford before returning to his alma mater. He spent eleven seasons as an assistant coach under Osborne and helped the Cornhuskers win seven conference championships and two national titles. Samuel had all the qualifications necessary when New Mexico State hired him as head coach in 1997.

Like so many others at New Mexico State, however, Samuel faced a daunting challenge in trying to rev up a program with a losing tradition that didn't have the resources of most major schools.

He smartly installed an option offense, which went against the norm of most Division 1A programs that were using the pro passing game. But it allowed Samuel to recruit the best high school option quarterbacks who were not drawing interest from the schools that were pass happy. In his third season, Samuel managed a 6-5 record, only the third winning season in thirty-two years for the Aggies. In 2002, Samuel won seven games, the most for the school since 1967. More significantly, Samuel increased the graduation rate among football players at the school to 76 percent, which ranked thirteenth best among Division 1A programs.

In the end, none of that was enough to save his job. After eight victories over the next two seasons, Samuel's contract was not renewed following the 2004 season when he compiled a 5-6 record. As if to certify the tough job Samuel had faced, his successor, Hal Mumme, went 0-12 the following season and 4-8 in 2006. Mumme never surpassed four wins in a single season and finished with an 11-38 career record before being fired.

Did the athletic administration really believe that Samuel underachieved? Maybe it was indeed time in 2004 for the school to make a change. But it remains to be seen if the change was for better or worse. Samuel spent the 2005 season as an assistant coach at Purdue and in 2006 was named head coach at Southeast Missouri State University, a Football Championship Subdivision program. After winning only 13 games in four seasons, Samuel's team jumped up to post a 9-3 record and claim the Ohio Valley Championship. It was the program's first winning season since 2002. For this turnaround performance, Samuel received the Eddie Robinson Award as the FCS National Coach the Year. He was also given a nice raise and new five-year contract which runs through 2016.

Degree of Difficulty: 10
Grade: B

(15) JERRY BALDWIN,
Louisiana Lafayette 1999-2001

You can read the gory details of Baldwin's tenure at Louisiana Lafayette in the next chapter, which will discuss how boosters can adversely affect a minority coach's chances for success. But in a nutshell, this was another case of a coach trying to do his best at a school on the outer limits of Division 1A and finding the task to be daunting. Baldwin's record of six wins and twenty-seven losses after three seasons led to his firing after three seasons. The man who took over his job, Rickey Bustle, had better support from alumni and the administration—but after compiling a 41-65 won-loss record was terminated at the conclusion of the 2010 season.

Degree of Difficulty: 10
Grade: D

(16) BOBBY WILLIAMS,
Michigan State 1999-2002

Bobby Williams had been the running backs' coach at Michigan State for nine years when, without warning in early December of 1999, he was asked to become interim head coach at the school five days after Nick Saban resigned to become head coach at Louisiana State. Less than a month later, Williams coached Michigan State to a Citrus Bowl victory over Florida and earned the permanent position.

But there was a catch. Williams was forced to retain every member of the Michigan State coaching staff, giving him less than total control over his situation. Ultimately, he perceived that's what undid him, even though he had a winning season in 2001 and won another bowl game. A coach needs to pick his own staff and call his own shots in that regard. Williams believes he wasn't given that opportunity. Still, during his first two years as head coach, his winning percentage was better than his most immediate predecessors—and better than the combined coaching record of all Michigan State coaches during the previous quarter century. But in 2002, Williams's team won just three of its first nine games. Impatient school administrators fired him.

The widely believed catalyst for this drastic move was a remark Williams made following his team's 49-3 loss to state rival Michigan. At his press conference afterward, Williams was asked whether he still had control of his team. Answering honestly, he replied, "I don't know." He was dismissed a few days later, finishing his Michigan State tenure with a 16-17 record. Williams's experience at the school is covered with great detail in the book *Innocence in the Red Zone*, written by his friend Roger Groves.

Williams subsequently worked as an assistant coach at LSU and with the NFL's Detroit Lions and Miami Dolphins. He is now on the coaching staff of the University of Alabama.

Degree of Difficulty: 4
Grade: C

(17) FITZGERALD HILL, San Jose State 2001-04

My time as head coach at San Jose State is also covered in another chapter. But if knew today what I didn't know in 2000, I never would have taken the job. I accepted the offer without even visiting the campus or checking up on the community support. My eagerness to prove myself as a head coach basically allowed me to be tricked into believing everything would be great. That's nobody's fault but mine. I accept full responsibility for my decision to try and lead the Spartan program.

Like any coach, I would love to have won more games. But I am not ashamed of my 14-33 record, especially since I have removed myself from that situation and can now examine the challenges objectively. We recruited very well and built a national awareness about the program. We just didn't win enough games, and I accept responsibility for that. Nevertheless, it was an awesome experience.

Degree of Difficulty: 10
Grade: D

(18) KARL DORRELL, UCLA 2003-07

When he was named head coach at UCLA, Karl Dorrell could not claim ignorance of the terrain. Dorrell had played wide receiver at UCLA. He knew about the Bruins' great football tradition. He also knew it is very hard to compete with crosstown rival University of Southern California, because the Trojans have even more tradition, more Heisman Trophy winners, more national championships, and more alumni support.

Dorrell did his best to meet those challenges. His first Bruins' team in 2003 finished the regular season with a 6-6 record before losing to Fresno State in the Silicon Valley Bowl. He went 6-5 the following season and then suffered a defeat to Wyoming in the Las Vegas Bowl. With two bowl losses to programs that Bruin fans considered inferior to UCLA, Dorrell was feeling the heat. With no NFL team in Los Angeles, the city's two major college programs there receive even more scrutiny than usual.

You would think that Dorrell's critics would have been satisfied with a 9-2 regular season in 2005. But because one of those two defeats was a crushing 66-19 loss to USC, not even a Sun Bowl victory over a good Northwestern team could hush the detractors. However, Dorrell did much to shut them up the following season when he coached the Bruins to a 13-9 upset victory over the Trojans, a defeat that kept USC out of the BCS title game. The Bruins finished 7-6, losing to Florida State in the Emerald Bowl. I can understand why UCLA fans expected more. But to my way of thinking, taking the Bruins to four bowl games in four seasons is a pretty good achievement.

Dorrell was fired after the 2007 season when he finished 6-6 and lost to USC by seventeen points. He still had a decent 35-27 overall record at UCLA and was interviewed for the vacant head coaching job at Duke University. He didn't get the offer. Dorrell landed with the Miami Dolphins as an assistant coach. Why do I get the feeling that if he is a head coach again, it will be in the National Football League and not the NCAA?

Degree of Difficulty: 3
Grade: B

(19) SYLVESTER CROOM,
Mississippi State 2004-08

It is impossible to overstate the importance of Sylvester Croom's hiring at Mississippi State. There were some of us who wondered whether we would ever see an African American head coach at a Southeastern Conference school in our lifetimes. All credit to the Mississippi State administrators for finally taking the step and giving Croom the opportunity he deserved.

That said, in my opinion, Croom really should have been hired a year earlier when a coaching vacancy cropped up at his alma mater, Alabama. Croom had played there under Bear Bryant on the Crimson Tide's national championship team of 1973. He was one of Bryant's first African American players and, by all accounts, was an inspirational player and the leader of the offensive line from the center position. Croom then served as an Alabama assistant coach for eleven seasons before moving on to a succession of NFL assistant coaching jobs. But in 2003 when Alabama needed a head coach, it hired less experienced Mike Shula after leading Croom to believe he was the leading candidate.

Croom would later express his belief that race did play a part in Alabama's decision, telling the Black Athlete Sports Network that he was very discouraged by the process. Croom said he had "great support from the former players and the fans there and even some people within the administration" but that "somewhere in the final process, somebody made another decision."

The following season, Mississippi State at last opened the door for Croom. And four decades after ending segregation on the playing field, the SEC finally had its first African American football head coach.

Croom compiled just three victories in each of his first three years at Mississippi State and owned a 9-25 record after his first three seasons. However, in the three seasons before Croom's arrival, the Bulldogs had won only eight games total under Jackie Sherrill. This may explain why Mississippi State's athletic director remained supportive, defending Croom after one defeat by calling him still "the right man for the job" and "the most positive thing that has happened in our athletic department since I took this job twenty years ago."

But we all know that you can't keep winning just three games a season forever. Croom knew that wasn't acceptable either.

Fortunately, Croom had a brilliant 2007 season. His team won eight games and made a victorious trip to the Liberty Bowl. He was named SEC Coach of the Year by both the Associated Press and his fellow conference coaches—the first time since 1970 that a MSU coach had won the AP honor. Everything seemed to be rolling his way. But the 2008 season was just the opposite of 2007. The Bulldogs lost eight games—including an embarrassing 45-0 defeat by rival Mississippi. Taking heat for his ineffective offense and with boosters withdrawing support, Croom resigned under pressure one day after losing the game to Ole Miss.

Worst of all, college football keeps losing men of Croom's character. In a recurring theme, he chose to continue his coaching career as an NFL assistant, coaching running backs for the St. Louis Rams. It's too bad he didn't get the chance to succeed at one of the SEC's more powerful programs such as Alabama, Auburn, or LSU. At the very least, why wouldn't one of those schools give Croom an opportunity as a coordinator? Many coaches also use those jobs to position themselves for a return to the head coaching ranks. That rarely happens to African American coaches.

Degree of Difficulty: 8
Grade: C-

(20) TURNER GILL,
Buffalo 2006-09,
Kansas 2010-present

What a tough deal Turner Gill cut for himself at the University of Buffalo. In 1999, after some success as a Division 1AA football program, the school ascended to Division 1A and began playing in the Mid-American Conference. But in the team's first seven MAC seasons, the Bulls never won more than three games. Gill was hired in 2006 to replace Jim Hofher, who walked out the door with an 8-49 record.

At the time of Gill's hiring, he was working in player development for the Green Bay Packers. But he must have wanted to become a head coach in the worst way. In college football, there aren't many more difficult tasks than the one Gill accepted.

Gill, who was an all-conference quarterback at Nebraska and later spent thirteen seasons as a Cornhuskers' assistant coach, has said all the right things about creating a winning environment. But here's the biggest problem: Buffalo is a program with very low attendance and miniscule television income. So to compensate financially, the team must play many revenue-producing road games against higher-level competition. In college football, these are often called "body bag" games. The players invariably come home beat up and injured—but the school receives a bag of money to keep football afloat as well as balance the budget. After my four years at San Jose State, when we did the same thing, I started calling this "athletic prostitution." And as I can tell you from personal experience, when you are getting your butt beat frequently and still look up to see those top programs on your schedule year after year, you, the alumni, and the fans become disenchanted about the direction in which you're headed.

In Gill's first season at Buffalo, for example, he won only two games. But among his ten defeats were money-producing trips to Wisconsin, Boston College, and Auburn. The 2007 schedule included games at Rutgers, Penn State, and Syracuse. When you begin each season perceiving that you have three near-automatic losses, it can be very discouraging. And the injuries in those "body bag" games often carry over into future games against more beatable competition. I personally experienced this during my tour of duty at San Jose State.

For Gill, there was one bright sign in the final game of the 2006 season. Buffalo defeated Temple, 9-3, before an announced crowd of twenty-nine thousand, the largest home attendance in school history. The progress continued in 2007 when Buffalo had its first-ever winning record in the MAC and finished the season with an overall 5-7 record. And the next season was a near-miracle. Buffalo won its MAC division and scored an upset of previously undefeated Ball State in the conference championship game. The Bulls then played in the International Bowl and finished with a 7-5 overall record.

You're probably thinking that after such a turnaround, bigger schools would be falling all over themselves to hire Gill. That wasn't the case. Syracuse did interview him but decided to hire Doug Marrone, a NFL offensive coordinator (New Orleans) with no head coaching experience. But what appeared to be the bigger injustice occurred a few days later when Gill interviewed for the head coaching position at Auburn—and lost out to Iowa State head coach Gene Chizik, who had accumulated an unimpressive 5-19 record with the Cyclones. Apparently, Chizik was "a comfortable fit" at Auburn because of his previous success as a coordinator there.

But let me repeat: Auburn decided to hire a guy who, in three years at a BCS school at Iowa State, did not even win as many games as Gill did in one season at Buffalo, a non-BCS program with a fraction of the resources that BCS schools possess. Auburn alumnus Charles Barkley called out his school for this decision. Not only that, but he stated the reason the non-hiring occurred at Auburn was because Gill's wife was white. I know, it sounds amazing that in 2009 that would affect such a decision at a school that says it is determined to win. But to quote Barkley: "You can say it's not about race, but you can't compare the two résumés and say [Chizik] deserved the job. Out of all the coaches they interviewed, Chizik probably had the worst résumé." Yet he was—as I mentioned earlier—the so-called "right fit."

The good news is, Gill wound up getting a raise and a contract extension to 2013. Before 2008, I thought that Gill would try to win four or five games during one season and then use his NFL connections to move on because it would be difficult to sustain the winning momentum he created. That became evident in 2009, when the Buffalo recorded a 5-7 record. I was thinking he ought to sneak out of Buffalo as soon as possible—and he did just that in December of 2009 by accepting the head coaching position at the University of Kansas. He was very deserving of this opportunity after his herculean effort at Buffalo. Gill exceeded my wildest expectations there. I hope to see him do the same at Kansas, where he posted a 3-9 record in his inaugural season.

Degree of Difficulty (Buffalo): 10
Grade: A

Degree of Difficulty (Kansas): 5
Current Grade: D+

(21) RON PRINCE,
Kansas State 2006-08

Prince looked to be a terrific hire for Kansas State. He had been an assistant coach at James Madison, Cornell, and Virginia (where he was the offensive coordinator) when he came to Manhattan. He was thirty-six years old and ready to rock and roll. But Prince was replacing the retiring Bill Snyder, who had revived the Kansas State program and taken it to eleven consecutive bowl games from 1993-2003. The school's football stadium is named after Snyder.

In other words, Prince had a tough act to follow. But he was up to the task in his first season, 2006. The Wildcats had a 7-6 record—their first winning season since 2003. Most impressively, Prince coached Kansas State to a 45-42 major upset of Texas, ranked fourth in the nation at the time. A loss to Rutgers in the Texas Bowl did not dampen too many spirits on the Kansas State campus.

Prince's second team at KSU had a 5-7 record, and he seemed to panic. Kansas State is the type of place where I think strategic and targeted recruiting of junior college players can yield great dividends. The previous head coach, Snyder, had demonstrated this while turning the "Mildcats" into true Wildcats. Prince attempted to do something similar. But he probably went overboard. His February 2008 recruiting class included nineteen junior college players—even though just fifteen of them were eventually eligible to enroll that fall. The other four had academic issues. That's also typical. But the school seemed to support Prince's vision in August of 2008 by giving him a contract extension through 2012. Three months later, on the way to another 5-7 season, Prince was fired after a 31-point (21-52) loss to cross-state rival Kansas. During the fourth quarter of that game, Kansas fans were heckling Kansas State fans by chanting: "Save Ron Prince! Save Ron Prince!"

No official reasons were given for Prince's firing. But the scuttlebutt on campus was that he had been "aloof" and treated his assistants badly. One of his assistant coaches had made mention of that. If Prince would have won more games, he could have been as "aloof" as he wished.

Still, what happened next at Kansas State surprised even me. KSU rehired Snyder, the man Prince had originally replaced.

Of course, this is college football, so the story got even stranger. In May of 2009, the school announced that it had discovered a "secret deal" that had been struck between Prince and former Kansas State athletic director Bob Krause—who had mysteriously resigned two months earlier. This "secret deal" was totally off the books at the university, at least according to news media reports. In addition, the Kansas State president claimed he knew nothing about it.

The arrangement had instead been sealed between Prince's agent and Krause, who signed the document on behalf of the athletic department. The payment was apparently part of Prince's exit package and required Kansas State to pay a total of $3.2 million to a corporation owned by Prince in a series of deferred payments starting in 2015 and ending 2020. When the school administration learned of the deal, it filed legal action to have the $3.2 million agreement declared invalid. Kansas State settled the lawsuit with Prince in May of 2011 for $1.65 million, after spending a reported $395,000 in legal fees.

After he was released from Kansas State, he was hired as the special teams' coordinator at Virginia for the 2009 season, yet was not retained after the firing of Al Groh. Prince served as assistant offensive line coach for the Indianapolis Colts during the 2010 season and remains in that same capacity as the 2011 season approaches. One day, he might be blessed with another try at a head coaching job somewhere. Odds are it will be in the NFL.

Degree of Difficulty: 5
Grade: C+

(22) RANDY SHANNON,
Miami 2007-10

I truly thought justice was served in December of 2006 when Randy Shannon was named as the Miami Hurricanes' new head coach. Shannon had worked for fifteen seasons as a Miami assistant coach. He was considered one of the country's top defensive coordinators. He was a Miami alum. He definitely deserved the job. But the hiring was still a little surprising.

Here's why: Miami had just fired Larry Coker, who was Shannon's boss.

Coker was dismissed because he had just completed a 6-6 regular season that was unacceptable by Miami standards and was marked by an ugly bench-clearing brawl that resulted in the suspension of thirteen Hurricane players. Often when a coach is fired under such conditions, a majority of his staff is fired. And when that happens, it's very seldom that one of the assistants is considered for the head coaching job.

Other candidates were reportedly interviewed to replace Coker. But when some of those top coaches shunned the Hurricanes, administrators turned to the forty-year-old Shannon. It made sense in so many ways. His technical coaching skills were never an issue. Shannon grew up in inner-city Miami. He played high school ball in South Florida. He was a starting linebacker on Miami's 1987 national championship team. And between his stints as a Hurricanes assistant coach at the school, Shannon worked three years for the Miami Dolphins.

But after two seasons, Shannon's record was 12-13 and the package was in need of a little rewrapping. Shannon had scored some big victories (upsets of Texas A&M in his first season, Virginia Tech in his second) and awful losses (routs by Virginia in his first season, Georgia Tech in his second). The Hurricanes reached the Emerald Bowl after the 2008 season but lost to the University of

California. Afterward, Shannon dismissed his offensive coordinator. His defensive coordinator left and took the same job at another university. Shannon retrenched and in 2009 led the Hurricanes to a 9-4 record while being ranked in the top ten in the early part of the season. After posting a disappointing 7-5 record in 2010, Shannon was fired after compiling a 28-22 record over four seasons.

Most minority coaches are given the keys to programs that have very low expectations, with the administration praying for miracles or hoping just to have the team be competitive. Not at Miami. The expectations are rightfully much higher. After a personal visit with Shannon during his tenure as the Miami head coach, I can tell you that he understood how his success at Miami could have been the catalyst for more African American coaches to be hired as head coaches at other BCS schools.

Shannon did not wish to be outspoken about race because he wanted to be judged solely as a coach, not as a minority coach. Besides, as he once told me, his situation was quite obvious anyway.

Degree of Difficulty: 1
Current Grade: C+

(23) DEWAYNE WALKER, UCLA 2007, New Mexico State 2009-present

Walker's first head coaching "opportunity" was barely a blip. When Karl Dorrell was fired at UCLA at the conclusion of the 2007 regular season, he was given the option of staying on to coach the Bruins in the Pioneer Las Vegas Bowl against Brigham Young. Dorrell declined. The interim duty was then given to Walker, who was UCLA's defensive coordinator under Dorrell. The Bruins lost the game in the final seconds when a potential game-winning field goal from twenty-eight yards away was blocked. Even if UCLA had won the game, in my opinion there was no chance Walker would have been named to the UCLA job on a full-time basis. After firing a young African American who'd never been a head coach until UCLA named him to the job (Dorrell), would the school then turn around and hire another African American without head coaching experience?

Nope. Instead, the Bruins went with the "safer" route, hiring alum Rick Neuheisel, even though he had committed NCAA violations at his two previous stops, Colorado and Washington, where he was fired by then-athletic-director Barbara Hedges. She dismissed Neuheisel in June 2003 after she claimed he had lied to her about interviewing for a job with the San Francisco 49ers. It should be noted that Neuheisel eventually received a $4.5 million financial settlement in a lawsuit that he later filed against the Washington and the NCAA for wrongful termination of his contract.

To Neuheisel's credit, after he was hired at UCLA, he recognized Walker's talent and retained him as defensive coordinator for the Bruins. But when New Mexico State came calling after the 2008 season, Walker could not turn down the offer. At age forty-eight, he no doubt realized it might be the only offer he was ever going to get. New Mexico State definitely falls in the "have-not" category of FBS schools. It is a member of the Western Athletic Conference and struggles mightily. The Aggies have not appeared in a bowl game since 1960. The campus, located in the pretty but very isolated small town of Las Cruces, is not on the must-see list of top high school recruits.

However, I would like to applaud New Mexico State for doing something that rarely happens at major college football programs. They found another qualified coach who happened to be African American. Walker is a friend. But I wish he wouldn't have taken this job. I honestly believe it is a dead-end street. I hope he can somehow win and then leave as soon as possible. Yet I am happy that New Mexico State is giving him a chance.

Walker is an intellectually gifted football coach and possesses "fire in his belly," as a NMSU official said in introducing him. But as he has discovered during his tenure at NMSU, a belly fire can be difficult to build into a winning blaze with the Aggies, where after two seasons he has won five out of twenty games.

Degree of Difficulty (UCLA): 3
Grade: B-

Degree of Difficulty (New Mexico State): 10
Current Grade: D

(24) KEVIN SUMLIN,
Houston 2008-present

I thought this was a perfect match when Sumlin was hired. And he is proving me correct. The University of Houston job opened up after Coach Art Briles left for Baylor. But in his final two seasons at Houston, Briles had compiled an 18-8 record and was leaving Cougar football in pretty good shape for Sumlin. I believe an African American coach should thrive at an urban school, and the Cougar program's status—good tradition and a member of the very winnable Conference USA—should open the door for success. Also, Sumlin's credentials were excellent when he walked in that door at Houston. He had been offensive coordinator at Texas A&M and Oklahoma. In his last season with the Sooners, Sumlin's offense had averaged forty-four points per game.

His first season at Houston was also impressive. He went 8-5, finished third in the conference, and beat Air Force in the Armed Forces Bowl. His second Cougar team was even better. Sumlin led Houston to a 10-4 record and won the Western Division of Conference USA. He posted a 5-7 record in 2010. Still, Cougar fans should be proud of what he has accomplished. Sumlin supposedly was a finalist for the Tennessee job—at least it was reported that he interviewed for the position—before the volunteers hired Derek

Dooley. Maybe someone should alert Charles Barkley to have another round of commentary at the ready when Sumlin interviews for future jobs at BCS institutions. Just like Turner Gill, Sumlin is married to a white woman. Will that eliminate him from hiring contention at certain schools? I'd like to believe it would not.

Degree of Difficulty: 5
Current Grade: A-

(25) MIKE LOCKSLEY,
New Mexico 2009-present

Who would have thought? During the 2009 football season, the state of New Mexico was the home for nearly one-third of the African American FBS head coaches. In December of 2008, Locksley was hired at the University of New Mexico a few weeks before DeWayne Walker was hired at New Mexico State. Of the two hirings, Locksley's received the most attention. He came to Albuquerque from his job as offensive coordinator at the University of Illinois. Before that, Locksley had been the recruiting coordinator at Florida. At both places, he had a reputation of going into a family's living room and being a very convincing salesman.

At both Illinois and Florida, Locksley worked the areas around Washington DC—his hometown—especially hard. At New Mexico, he will have to set his sights on Southern California and Texas, but I imagine he will also go back to his familiar territory and try to convince some eastern kids that life in the southwestern desert can be awesome. I wish him luck.

Particularly in Southern California, I am guessing that New Mexico's Locksley and New Mexico State's Walker will be going after many of the same recruits. New Mexico is theoretically the bigger and better program, because the Lobos are in the Mountain West Conference, considered a better league than the WAC of New

Mexico State. But on the flip side, it will be much harder for Locksley and the Lobos to win recruits and games against the likes of TCU and Utah.

If given time, Locksley should be able to recruit enough athletes to eventually be competitive in the Mountain West and finish above .500, which should get him to a bowl game every couple of years. However, there was a troubling report out of Albuquerque less than six months after his hiring. Locksley was accused of sexual harassment and age discrimination by a female executive assistant who filed a complaint with the state's Equal Employment Opportunity Commission. Locksley issued a statement essentially denying the accusation, saying he has always treated everyone with respect and added, "Change and transition is always tough on everybody."

Remember, an accusation also does not mean guilt. At the same time, no accusation can be tossed aside without examining the facts. It was reported that New Mexico did a thorough job of this. But it's always more worrisome when an African American coach is accused of something such as sexual harassment. As I have mentioned many times, black coaches tend to be judged collectively, not individually. When a black coach does something negative, I've talked to enough people to know that it affects the chances of other black coaching candidates everywhere.

And I know for sure that it rarely works the other way. For example, in 1999 when Alabama head coach Mike DuBose spent $300,000 to settle out of court after his secretary accused him of sexual harassment, no one thought it reflected on all white coaches. Alabama obviously didn't, because three years later, Mike Price was hired to coach the Tide. Price was then fired before ever coaching a game. He became intoxicated during a summer golf outing for boosters and allegedly had a sexual liaison with a stripper (Price denied the stripper encounter but not the intoxication).

Even after all of that, I never heard an Alabama fan say: "Maybe we should think about not hiring another middle-aged white guy."

In fact, the University of Texas El Paso didn't have any problem with the accusations filed against Price, because UTEP hired him as head coach following the 2003 season. If Mike Price would have been black, my research leads me to offer the following opinion: (1) he would have not been hired at Alabama; (2) after being terminated at Alabama for misconduct, he would not have resurfaced at a BCS institution; and (3) as an African American, his head football coaching opportunities would probably have been limited to historical black colleges and universities.

Locksley did emerge from his harassment case with his job still intact. According to the university, Locksley resolved the legal issues with his former football administrative assistant by claiming the sexual harassment allegation did not fit the situation. Unfortunately, this was not the only ugly incident that he had to deal with in his first season, during which he recorded just one win and eleven losses. Locksley was suspended for ten days in midseason by University of New Mexico administrators as punishment for his role in a fight with an assistant coach who was also black. This is an episode of what I call black-on-black crime in coaching. I'll discuss that phenomenon in greater detail in another chapter of this book.

It appears that Locksley simply developed brain lock during a staff meeting. At least he took responsibility for it, saying at a press conference: "I'm the leader of the team and my staff. I should have used better judgment. I showed poor leadership, and I won't let it happen again. I've learned some harsh lessons, lessons that I feel will make me a better leader."

That error in judgment cost Locksley a reported $29,000 of his $750,000 annual salary. Locksley did not come out of the blocks with several wins as he had hoped. In addition, the former assistant coach who accused Locksley of attacking him filed a lawsuit right before preseason practices for the 2010 football season. Although the New Mexico administrators clearly want to be fair, they won't be stupid. After two seasons of leading the Aggies, Locksley is 2-22 as head coach and the buzzards are circling. I'm sure there are some boosters in New Mexico who didn't like this experiment from the start. As good a guy as athletic director Paul Krebs appears to be, I don't think he will jump on a grenade to protect Locksley.

Degree of Difficulty: 7
Current Grade: F

(26) RON ENGLISH,
Eastern Michigan 2009-present

This doesn't look promising. Eastern Michigan is one of those schools on the fringe of the FBS. It is located just down the road from the much bigger University of Michigan and rarely has been a factor in the Mid-American Conference. The Eagles have had thirteen straight losing seasons. Coaches go there for their careers to die. I hope Ron English doesn't suffer the same fate.

On the other hand, I originally had the same opinion about Turner Gill and the University of Buffalo. And look what happened. Gill succeeded. So I may again be totally off base. English played football at the University of California and worked his way up through the ranks at San Diego State and Arizona State before he was named defensive coordinator at Michigan under Lloyd Carr before the 2006 season. English had already accepted a job as a Chicago Bears assistant before Carr talked him into staying in the college ranks. I wonder if English regrets that decision. A year later, Carr and his entire staff were out of work and English caught on as the Louisville defensive coordinator until Eastern Michigan made him an offer to become its head coach.

It's going to be a difficult task for English to find enough good players to win at EMU. Institutional support is also in question. But I do know that Derrick Gragg, the athletic director who hired English, will do his best to support the coach. I hope that Gragg will not prostitute the program by playing "body bag" away games for big paychecks in order to balance the budget. I recommend that English line up a few wins each year for confidence purposes. It can't help that Michigan was one of the hardest-hit states by the 2007-08 economic slump. Donations and resources are bound to be down. Many families have been forced to move out of state; some of those families have good high school football players.

Bottom Line: If English wins seven or eight games in a season, any season, he should be coach of the year—or maybe coach of the millenium. Why do I say that? Because in his inaugural season of 2009, he went 0-12. He then posted a 2-10 record in 2010. That's a long two years. With all those losses comes a lot of doubt—and little if any support from prospective donors. I am hoping that Coach English can do an about-face with the program in 2011.

Degree of Difficulty: 10
Current Grade: F

(27) MICHAEL HAYWOOD, Miami (Ohio) 2009—10

The hirings of English at Eastern Michigan and Michael Haywood at Miami were doubly great—because they proved my point about how perception and image are so very important. It is no coincidence that, after a season in which Turner Gill turned around the Buffalo football program and took it to a Mid-American Conference championship, two schools from the same league as Buffalo also decided to hire African American coaches. The success of Gill allowed the presidents and athletic directors at Eastern Michigan and Miami to sell the concept of an African American football coach to fans and alumni. Those fans and alums have now seen a black man on the sidelines—Gill—taking a team to a championship in their league.

It's not a question mark for them anymore. They are eager to imitate a champion. English and Haywood look like that champion.

Between the two men, however, Haywood had far better odds of winning in the long term. Miami has far more football tradition than Eastern Michigan. Miami is the tenth oldest public university in America and has fielded football teams since 1888. The school has produced such great coaches as Paul Brown, Bo Schembechler, and Ara Parseghian. The school's athletic program is well supported by the administration. Ohio athletes who are not good enough to play at a BCS school know that among the non-BCS options for them, Miami is an excellent one. The Redhawks have played in two bowl games since 2003. Shane Montgomery had to resign after the 2008 season because the administration found his four-year record of 17-31 to be unacceptable.

Haywood, therefore, walked into a challenging but workable situation. I know Mike personally. We recruited against each other very often when I was an assistant at Arkansas and he was employed at LSU. Haywood had the experience needed for the job. He has held BCS-level assistant positions at LSU and Texas and was the offensive coordinator at Notre Dame before taking the head coaching position with the Redhawks. His recruiting contacts in the Midwest should have been solid after four seasons in South Bend.

In 2009, Haywood posted a 1-11 record with a very brutal nonconference schedule that included three BCS teams (Kentucky, Cincinnati, Northwestern) that went on to play in bowl games—plus Boise State, which went on to win the Fiesta Bowl. However, Mike then proceeded to do the incredible at Miami in 2010. He went from the outhouse to the penthouse by going 9-4 overall, 7-1in conference play, and winning the Eastern Division of the MAC. The Redhawks subsequently showed the football world they were for real when they upset twenty-fourth ranked Northern Illinois 26-21 in the MAC championship game to win the conference title. This caused Mike's coaching stock to soar and he was offered the head coaching job at the University of Pittsburgh, a member of the Big East conference.

The MAC is a showcase for coaches trying to make a name for themselves and jump up to the next level. That's exactly what happened to Mike. But his Cinderella story had an awful ending for Mike's head coaching career. In my opinion, it will subconsciously have a detrimental effect on future employment opportunities for prospective black head coaching candidates at Pitt, regardless of how his case is eventually resolved.

After Pitt made a bold statement by giving a minority candidate a deserved opportunity, the school fired Haywood before he ever landed a recruit, held a practice or coached a game. Less than three weeks after he became employed at Pitt, Haywood was arrested on a felony domestic battery violence charge in the presence of a minor. The incident occurred at the home Haywood still owned in South Bend after his time at NotreDame. The local police reported that the alleged violence was sparked after a custody issue developed between Haywood and a woman who is the mother of Haywood's child. She accused Haywood of grabbing her by the arm and neck and shoving her when she attempted to leave the home.

This was not good. Haywood's hiring by athletic director Steve Pederson had not been greeted with a great amount of enthusiasm by fans, booster, alumni and students. I surmise that Mike's profile was not the one those Pitt followers had envisioned when Dave Wannstedt was forced to resign following a disappointing 7-5 regular season. Pitt has a long tradition of hiring great coaches, including Pop Warner, Johnny Majors and Jackie Sherrill. Haywood was joining great company until his unfortunate incident. It all worked out poorly for Pitt and Haywood and, in my mind, other minority coaching candidates in the future. Black coaches in leadership positions *cannot* live up to the negative stereotypes from which we are frequently evaluated. It's not fair. But it is what it is.

Degree of Difficulty (Miami Ohio):7
Current Grade: A

Degree of Difficulty (Pittsburgh):3
Current Grade: Expelled

(28) RUFFIN MCNEILL,
Texas Tech 2010,
East Carolina 2010-present

I keep a journal of all hirings and firings of FBS coaches. My journal after the 2009 season was quite extensive because of the six African American coaches who joined the Lonely Twenty-Seven to make it the Lonely Thirty-Three. This was by far the highest number of new black head coaches hired in any offseason—and it doesn't include Turner Gill, who left one FBS school for another.

Of all the coaches who moved up, however, Ruffin McNeill had to take the strangest route. In late December of 2009, he was minding his own business as the defensive coordinator at Texas Tech, preparing his unit to compete in the Valero Alamo Bowl against Michigan State in five days. McNeill was in his tenth year as a Tech assistant, working for Coach Mike Leach. Suddenly, on the morning of December 28, all craziness broke loose. Leach was suspended and then fired by university administrators after a controversial accusation that he had mistreated one of his players. McNeill was asked to step in as the interim head coach for the bowl game.

What else could McNeill do? He said yes. And he somehow managed to pull together the Texas Tech team through the chaotic situation and steer the Red Raiders to an impressive 41-31 victory. As he walked off the field at the Alamodome and did a live interview with ESPN, McNeill made his case to stay on as Tech's permanent head coach, saying he was ready for the job. Seven days later, school administrators politely rejected that case and hired Tommy

Tuberville—who five days later promptly fired McNeill as defensive coordinator. Texas Tech's president did offer McNeill a vague position involving fundraising if he wished to stay with the school. Fortunately for McNeill, he didn't have to accept it.

Why? Because on the very same day that Tuberville dismissed him, the head coaching job unexpectedly opened up at McNeill's alma mater, East Carolina University. Skip Holtz announced he was leaving the school to become head coach at the University of South Florida. McNeill applied for the vacancy and was hired at ECU a week later. The fifty-one-year-old McNeill, who had been a team captain as an East Carolina player, built a strong résumé after leaving the school. He spent time at Austin Peay, North Alabama, and Appalachian State. He then worked as the defensive coordinator at the University of Nevada Las Vegas before Leach hired him at Texas Tech.

In his first year at East Carolina, McNeill finished 6-6 and lost a bowl game, a pretty good start. He will need to keep the momentum going by recording a few signature victories along the way and competing for the Conference USA title on a regular basis. Although he was accepted at ECU as an African American student-athlete, leading the university's football program is a different experience and hiring McNeill as head coach in North Carolina was bold. I'm grateful the ECU administration was willing to give McNeill an opportunity to either succeed or fail based on the results he produces. The past terminations of African American head football coaches at predominantly white institutions indicate that McNeill needs to win a lot and as soon as possible.

Degree of Difficulty (Texas Tech) : 3
Grade: A

Degree of Difficulty (East Carolina): 6
Grade: B-

(29) WILLIE TAGGART,
Western Kentucky 2010-present

I could see this one coming. Willie Taggart had been working as the running backs' coach at Stanford since 2007, but every other year of his coaching life had been spent as an assistant at Western Kentucky, where he had been an All-American quarterback as a player from 1995-98 and had his jersey retired. So when the Western Kentucky head coaching job opened up following a winless 2009 season, Taggart quickly offered up his candidacy. He interviewed well and won the job. It could not have hurt that Taggart had spent the previous two seasons coaching Stanford running back Toby Gerhart, runner-up for the Heisman Trophy.

Taggart doesn't have that sort of athlete to work with at Western Kentucky. The Hilltoppers have recently moved up from the Football Championship Subdivision (the former Division 1AA) to the much tougher FBS classification. But the trouble is, there aren't many FBS athletes in Kentucky to recruit. Taggart will have to use his recruiting budget wisely and seek out under-the-radar players in southern states, including his native Florida. Taggert's first season was just as difficult as expected. He did squeeze out two victories in 12 games. Hopefully, 2011 produces sweeter results.

Degree of Difficulty: 10
Grade: D-

(30) LARRY PORTER,
Memphis 2010-present

Much like Taggart, Porter returned to his alma mater and tried to lift a non-glamour program into a higher national profile. Unlike Taggart, Porter is at a school with more resources, located in a more productive area for high school football players. Still in his late thirties, Porter has a lot of energy and will need it. He was known as an excellent recruiter at LSU, his previous stop—but of course, recruiting players to LSU in the Southeastern Conference will always be easier than recruiting at Memphis, a Conference USA school.

Porter was eager for the challenge, however, telling supporters at his first press conference that there is so much excellent talent in the surrounding area that if he can simply coax enough of those players into becoming Memphis Tigers, all will be well. Porter's exact quote: "There are a lot of kids that really want to stay home. I've basically identified about ten guys, five of which I know have legitimate BCS and SEC offers, that are very, very open to coming to the University of Memphis. The other five...I know there's a chance we can get them on visits."

The recruiting class did not yield immediate results, though. The Tigers were a disappointing 1-11 in 2010 and were not competitive. Things will have to get better...quickly.

Degree of Difficulty: 5
Grade: F

(31) MIKE LONDON,
Virginia 2010-present

This hire reveals the value of having diversity at the Football Championship Series (FCS) level. Mike London was head coach at the University of Richmond for two seasons, compiling a 24-5 record and winning the 2008 FCS national title. He had previously worked six seasons as an assistant coach at Virginia, so he knows the territory in Charlottesville. And he's a native of the state—or commonwealth, as the citizens call it—so the residents of Virginia ought to have his back.

But winning consistently with the Cavaliers has been problematic. The university has high academic standards. And even though

London says he will embrace the challenge of finding students who can excel in the classroom and excel on the field, history shows that it isn't simple to make that formula equal a BCS bowl trip. There's a much smaller pool of those types of athletes. And there's heavy competition to recruit them from other such programs as Stanford, Northwestern, and Vanderbilt.

His hiring, though, was a positive move for football in general and black coaches specifically. It was also relatively unique. Rarely does an African American athletic director have the guts to hire an African American football coach because of what I think equates to self-preservation. Particularly at a school below the Mason-Dixon line, I am convinced that boosters keep a wary eye on a black athletic director's moves. I commend the courage of Craig Littlepage, the first African American athletic director in the Atlantic Coast Conference, for reaching out and finding another qualified minority. In the ACC, that amounts to a monumental breakthrough. In 2010, London's first season, Virginia recorded a signature win over nationally ranked Miami en route to a 4-8 record.

Degree of Difficulty: 5
Grade: C-

(32) CHARLIE STRONG,
Louisville 2010-present

I've expressed on numerous occasions my admiration for Strong, who in my opinion deserved a major college head coaching opportunity a long time ago. Strong was doing awesome work as Florida's defensive coordinator. Finally, a school such as Louisville had the courage to hire him. Strong had some shoring-up work to do. Competing in the Big East conference is easier than competing in the SEC or Big 10. But the pressure to win at Louisville is greater than you might think, especially with a stadium expansion under way.

Strong brought his jumper cables with him and spark-started the Cardinals in his first season. He won seven games and lost six, with a victory in his first bowl appearance. His team could have easily been 9-4 or 10-3. On the surface, 2011 looks promising because his athletic director has scheduled wisely. It is obvious that Louisville wants to win and it appears the school is following a strategic plan to do so.

Degree of Difficulty: 3
Grade: B

(33) JOSEPH "JOKER" PHILLIPS,
Kentucky 2010-present

This is another alum trying to make his old school proud. His unusual nickname came about because his father is also named Joe, so the family wanted a way to lessen the confusion when talking to both of them. Some of the Internet blogs have implied that his hire was a joke — but at least he has the opportunity to prove the naysayers wrong. I always thought former Kentucky Coach Hal Mumme had the right idea in Lexington, by creating a real identity as a pass-happy team that lured some skilled players to the campus. Rich Brooks played the game more conventionally and won some games but didn't create a lot of excitement.

No matter what, at Kentucky, it's always going to be basketball first, second, and third. But Phillips' first year was definitely no joke. The Wildcats were very competitive and had a huge win over No. 10 ranked South Carolina while also qualifying for a bowl, where they lost and wrapped up a 6-7 campaign.

Degree of Difficulty: 5
Grade: C+

(34) JON EMBREE,
Colorado 2011 – present

A dream came true for Coach Jon Embree when he was tapped to replace Dan Hawkins, who was fired after posting a 19-39 record in four-plus seasons in Boulder. "It's a dream job with it being my alma mater and growing up there," said Embree, who spent ten years as a Colorado assistant under former coaches Bill McCartney, Rick Neuheisel and Gary Barnett. It appears that McCartney was instrumental in working behind the scenes to prompt the Buffaloes to hire a minority for the first time to lead their program. If Embree is smart, he will follow McCartney's philosophy of shooting high for the best recruits, especially with Colorado joining the Pac 10 conference to make it the Pac 12. The California recruiting ground is fertile and there are many student-athletes who will want what Colorado has to offer. Embree has never been a head coach but brings a wealth of experience. If he can show improvement each season toward the goals and objectives established by the administration, he can have a great career in Boulder.

Degree of Difficulty: 3
Grade: Incomplete

(35) DARRELL HAZELL,
Kent State 2011 – present

Darrell Hazell became head coach at Kent State in December of 2010 after previous coach Doug Martin resigned following seven years of struggles and a 28-53 won-loss record at the Mid-American Conference school.

Kent State is a typical lower-tier Football Bowl Subdivision program. It faces resource and recruiting challenges that make it difficult to be successful. The Golden Flashes have not been to a

149

bowl games since 1972. It is just the sort of program where African American coaches are frequently given an opportunity—often in the what-the-heck-do—we-have-to-lose philosophy of hiring.

Hazell probably falls into that category, although he was a solid candidate for a head coaching job by any estimation. At age 47, he had accumulated the proper resume to be considered strongly by the Kent State administration. Hazell played small college football at Muskingum College and then began his coaching career at Oberlin College, another Division III school in Ohio.

Following that, Hazell worked his way up through the assistant-coaching ranks at Eastern Illinois, Penn, Western Michigan, Army and West Virginia before settling in for three years at Rutgers. He then joined the Ohio State staff and for five years served as assistant head coach under Jim Tressel while also coaching the Buckeyes' wide receivers. After Martin stepped aside, Kent State made a phone call to Columbus and landed Hazell without much competition.

Degree of Difficulty: 10
Current Grade: Incomplete

(36) DON TREADWELL,
Miami, Ohio 2011 – present

ESPN.com's Adam Rittenberg wrote that Michigan State will be sad to see Don Treadwell leave, but there were few men more deserving of being selected as head coach. During the 2010 football season Treadwell, was able to display his head coaching potential by filling in for Michigan State's Mark Dantonio as acting head coach for two games after Dantonio suffered a mild heart attack. Treadwell won both games. "It's a dream come true to return to my alma mater, Miami, as head football coach," Treadwell said.

Here's another significance of this hire: After Mike Haywood left Miami (Ohio) for Pittsburgh, the administration made a bold statement by replacing an African American football coach with another African American football coach. This rarely happens because of the collective evaluation of coaches of color. Give Haywood credit in paving the way for Treadwell.

Degree of Difficulty (Michigan State):4
Grade: A+

Degree of Difficulty (Miami Ohio):7
Grade: Incomplete

(37) JAMES FRANKLIN,
Vanderbilt 2011 – present

In July 2010, Vanderbilt head football coach Bobby Johnson announced his retirement. The university initially tapped Robbie Caldwell as interim head coach. But before the season started Vanderbilt officially dropped the interim tag and decided that Caldwell was their man and they didn't need to look any further. Caldwell subsequently resigned after posting a 2-10 record and saying the program needed change. Vanderbilt stepped out of its comfort zone and hired a search firm to help find its next head coach. The private institution selected 38-year-old James Franklin, who will be the first black coach of any major sport at Vanderbilt and the only third black coach in the SEC. According to Vice Chancellor David William, the hiring of Franklin is part of an effort to instill a winning culture. The initiative includes improving facilities, which at Vanderbilt currently don't match up to other SEC schools.

Franklin was assistant head coach and offensive coordinator at Maryland and had been in line for several years to succeed Ralph Friedgen. However, Kevin Anderson was introduced as Maryland's new athletic director in September of 2010 and told Franklin that he couldn't guarantee him the job if Friedgen left. The Vanderbilt opportunity was one that Franklin couldn't pass up — but I hope he did his homework and comprehends how history has proven it will be difficult to win at Vanderbilt.

Degree of Difficulty: 8
Current Grade: Incomplete

(38) DAVID SHAW,
Stanford 2011 – present

When Stanford promoted David Shaw to replace Jim Harbaugh, who left to take over the San Francisco 49ers, it became the first FBS institution to hire three African Americans to lead its football program.

"Since the day I started coaching, this is the job I always knew that I wanted," Shaw said at his opening press conference. "I will do what I can to help this place be successful. Two years of good football is not enough."

Athletic Director Bob Bowlsby said he interviewed four in-house candidates and visited at length with three others from outside the program before choosing Shaw, who had been a Harbaugh assistant with the Cardinal and is a Stanford alum.

"His contribution to the current state of affairs of our football program is immeasurable," Bowlsby said of Shaw. "This is, in my estimation, the most logical step that we can take. He is the guy who is going to lead Stanford football for a long, long time."

With Shaw as part of the coaching staff, Stanford improved each season under Harbaugh, making a bowl game in his third year and going 12-1 in the 2010 season with a dominant 40-12 victory over Virginia Tech in the Orange Bowl. Stanford finished fourth in the final AP poll, its best ranking since the unbeaten 1940 team that finished No. 2. Consequently, expectations are high and Shaw will be expected to feed the monster.

Degree of Difficulty: 5
Current Grade: Incomplete

Bits and Pieces

So that's the list. When you examine the situations of these thirty-eight men, you find some commonalities. Almost all have worked—or are working—for programs either in dire distress or in a perpetual rebuilding situation. There have been notable exceptions—Willingham at Notre Dame and Washington, Blake at Oklahoma, perhaps Dorrell at UCLA and Shannon at Miami—but they are the exceptions to the rule. If you average the "degree of difficulty" numbers above, then the average African American coach faces a 6.4 average degree of difficulty when he walks through the door on his first day of work.

I am certain that some of these men, given a choice, would have preferred to wait until better jobs came along. But they can't. The opportunities for African American coaches pop up so rarely that those coaches feel as if they need to take any head coaching job, anywhere. Why am I so sure of this? Because I was there once. I knew San Jose State was not an ideal situation. But I thought it might be the only college head coaching job I would ever be offered. And because I did, in fact, accept the job, and did not win more football games than I lost, SJSU was my first and last major college head coaching opportunity.

Throughout the 2010 football season, Willingham was the only African American coach who has reached a BCS bowl game. He and his Stanford team lost the 2000 Rose Bowl to Wisconsin. I want to be optimistic that coaches such as Charlie Strong at Louisville or Turner Gill at Kansas will one day take their teams to another BCS bowl. But my biggest concern, as I examine the travails of the Lonely Thirty-Eight, is that too many talented men of integrity are leaving NCAA football and migrating to the NFL after their experiences as college head coaches.

It is very striking to me how many of the Lonely Thirty-Eight—including Nunnely, Caldwell, Dorrell, and Croom—have ended up in pro football following their unpleasant college experiences. I understand completely. They probably perceive that the path to becoming a head coach in the NFL has fewer potholes, even though there are theoretically fewer head coaching opportunities. Plus, as bad as the Cleveland Browns or Houston Texans have been over the years, it is still easier for them to be competitive among their peers than it is at New Mexico State or Louisiana Lafayette or Eastern Michigan.

I grant you that the records of most African American head coaches in the FBS have not been stellar. But remember the sample size. If more African American coaches were given a chance, particularly at BCS schools, those results might change rapidly. Prince and Dorrell have proved that an African American coach can have winning seasons in a BCS conference. Gill has proved that an African American coach can turn around a moribund non-BCS program.

Yet of the 120 current Football Bowl Subdivision schools, through the 2011 season, eighty-four have yet to hire an African American head coach. I want to note one more time that I am not advocating the hiring of a head football coach simply because he is black. However, I am proposing that programs do not eliminate qualified coaching candidates who are black. It is my dream that more black coaches can be blessed with as many opportunities to succeed or fail as Lane Kiffin, currently the head coach at the University of Southern California. Prior to that, Kiffin was fired by the NFL's Oakland Raiders early during his second season as their head coach after he had lost 15 of the 20 games he coached. Nevertheless, when Tennessee decided to replace Phil Fulmer after the 2008 season, the school hired Kiffin, who posted a mediocre 7-6 record leading the Volunteers. Yet a few months later, Southern Cal asked Kiffin to replace Pete Carroll after he ran away to the NFL's Seattle Seahawks.

Kiffin, in other words, received two great opportunities in the college game after flopping as a pro head coach. I'm not hating on Coach Kiffin. In fact, more power to him. But my research suggests with a high level of certainty that if Kiffin had been a black coach with similar coaching credentials, the odds of his being hired by a college program with the tradition and national prominence of Tennessee or USC would be less than one in twenty. This reflects how employment opportunities at predominantly white colleges and universities remain color coded. Nearly 50 years after civil rights legislation was passed, employment opportunities for black football coaches at BCS, FBS, Division II and III have definitely improved. But I can confidently say that, at predominately white institutions, head coaching opportunities are still restricted for black football coaches.

If Dr. King's dream is one day truly fulfilled and black coaches are viewed in the same light as their white peers, maybe one day the thirty-eight men in this chapter won't be quite so lonely.

CHAPTER SIX

-BOOSTERS-
THE PERPETRATORS
OF THE CRACKBACK!

When people discover that I have spent the last two decades re-searching the issue of black football coaches and their struggle to get a fair shake at the college level, I am usually asked one or all of the following questions:

- No matter what color you are, isn't the job still just coach-ing and teaching and winning and losing?

- Don't white coaches have to deal with the same problems and challenges?

- Is it really so different being a black coach?

In response to all those questions, I tell a story.

It has nothing to do with a touchdown, nor with a halftime adjustment or a videotape session. That's real football stuff. No, this story is about the most critical constituency a college coach has to please: boosters. These are the fat cats who support football teams at universities across the country, often in a big way—by writing out big checks.

A few months after the 2003 season at San Jose State, the ath-letic department held a gathering of our major financial contribu-tors—people who donated $2,000 or more to the athletic programs on an annual basis. The gathering was held at a downtown San Jose hotel. The mood was upbeat, even though we had finished the season with a disappointing 3-8 record. In spite of the results, we were making progress. Our home attendance was up. Our players' academic records had improved.

In my first three years as head coach, we had won twelve games and lost twenty-four. Not spectacular, I'll admit. But the record books reflect the challenges my predecessors, John Ralston and Dave Baldwin, and I all faced. Like me, they struggled to make San Jose State a winner. Ralston, a College Football Hall of Fame inductee, had a 10-25 record in his first three seasons with the Spartans. Baldwin was 11-22 in his first three seasons at the school.

Despite this history, I really felt better days were ahead for our program. Thanks to generous contributions from a few boosters, I had been able to hire a top-notch new defensive coordinator for the 2004 season—Keith Burns, the former head coach at Tulsa and someone I had worked with on the coaching staff at the University of Arkansas. Keith was a white guy; I didn't think his color mattered.

As the evening progressed in the hotel ballroom, several of our boosters enjoyed glasses of wine. No problem on my account. This was supposed to be a relaxed and informal occasion. At one point, a booster carrying a glass of wine came up to me and started a conversation. He was trying to be complimentary about Burns's hiring but wound up making a comment about the racial makeup of our entire staff. The booster said he was just trying to be honest with me and that he and some of his booster friends believed I would have been more successful during the 2003 season if I had hired fewer black assistant coaches. At the time, there were four. After thanking him for his candor, I asked if by "successful" he was referring to wins and losses—because in all other areas, the San Jose State program had definitely improved. The booster agreed. "Well," I said, "then I assume you must have also told Coach Baldwin and Coach Ralston that they didn't do better because they had too many white coaches.

Because, you know, they won fewer games than I did in their first three years here."

"I didn't know that," the booster replied.

I then talked about how black coaches often deal with the belief that they are unqualified simply because of their skin color. White coaches, just the opposite. They are often deemed qualified simply *because of* skin color. This, I told the booster, wasn't fair to either party. And that pretty much ended our discussion.

If he had wished, though, I'd have gladly continued the conversation with him, acknowledging that boosters have always been part of college football. In the beginning, they were the fans and alumni who showed up in their raccoon coats to cheer their favorite teams. The most prominent and passionate of these folks evolved into well-organized groups that raise thousands or millions of dollars for their schools. As such, boosters are often described as the "lifeblood" of the sport. I would have noted, however, that the "lifeblood" always has a lot more white blood cells in it than any other kind. From coast to coast, booster club members are overwhelmingly males—and overwhelmingly white. That could change one day. But right now those are the unabashed facts. And as the evidence bears out, it is definitely a factor when athletic directors and school presidents make coaching decisions.

I could have also pointed out to this booster how Mack Brown of Texas and Frank Beamer of Virginia Tech, who are both white, probably never had their qualifications questioned because of skin color even as they struggled early in their head coaching careers. I could have explained that while Brown has been very successful at Texas, he compiled an 8-24-1 record in his first three seasons as North Carolina's head coach, including back-to-back 1-10 seasons. I could have expressed my admiration for Beamer, who has built Virginia Tech into a top program but, during his first three seasons there, lost twenty-one of his first thirty-four games. It's probably a stretch to think that Virginia Tech would have hired Beamer if he had been black. But let's pretend he had been African American. Could the school have withstood pressure from boosters to dump him after losing two-thirds of his games? I don't know for sure, of course. It's a hypothetical question.

But I know what my gut tells me.

Actually, I don't even need my gut instinct. I just need my eyes. Look what happened at Notre Dame, where Ty Willingham was fired after three seasons with a better record than previous Notre Dame coaches—all of whom were white—had posted after their first three seasons in South Bend. Notre Dame proved that membership has its privileges. The membership I'm talking about has nothing to do with American Express. It is the membership that comes from being born white.

Six months after my conversation at the booster gathering, I received an e-mail from another San Jose State booster following our team's loss to Southern Methodist University. This booster asked me to resign and turn over our program to Keith Burns—the defensive coordinator I had hired the previous winter. Again, Keith is white. Obviously, I think he's an excellent football man. That's why I wanted him on our staff. But when Burns was the head coach at Tulsa, his teams had posted a 7-28 record—and in our head-to-head encounters, I had won both games. Just like me, Burns had struggled in building his program. We often spoke about the challenges he faced with similar limited resources. I concluded that there is only one thing worse than being an unsuccessful football coach—and that is being an unsuccessful black football coach.

I also concluded that in terms of the machinery that creates this situation, boosters provide much of the fuel for both black and white coaches. Many of them are well-heeled professionals who are accustomed to having influence at work. So they naturally expect to be influential when they fork over sizable donations to their favorite schools or favorite teams.

And where does that influence count most? The NCAA has strict rules about what boosters can and cannot supply to student-athletes. Although the rules are violated by some schools, most make a strong effort to enforce them. So the boosters know they can't simply hand over a bundle of money to the starting quarterback. They can, however, hand over bundles and bundles of money to athletic departments. Boosters can also designate where and how they want the money to be used. They can have it pay for part of a new stadium or other athletic facility—and have a building or room named after them. Or they can make a contribution to a special foundation that is used to augment the salary of coaches.

They can also make contributions to endow scholarships for football players. In 2007, a *Sports Illustrated* story reported that at Ohio State, more than a hundred boosters had underwritten athletic scholarships to the tune of $36 million. Gene Smith, the Ohio State athletic director, told the magazine that if not for those endowed scholarships, "I might have to cut travel and recruiting and equipment."

There are no rules against any of this. And the boosters are not dummies. They realize that their money buys them access, power, the ears of the athletic directors and presidents—and the ability to tell inappropriate, racially oriented jokes at public gatherings with impunity.

Yes, that really happens. I experienced it firsthand during my coaching career. Boosters often feel enough at ease to crack jokes with blatant racial overtones at university gatherings. And I'm ashamed to admit that I never uttered much of a protest. It made me feel half dead, not having the courage to pull aside the offending boosters and tell them: "You know, those jokes might be funny to you. And please don't think I'm overly sensitive or that I have a chip on my shoulder, but they are not acceptable around me. I ask that you refrain from cracking racial jokes—or at least, don't tell them around me if you feel the need to continue getting your laughs that way."

Of course, it would help if the school presidents and athletic directors confronted such boosters with the same sort of advice. But I'm also ashamed to say that many administrators go right along and laugh at the jokes, even though they're not funny.

Here's another story, courtesy of an African American former assistant coach at a Conference USA school: One night during the 2007 season, this assistant coach was sent to represent the head coach at a beer-and-chicken-wings gathering of boosters at a popular restaurant. The assistant coach wound up sitting in a large booth with several people, including the owner of a local company, a man who was a major donor to the athletic department. This man was at the opposite end of the booth.

"As we're sitting there," the assistant coach told me, "this guy starts talking about things at work. He says, 'I am so tired of these niggers I have who show up late and leave early—I'm going to fire them all.' I mean, I heard this with my own ears. I got up and walked over past him and made sure he saw me. This guy's friend later pulled me aside and apologized, saying his friend was just mad and didn't mean what he'd said. Then the guy himself comes over and offers to buy me a drink. He didn't apologize, just offered to buy me a drink. I didn't take up his offer."

If that particular booster had been brazen enough to use such offensive racial language in the presence of an African American assistant coach, don't you think the booster has probably used that language in the presence of white administrators? Why would administrators put up with that? Why would they even want his support?

I'll tell you why: those administrators too often see only one color—green. Money will make you sell your soul, eat cheese, chuckle, smile, and grin at things that you don't like or things that make you feel uncomfortable. The administrators probably feel they are taking one for the team so that they can collect those booster checks for the school or athletic department.

But let's connect some dots. What happens when those booster checks are used to directly pay for a football coach? Typically, when a university makes a head coaching hire, the new man receives part of his compensation package as a "contribution" from a foundation that is funded by the booster club. Often, that "contribution" effectively doubles or triples the coach's listed salary. Without that "contribution," a university would not be able to hire any of the top people in the field.

You know what the real problem is? The system allows it to happen, and boosters know how to play the system; they maximize their influence by pledging literally millions of dollars to the school over a ten- or twenty-year period, spreading out their donations over those years. That financial commitment buys the boosters long-term influence. It can also buy them entry into exclusive areas—comically so, at times. I have personally witnessed boosters being given sideline passes and allowed to dress as coaches. Believe it or not, while coaching at Arkansas, I even heard a booster suggest a play that should be called during the critical moments of a game. You can't buy that kind of access in the NFL, which is precisely my point. Pro football's culture doesn't include boosters who can sidle up to the top decision-makers and lobby for—or against—a black head coach.

I know what you're thinking: college football's booster dynamic surely affects the hiring of all coaches, no matter their color. You're right. But it's clear to me that African American head coaches are affected more than any others.

Let me share another experience with you.

Don Kassing became president of San Jose State in 2004 during my fourth season at the school. He was elevated to that position from his previous job as vice president of finance and administration. Kassing had been one of my biggest supporters during my first three years at San Jose State. One time, he stood in front of a booster group at a "Quarterback Club" meeting and backed me to the hilt

in a situation that involved gross negligence by the school bureaucracy. Because of this negligence, our coaching staff was stunned just
twenty-four hours before our 2004 season opener against Stanford.

Here's what happened: As we sat down to review our game
plan on Friday morning, an administrative official informed us
that several of our key players who had supposedly been certified
as academically eligible by the school were, in fact, not eligible to
play the next night. It was a paperwork issue, not a grade-point or
scholastic issue. University officials said they needed more time to
certify the players' records—even though I knew that other football
programs always seemed to get this work done with no problems
and no delays. But that did us little good. We were in a train wreck
of a situation. Without the key players in uniform, we would be
forced to play Stanford with backups who had not even been prac-
ticing the game plan.

After consulting with my staff and athletic director, I made a
drastic decision. I said we would not play the game at all. I knew
this would cause a stink. But I was fed up. During the previous three
years, I had been confronted with similar issues and had suppressed
my anger. I wasn't going to do it again. I also knew our chances
to beat Stanford were very slim with those backup players on the
field—and it wasn't fair to them either. Against our biggest neighborhood rival, these players would be asked to perform without
proper preparation. In that situation, I would rather forfeit.

President Kassing caught word of my plan. Six hours prior to
kickoff, he came to our hotel and asked us to play the game. And
because I trusted him, we did. We lost, 43-3. But I really believed
in Kassing. I thought that with him as president, things would be
better for me and our program. I was wrong.

After the Stanford debacle, Kassing and I had a frank discussion. We agreed that the bureaucratic messes couldn't continue. Trying to battle a schedule of tough Division I opponents was difficult
enough. I didn't need to also battle my own school. Kassing told

me he understood the challenges facing me. He said, forcefully and boldly, that I could count on him to correct the problems. Because I felt he was an open, up-front guy, I had faith in him. But about a month later, Chuck Bell, my athletic director, came to me with some unsettling information. He'd been informed that a meeting had been called by a group of influential boosters, including the late Bill Walsh, the former 49er head coach, a San Jose State alumnus. This meeting was said to have been held at Stanford University, where Walsh worked. Kassing was supposedly not involved with the group—or at least that's what he told Bell.

That fact seemed important, especially after I learned that the upshot of the Stanford meeting was that the boosters wanted to fire Bell and me. I figured that with Kassing in our corner, we were safe. But since Bell and I are now no longer employed at San Jose State, I would have to assume that I was incorrect—and that Bell's source was a credible one.

Within weeks after this discussion, Kassing met with Bell. Then he met with me. He more or less pushed us into resigning after the institution found money to pay off the remainder of our contracts. Obviously, in his new position, Kassing had somehow found money that we were told the institution didn't have—and the money wasn't merely used to fund the contract buyouts for Bell and me. Kassing hired a new athletic director, who subsequently hired my replacement. Kassing approved a contract that doubled the compensation I'd been paid. The boosters raised more money so that the school could hire more experienced assistant coaches.

Previously in my relationship with Kassing, he had assured me that any influence pills he swallowed from the booster club would have a placebo effect on him. But I guess he, too, fell victim to "boosteritis," a virus that plainly affects the hiring and firing of football coaches.

One might ask: "Coach Hill, with your 14-33 record, how did you expect President Kassing to fight off the boosteritis virus?"

My answer—and my prescription to fight off the virus—was very simple. I wanted the opportunity to do my job with the same support and resources given to my successor. Nothing more, nothing less. But I never was given that chance. These things happen to white coaches, too. But my research suggests it happens to black coaches more frequently.

Kassing would retire as president of San Jose State during the summer of 2008 but would return on an interim basis in August of 2010 through the summer of 2011. I remain disappointed about my experience with him, but I forgave him and moved on a long time ago. I honestly believed that Kassing had my back, because he frequently applauded my leadership skills and lunched with me regularly; Kassing had supported my idea to stage a home football game with Grambling State that would benefit the cause of literacy. It drew the largest home crowd in the history of San Jose State's football program.

Before the 2002 season, Kassing had even sent me a book called *Good To Great* by Jim Collins. Inside the book, Kassing wrote: "You're a natural leader, so you will relate to the ideas in this book. Check out particularly the 'Level Five' leader, because I think you have many of those characteristics."

You think Kassing ever mentioned that to the boosters?

If the boosteritis virus could infect San Jose State, which hardly leads the nation in booster contributions, then just imagine what the virus does at places such as Notre Dame or USC.

You'll never find an athletic director or university administrator who will openly admit that the boosters influence a decision whether to hire a football head coach of color. Despite that story involving the "n" word from my friend at a Conference USA school, racism in this day and age is usually not out in the open. It is not a roomful of people in white hoods, nor a sign on the wall above a drinking fountain. Racism today is more often something you can feel but can't see—just like humidity or a cool breeze on a summer day. But I can think of at least two instances where the humidity was thick—and the breeze was downright chilly.

Consider the curious case of Doug Williams, the former quarterback of the Washington Redskins and Super Bowl MVP. In 1998, Williams took over the football program at Grambling, a Division 1AA program, where he proceeded to win fifty-two of his first seventy games. In short, Williams had an ideal profile for a major college coaching job. He had done everything possible to earn that consideration: with an NFL pedigree and a proven record as a college head coach, he related well to young people and obviously knew the game.

After the 2002 season, the athletic director at the University of Kentucky called and asked him to be a candidate for the school's vacant head coaching job. The phone call was a potential history-maker, because at that time, no school in the Southeastern Conference had ever hired a black head football coach. Kentucky could have made Williams the first. He had a great interview with athletic director Mitch Barnhart...or so Williams thought.

A few days later, Barnhart told Williams the school wanted to go in a different direction. Kentucky ended up hiring Rich Brooks, the former University of Oregon head coach who was looking for a place to land after two unsuccessful seasons in the NFL with the St. Louis Rams.

How did Brooks do? Before retiring in 2009, he compiled a 39-47 record in seven seasons as Kentucky's head coach, although he did win three bowl games and finish 7-6 in his final season. I guess that's not terrible. But in my opinion, Williams was just as deserving of the opportunity. It's obvious to me that given a choice between a retread such as Brooks or a fresh face and a proven winner like Williams, it would have made sense for Barnhart and the school to select a proven winner like Williams. However, Kentucky went with the retread. Why?

After being told by Kentucky that he'd been eliminated as a candidate, Williams asked Barnhart the same question. "He told me that he was more 'comfortable' with hiring Coach Brooks," Williams said in August 2003, eight months later, when he appeared at a seminar about minority coaches that I helped organize. And how did Williams respond to that remark from Barnhart? "I didn't know how to respond," Williams said. "I still don't know what that means."

Here's what I think it means: most athletic directors don't believe their mostly white boosters are going to be wildly enthusiastic about seeing a black face representing their school on the sidelines. In my opinion, the only thing Doug couldn't adjust on his résumé, the only thing that kept him from being selected as a head football coach at Kentucky or a major institution, was his skin color.

Here's what else I think Barnhart meant: If he had hired Williams, Kentucky would have been the first SEC institution to simultaneously employ black head coaches in both of the major revenue producing sports. Tubby Smith, the Wildcats' basketball coach at the time, is also an African American. In 2009 when Brooks retired, I had to give Kentucky some credit for tapping Joker Phillips, an alum of the university who is African American, as Brooks's replacement. Two years earlier, Phillips had been named as the school's "coach in waiting" as preparation for Brooks's departure. It could be that in the years that passed since the Kentucky folks snubbed Williams, those folk had become more open to a minority hiring. Or, it is also possible that the mysterious "comfort factor" developed because Phillips was a familiar face at the school.

Nevertheless, since nondiscrimination and equality are my goals, I must be consistent and criticize the "coach in waiting" handoff approach. At Kentucky or anywhere else, it is hardly fair for other coaches—of any color—who might want to interview for the job. Also, as I was pondering the Phillips "coach in waiting," I remembered the following: Tubby Smith is now the head basketball coach at Minnesota. The Kentucky basketball team is currently led by John Calipari, a white coach. What does that mean? There will not be two African American faces simultaneously leading the university's two most prominent sports teams.

If boosters aren't afraid to question whether a school has too many black assistant coaches, you can bet that administrators hear the rumbles about too many black head coaches. I know that Bell, my athletic director at San Jose State, heard rumblings from the school boosters there. Some complained about Bell's efforts to hire the most talented coaches based on their résumés and their qualifications rather than their race. Nearly half of the head coaches hired by Bell during his tenure at San Jose State were people of color.

Do the vast majority of boosters not feel "comfortable" with minority coaches? I'm not sure. It is quite possible that many athletic directors are just assuming the boosters feel that way and never bother to ask. Regardless, the result is the same.

There are both funny and sad aspects to all this. College football purists often gripe that their sport is becoming too much like pro football in terms of commercialization. But if college football were more like pro football in terms of a business model, there would be no boosters or donors or "influential supporters" in the college game. In the NFL, owners and general managers hire coaches without having to worry about how the alumni are going to like the decisions. The mission is to win games and fill up seats. And if you do the first, the second follows. It's brutally competitive. But it's not complicated.

Pro football owners only have to worry about television ratings and selling tickets and luxury boxes to corporations and fans. The owners don't have to worry about romancing a select group of those fans in the hope that they will donate $25,000 or $50,000 to help keep the "franchise" afloat—or play host to back-slapping cocktail parties where the head coach is supposed to be the meet-and-greet star.

As an illustration, let's look at John Tyson, the former CEO of Tyson Foods, which is based in Northwest Arkansas. Mr. Tyson wanted to help my own beloved University of Arkansas to reach its goal in a $1 billion fundraising campaign. So he made a $7 million gift to the school. I've met Mr. Tyson personally. He is a great man of vision who exemplifies hard work. These are reasons why Tyson Foods is so successful. But I also have heard from reliable sources that Mr. Tyson speaks frankly with university officials about issues surrounding the head football coaching position with the Arkansas Razorbacks.

The booster tentacles can reach even higher up the food chain. When John White was serving as the University of Arkansas chancellor—he's now retired—some very credible and reliable sources told me that White wanted to remove Frank Broyles as the school's athletic director. A very similar thing had happened at the University of Georgia to Vince Dooley, the school's longtime beloved football head coach who moved up into the athletic director position and stayed there for twenty-five years—until the school's president soured on Dooley and demoted him.

At Arkansas when the same plan was afoot, a few key board members—the ultimate boosters—got wind of White's intention. I was told the board members told White that he would be dismissed himself if, in fact, he decided to fire Broyles. But things can change, and here's the kicker: In 2007, about ten years after White's initial plan was foiled, word on the street is he did indeed force Broyles to step down and move into a fundraising position with the Razorback Foundation. Who do you think gave White the authority to initiate what he originally wanted to do with Broyles? Very credible sources revealed that it was the board of trustees—many of whom were also big athletic boosters.

This just shows how the hiring process at universities is influenced by people of power—who usually are the people with money. These relationships set the table for a dinner of gourmet hypocrisy.

How so? In 2001, a survey was administered by the American Football Coaches Association. The organization sent a questionnaire to the athletic directors at all Division I football schools. The athletic directors were asked to list the qualities they most sought when searching for a new football coach at their school. According to the survey results, "integrity" was the number-one attribute that athletic directors wanted. The second most important quality was "football knowledge and intelligence." There was no mention of "winning record." Of course, if you pay attention to the sports headlines every December, plenty of coaches with "integrity" and "football knowledge" are fired. But that's not why I found the AFCA survey so fascinating.

When I looked farther down the list of qualities that athletic directors sought, I saw such items as "salesmanship" and "fundraising." I don't imagine an NFL owner is concerned too much about these things. If so, such great coaches such as Mike Ditka and Bill Parcells would have probably never been hired. Imagine asking Bill Belichick of the New England Patriots to be more people friendly and have a few drinks with sponsors and potential fans so they will buy more tickets or lease more skyboxes.

The truth is, if you are a head coach in college football, it is far more important to have the support of your school's board of trustees than the support of your athletic director—or even your school president. Just ask Ty Willingham about that. During his three seasons at Notre Dame, no one ever questioned his "integrity" or ability to endure criticism with class. In 2003, a court case later revealed, a Florida man who said he was a Notre Dame fan called up Willingham and left a threatening message on Willingham's voice mail. The message included racially charged language and a threat to burn a cross in Willingham's front yard. The Florida man, Andrew French, eventually pled guilty to a misdemeanor charge and received a year's probation and $2,000 fine.

Willingham never uttered a peep about the case, either when it occurred or when it was settled. And yet Willingham's unquestioned "integrity" and ability to work well with the athletic director at Notre Dame didn't help him one bit when it came down to deciding his future at the school in December of 2004.

The full and gory details of Willingham's experience at Notre Dame may never be made public. But when he was fired as the Fighting Irish head coach in spite of his overall winning record, there was no question about who pushed Willingham out the door. In the days following Willingham's departure, Athletic Director Kevin White admitted that he had not been in favor of the move. Even more incredibly, the school president said the same thing. Father Edward Malloy had only a few months left in his tenure when the Willingham decision was made. For this reason, Malloy decided he would sit out the deliberations on football's future at the school. But when he was asked a week after Willingham's firing to comment on the decision, Malloy unloaded.

"In my eighteen years here, there have been only two days that I've been embarrassed to be president of Notre Dame—Tuesday and Wednesday of last week," said Father Malloy. "Notre Dame will get a new coach. I hope the person does well. But I think the philosophical hit that we've taken is a significant one. I am not happy about it, and I don't assume responsibility for it."

If the athletic director and school president didn't want Willingham fired, who did? According to published reports, the decision was made by two members from the board of trustees and five other Notre Dame administrators.

I think the AFCA sent its survey to the wrong people.

Willingham's treatment received much attention because of Notre Dame's elevated visibility. But that exact scenario—a small group of boosters wielding an inordinate amount of power—plays itself out every year at far less prominent schools. And if you think race doesn't play a factor for black coaches when such decisions are made…well, let me have you sit down with Jerry Baldwin.

From 1999 through 2001, Baldwin was the head coach at the University of Louisiana-Lafayette in the Sun Belt Conference. He had been a successful assistant coach at Louisiana State University. Our paths crossed often while recruiting student-athletes when I was an assistant at Arkansas. But at ULL, he won a total of only six games in those three seasons and was fired. Baldwin, a minister and a man of strong faith, filed a lawsuit, alleging that the university discriminated against him by not providing him the same support or offering the same treatment it offered his white successor.

After I agreed to serve as an expert witness based on my studies of black football coaches at predominantly white colleges and universities, I was flown down to Baton Rouge by Baldwin's attorney. I was never called to testify but did sit through a day of proceedings. In the end, the jury found Baldwin's race was indeed one of the reasons for his dismissal, if not the only reason. Baldwin didn't get his job back, but he won a $2 million judgment. According to the jurors, university officials broke Baldwin's contract and inflicted emotional distress through negligence. The university appealed the decision and litigation continued.

In my discussions with Baldwin, he made no bones about the fact that many important school boosters were not on his side, even before he coached a game.

"You can say there is racism among athletic directors," Baldwin told me, "but really, athletic directors are controlled by the support people. Athletic directors may not be racist, *per se*. But they are moved to do things in a racist manner because of the people who support the program. And I never experienced a huge level of alumni support."

According to the lawsuit, ULL President Ray Authement told Baldwin that he was not "a popular choice" with the community and that he supported the decision to terminate Baldwin because he "could no longer take the pressure" of having a black coach. Two deans on the football coach selection committee told Baldwin that Athletic Director Nelson Schexnayder did not want Baldwin as head coach because of his race. Baldwin was also told that one booster asked Schexnayder, "Why do we have to have all of the black coaches?" This booster was referring to the fact that the men's basketball team at ULL also had a black head coach.

It was interesting to observe this case and visit with Baldwin as the court sorted through all the accusations and listened to the testimonies of university officials. But having been where Baldwin was, I can say without hesitation that where there's smoke, there's probably fire. My research has shown, and my personal experience has borne out, that there is a pattern in the way black coaches are managed by their superiors. I can only hope that Baldwin's willingness to address the issue head on will create a higher level of sensitivity toward the hiring and firing of black head coaches.

So it was confusing to Baldwin, he told me, when he felt shunned by the Black Coaches Association (BCA) because certain black coaches thought his lawsuit would ruin advancement opportunities for them. In fact, Baldwin believed just the opposite—that his lawsuit was aimed precisely at creating a better employment climate for African American coaches.

Baldwin testified during his case that Schexnayder, the athletic director, pulled out on a plan to have the school's games televised, canceled the head coach's weekly TV show, eliminated a marketing position in the athletic department, cut the football equipment budget, and took $25,000 that was donated to the football program and used it for other purposes.

That story sounds very familiar. I never had a television show during my head coaching tour of duty at San Jose State. Dick Tomey, who replaced me, did a television show after the new athletic director found a sponsor to underwrite it. While I coached at SJS, the marketing director's position was eliminated. So was the position of my personal secretary.

In the academic arena, I am embarrassed to mention the lack of support my student-athletes received in the critical areas of university-funded tutors and support personnel. But two years after my resignation, San Jose State Athletic Director Tom Bowen (who had replaced Chuck Bell) blamed me for the Academic Progress Rate scores of the football team. I wonder if Bowen even knew that in 2004 there had been such a lack of funding for academic matters that during spring semester my staff and I were forced to personally serve as tutors for our players. Today, there are four additional academic support personnel available to the football team and a learning specialist position funded out of the school president's office.

During my tenure, there were limited funds to hire assistant coaches. But after I resigned, Bowen organized a "Coaches Circle" of donors. These people contributed an additional $200,000 to help supplement the salaries of Dick Tomey's assistants. I want to note that this sort of thing is not unique to black coaches. White coaches are also fired and then see their successors receive superior resources. But the net effect is far greater on black football coaches when this situation occurs—because employment trends indicate that only rarely will black coaches be recycled as head coaches in the same manner as their white peers.

I can only speculate as to the motivation behind all of these machinations that took place after I left San Jose State. But I believe that in the subconscious minds of those same boosters who felt that I had hired too many minority assistants, there was an assumption that Tomey would not hire as diverse a staff. In the 2009 season, Tomey employed one African American and one Samoan American.

Tomey retired at the conclusion of that 2009 football season with a 25-35 record at San Jose State. His final team recorded a 2-10 record. I really hope that during his time with the Spartans, Tomey didn't endure through the same wrenching process I went through when trying to hire assistant coaches. As I mentioned earlier, I did have a single school booster in Chuck Davidson whom I could rely on for support. Davidson assisted me in bringing aboard Keith Burns as our defensive coordinator. At that juncture, I was told that all California state universities were under a hiring freeze and that funds were not available to hire Burns. I still fought tooth and nail to try and get him to come to San Jose State. Finally, my athletic director told me that I could receive financial help to pay for a chunk of Burns's salary from a certain group of boosters—if I hired "the right guy."

I knew what that meant. The boosters didn't want me to bring in another black coach. So when I brought in Burns for his campus visit, I took him to meet my top boosters. Why? Because those boosters were going to fund a portion of Burns's paycheck, and I needed the boosters' tacit approval to hire him. Otherwise, I would have to abide by the hiring freeze that I assumed was in place at our sister institutions. As it turned out, Fresno State and San Diego State were able to ignore this hiring freeze because they could count on the more generous contributions of their booster clubs and foundations.

That brings me back to Coach Jerry Baldwin at the University of Louisiana Lafayette. Not surprisingly, Baldwin was succeeded by a white coach, Rickey Bustle. According to Baldwin's legal claims, Bustle was immediately given a television show and the benefit of a new athletic department marketing man. Looking back, Baldwin believes his undoing began when one particular financial supporter of the university—who had also been one of Baldwin's biggest supporters—died during Baldwin's last season. Baldwin also cannot forget those booster meetings where, try as he might, he always felt out of place.

"One, I'm African American," said Baldwin. "And two, I'm a Christian. I didn't drink, party, and do all that stuff. Some of those guys didn't know how to relate to someone like that. The booster meetings weren't crowded, I can tell you that. They were casual and uncrowded. Racism and discrimination is not overt now. It manifests itself in other ways—you know, by people who don't come to booster club meetings or don't volunteer for something they would have volunteered to do if the coach was white."

All right, so put yourself in the athletic director's place at a Football Bowl Subdivision school. The athletic director must satisfy his core constituency of boosters. But if he or she hires a black football coach, there is a chance some of those volunteers won't be volunteering their time or their money. Do you think this crosses the athletic director's mind while he or she assembles a list of candidates for a job opening? Do you think the board of trustees and the school president ever bring up the topic?

"I guarantee you," Baldwin said, "that in those closed meetings, they discuss it all from a racial perspective. But they can't ever talk about it openly, because it would be admitting some of their boosters are racist. And they're really counting on the fact that African American coaches aren't going to say anything because it might give them a label of being malcontents, and maybe they've got a family and are afraid of losing their jobs and not being hired somewhere else."

Ultimately, Baldwin said, that's why he filed his lawsuit. Just like me, he's no longer a coach. He works for the state of Louisiana and is also a church pastor in Ruston. Through his lawsuit, he focused as bright a light as possible on this topic—but even in Louisiana, very few people realize that Baldwin won his lawsuit to right a wrong. In the minds of the university leaders and boosters, their actions were not inappropriate. They simply believed that Baldwin wasn't the right coach for them. Bottom line: they believed that their lack of support played no part in his 6-27 coaching record.

You know the great irony here? In the NFL, unlike an academic institution, the powers that be have put the racial issue front and center and are never afraid to address it. This has led to more

African American coaches being interviewed and hired in pro football. Meanwhile, the alleged educators of our nation, who should be in favor of dialogue on the issue, are running away from it like a freshman cutting a tough chemistry class.

Baldwin wasn't surprised.

"Come on," he told me. "Educators don't run universities. Politicians do. You've got some alum out there who is, say, successful in the construction business but maybe didn't get his college degree. He didn't finish school. But now he's got money. So he's got a voice."

I am wondering how many black coaches have heard the same voices at other schools in other parts of the country. Even worse, I am wondering what some of those voices say when we are not around to hear them.

You know what, though? Every December, when universities fire and hire football coaches and I see excellent minority candidates not even receive interviews, I hear the voices of those boosters without them saying a single word.

CHAPTER SEVEN

WHY SOME BLACK COACHES APPEAR QUIET AND ANGRY

The morning of February 28, 2007, was among the more satisfying experiences of my professional career. I was in Washington DC, sitting before a congressional subcommittee that had asked me to testify and briefly present my research about the lack of black head coaches in college football.

Among others scheduled to testify that day were the now deceased NCAA president, Myles Brand; the Reverend Jesse Jackson; and Floyd Keith, the executive director of the Black Coaches Association. My friend, Dr. Richard Lapchick, was also there to speak about the empirical data he had gathered on minority hiring in sports. I had waited a long time to speak before such an audience.

I arrived early in Room 2322 of the Rayburn House Office Building, where the Committee on Energy and Commerce holds its sessions. I was appearing before the Subcommittee on Commerce, Trade, and Consumer Protection. That may sound like a strange group to be overseeing an issue involving college football coaches, but I guess it makes sense. College football is definitely big business these days. And if other big businesses in America had the same minority hiring record that athletic departments do regarding head football coaches, I would hope that a congressional committee might investigate.

Before sitting down at the witness table, I felt a mixture of nervousness and excitement. When my turn came, in my limited minutes, I tried to make my strongest points. I mentioned my own research, of course. But to put things on a more personal level, I tried to explain how frustrating it can be for qualified coaches and educators to continually see less qualified people be hired or promoted with skin color being the only apparent deciding factor.

Although Brand, who testified before me, had acknowledged that the hiring situation was not to his liking in college football, he had also stated that the NCAA is not legally empowered to force schools to hire minorities. This is true. But the NCAA, which is made up of its member institutions, could certainly pass legislation that requires schools to broaden their interview process when a coach is being hired. That's what the NFL has done with its Rooney Rule, which compels teams to speak with at least one minority candidate before filling a head coaching vacancy. Furthermore, I suggested that if the NCAA did not want to pass legislation that brings more equality to the hiring process, the US Congress might want to get involved, just as it did with Title IX to mandate equality in women's athletics. As I pointed out, if we simply wait around for people to do the right thing, we'll be waiting a very long time. In America, people didn't just spontaneously allow integration from coast to coast. It was mandated by law. I also submitted a written report in which I made the same recommendations you will read later in this book.

Bobby Rush, the Democratic congressman from Illinois who chaired the subcommittee, was very complimentary of my remarks and obviously supportive of diversity in key leadership positions on college campuses, especially football coaches. My own congressional representative from Arkansas, Mike Ross, also had some very nice things to say about my testimony, which I appreciated. After I finished speaking, I felt both relieved and gratified. But as I listened to the rest of the witnesses and sensed that the legislators were going to do nothing more than nod and express their wishes that things would get better, it was hard not to stay discouraged.

As the hearing progressed that day, there was much talk about holding seminars and meetings and study groups to discuss the issue and create awareness. But we've already done that over and over again. So what's the use of holding more meetings and seminars? I'm all met and "seminar-ed" out. It's like taking Pepto-Bismol for a headache—the wrong medicine for the problem. Every year at the NCAA and Black Coaches Association conventions, the same issues and topics are discussed. But nothing rarely happens. Awareness is raised for a few days. But without some type of enforcement, the awareness quickly fades away.

A few days after I returned home to Little Rock from Washington, I heard some talk radio callers discussing my testimony—and not all of it was a positive buzz. No problem there. My mission is always to get dialogue going on this topic. But many listeners were calling in to complain that there was no real reason for Congress to even hold such a hearing. They implied that African American coaches have nothing at all to gripe about and that opportunities are available to the most qualified candidates, regardless of color.

One caller said that you never hear white athletes gripe about having so many black players on college teams—which in an odd way makes my point. Players of all colors have the opportunity to earn a starting position on a team. And the best players will win those starting positions, because if they don't, the team won't be successful. There is also an easy way to judge whether one player should start over another player. You put them on the practice field and see which one performs the best.

The problem when coaches are competing for a job is that it is often difficult to examine their abilities and leadership skills. You can't put three or four coaches on the sidelines with the same players and determine which one does better in the same situation. Instead, the procedure is entirely subjective. And if an athletic director is a friend of the candidate, or if a big-money booster endorses another candidate, that can influence the "competition."

There were other callers on the talk show who expressed puzzlement and annoyance about my trip to Washington. I guess they wondered how somebody like me—who had been given an opportunity to lead a Division 1A program at San Jose State and had then produced a 14-33 won-loss record—could be critical of the hiring process regarding minority coaches. In a nutshell, the callers' questions boiled down to these two: If there really is a problem with minority advancement among college football coaches, why are so few speaking out about it? And why do the coaches who choose to speak out sound so angry?

I'll be happy to answer both questions.

But first, please do this: Pause for a few seconds and think about something that might frustrate you greatly in your own particular line of work. Maybe it is the way you're treated by your boss. Maybe it is bad delivery service or incompetent clerical help. Maybe it is inadequate equipment. Whatever.

Now, after thinking about that frustration and how much it bothers you, do something else. Imagine you cannot speak about that frustration to anyone. Ever. In fact, you cannot even bring up the topic without someone accusing you of being "too racially sensitive" or "irrational" or "militant." Unlike people in other professions who can let off steam about their frustrations or publicly take action to address their predicaments, you must keep your mouth shut and your anger bottled up.

My research indicates that's how many black college football coaches feel. They begin feeling it their first day on the job. And they keep feeling it until they no longer are in the profession.

How do I know? Because I once was one of those guys who felt that way.

Ellis Cose did an excellent job describing this emotional state in his book, *The Rage of a Privileged Class.* Cose interviewed dozens of African Americans who have attained what would be considered a comfortable station in life—middle class or upper class citizens with nice cars and homes. He discovered many of them were still dismayed and silently furious because, even though they have played by the rules, the things they were promised have not been completely delivered.

As Cose writes:

> Again and again, I heard the same plaintive declaration, always followed by various versions of an unchanging and urgent question. They say: "I have done everything I was supposed to do. I have stayed out of trouble with the law, gone to the right schools, sought professional development and worked myself nearly to death. Why in God's name won't they accept me as a full human being? Why am I pigeonholed in a 'black' job? Why am I constantly treated as if I were a drug addict, a thief or a thug? Why am I still not allowed to aspire to the same things every white person in America takes as a birthright?"

Cose could easily be talking about African American coaches, especially those who serve as assistant coaches in Division 1A programs or head coaches in the lower divisions. They understand that, compared to many people in society, they have it pretty good. They get to work with young people and spend their weekends outdoors in an exciting environment. There is no heavy lifting involved. And occasionally you get a bowl trip to Orlando or Tucson.

But these coaches, like their white counterparts, also want the chance to maximize their skills and ambitions. So when the black coaches are shut out of the opportunity to even apply for a promotion or a head coaching position that goes to a white coach with a weaker résumé, it creates resentment. When you couple this resentment with the other element mentioned by Cose's interviewees, the exasperation starts gurgling even louder in the coaches' stomachs. When they drive through predominantly white neighborhoods on recruiting trips, how many of them have been stopped for DWB (Driving While Black)?

And even when the NCAA administrators think they are doing the right thing, it can create resentment. Each year, the NCAA
holds education programs for an invited group of black coaches who
attend a series of meetings and workshops to "educate" them on
how present themselves as head coaching candidates. In effect, these
programs suggest to African American coaches that they are not
qualified for jobs unless they have such extra training. How do you
think that makes people feel? There are no such special programs for
white assistant coaches. In effect, the NCAA is sending a message
that black coaches cannot thrive without remedial help.

The black coaches' discontentment tends to peak every year
during the late autumn "Hurricane Hiring Season," when college
head coaches are fired and rapidly replaced. In many instances,
African American candidates who seek those jobs often cannot
even fight their way through the storm to get inside the door for a
legitimate interview.

And sometimes the disgruntlement arises from what does not
happen rather than what does happen. For example, in December of
2004, Tulsa Coach Steve Kragthorpe finished up a disappointing 4-8
season. School officials awarded him a six-year contract extension.
In December 2005, Southern Methodist Head Coach Phil Bennett
ended his fourth season at the school with an 11-35 overall record.
He received a four-year contract extension. Meanwhile, during this
same time frame, Ty Willingham of Notre Dame was fired in spite
of an overall winning record of 21-15. Karl Dorrell was terminated
from UCLA with a 35-25 record after five seasons. Kragthorpe and
Bennett are white. Willingham and Dorrell are black. I understand
that expectations are different with each program; nevertheless,
based on the past hiring practices at predominantly white colleges
and universities, if you are an African American assistant coach with
ambitions of becoming a head coach one day, wouldn't these hirings
and firings affect your perceptions of equality?

When these things happen, a few newspaper columnists express their outrage—but usually just once a year, in the days after the hirings and firings take place. Like the "Hurricane Hiring Season" itself, the outrage blows in and blows out quickly, doing damage to the hopes and dreams of coaches, particularly African Americans. If I could sum up what I've learned over the years, it is this: race defines space. It is apparent that in college football, there are a finite number of jobs available to minority coaches. And as soon as those jobs fill up, there is usually no more room.

My interviews with white coaches have turned up some antipathy on their side of the racial divide as well. Coaching can be a cutthroat business. And white coaches, just like black coaches, grow frustrated when they aren't promoted or hired for better jobs. Frequently, those white coaches make accusations about a quota system that favors African American candidate for certain jobs. Guess what? There might indeed be a quota system—but it mostly works against African American coaches, not in their favor.

Let's say a school feels comfortable with two or three black assistant coaches on a twelve-person football staff. That means all of the African American candidates are applying for those two or three positions—while all the white candidates are applying for the other nine or ten jobs. And this is supposed to be a drawback for white coaches? I'd rather have a nine-in-twelve chance of getting a job than three-in-twelve any day. But I have heard many white coaches attempt to compare the percentages of jobs being held by white and black coaches with the total number of white and black coaches in the profession. Although I truly understand their perspective, I must refer those individuals back to the race blind society that they frequently claim exists. So if, in fact, the coaching profession is actually a color blind environment, I have to continuously ask the question why so few qualified African American coaches are given fewer opportunities to lead collegiate football programs at predominantly white colleges and universities?

At the head coaching level, the quota system takes a slightly different form—the "one and done" syndrome. It works this way: During the "Hurricane" season, a subtle mood of tension arises as Football Bowl Subdivision programs with coaching vacancies wait to see whether an institution will hire a minority. If and when it happens, it appears everyone else feels relieved, because it takes the other schools off the hook. They can go back to business as usual and evade considering qualified African American candidates.

And here's the maddening part: people in coaching talk about this stuff behind closed doors *all the time*—but never in the open. I can't tell you how many times I have heard my coaching colleagues murmur in a semi-whisper: "That job has to go to a minority." Or: "They've got enough minorities on their staff, so a white guy will get that job." Yet out front, with their public statements, athletic directors and school administrators won't say any of this. They maintain that every job is open to all qualified candidates. If that's true, why are there just fifteen African Americans among the 120 FBS head coaches entering the 2012 season? Why has the NFL been far more progressive and given so many more chances to minority coaches? Did only fifteen African Americans apply for those fifteen college jobs?

You seldom hear black coaches complain on the record about this, of course, because a coach who speaks out is usually labeled a malcontent. And if a black coach merely expresses his concern about the situation to his fellow staff members, the first thing white administrators or head coaches say in response will be: "You're angry." And then, "We're not going to promote (or hire) someone who is angry all the time." That's when your survival skills kick in. You shut off the visible frustration. In the worst-case scenario, black coaches grow so discouraged that they simply stop applying for better jobs.

I am constantly fascinated that a black person speaking out against an injustice is called "angry" by the establishment, while, in the African American community, the same person is frequently perceived as a strong leader. It's because black people are happy to find someone who speaks the truth about their common experiences.

African Americans are frequently told to be patient, told that if we just calmly wait out history, things will change. But how long is long enough? In 1964, Title VII of the Civil Rights Act was passed. It was intended to address discrimination issues relating to employment. We are over a decade into the twenty-first century. Progress has been made in many areas. But in college football, even with recent gains, coaching opportunities are still not happening with all deliberate speed for qualified coaches of color.

If I am perceived as being an "angry" or "militant" black man because I want African American coaches to receive more of a fair shake, fine. I will accept that label. But truth be told, I am neither angry nor militant. Frustrated? Yes. Irritated about how the same plot keeps repeating itself year after year? Absolutely. Am I eager to see some sort of action plan that will help rectify the situation, as the NFL has implemented? Totally.

To give you a more concrete example of how my frustration developed over the years, I have made my collegiate head football coach diary available at www.crackback.us. I encourage you to visit my website. In 2006, I began keeping an informal journal of the coaching changes at FBS colleges during the "Hurricane Hiring Season." That year, the "season" began on October 23 when North Carolina announced that Head Coach John Bunting would not return as the Tar Heels' football coach. It ended on January 29, 2007, with the hiring of Stan Brock at Army. As coaches came and went, I jotted down my thoughts—and did so for the five "seasons" that followed, through 2010. I tried to place things in perspective. I drew upon the knowledge and experience I've gained over the years about how schools in different parts of the country conduct their business. I wanted to provide real-world illustrations of the sociological forces that I speak about in other chapters of this book.

If you decide to read my diary try to put yourself in the mind-set of an eager and ambitious young African American football coach as the days pass in each "Hurricane Season," and he watches these jobs open and quickly close. In going back over these entries myself, I sense how my own frustration built strictly as an observer—even during the so-called "breakthrough" of minority hires following the 2009 football season. That frustration is probably multiplied times five for the coaches who are trying to gain one of these jobs. Here is listing of the entire BCS job vacancies from 2006 through 2010:

Hurricane Hiring Season 2006

Coaching Vacancies: 23 (Air Force, Alabama, Arizona State, Army, Boston College, Central Michigan, Cincinnati, Florida International, Idaho, Iowa State, Louisiana Tech, Louisville, Miami, Minnesota, Michigan State, North Carolina, North Carolina State, North Texas, Rice, Stanford, Tulane, Tulsa)

African American Hires: 1 (Randy Shannon—Miami)

Other Minority Hires: 1 (Mario Cristobal—Florida International)

Hurricane Hiring Season 2007

Coaching Vacancies: 18 (Arkansas, Baylor, Colorado State, Duke, Georgia Tech, Hawaii, Houston, Michigan, Mississippi, Navy, Nebraska, Northern Illinois, Southern Methodist, Southern Mississippi, Texas A&M , UCLA, Washington State, West Virginia)

African American Hires: 1 (Kevin Sumlin—Houston)

Other Minority Hires: 1 (Ken Niumatalolo—Navy)

Hurricane Hiring Season 2008

Coaching Vacancies: 22 (Army, Auburn, Ball State, Boston College, Bowling Green, Clemson, Eastern Michigan, Iowa State, Kansas State, Miami, Mississippi State, New Mexico, New Mexico State, Oregon, Purdue, San Diego State, Syracuse, Tennessee, Toledo, Utah State, Washington, Wyoming)

African American Hires: 3 (Mike Haywood—Miami [Ohio], Mike Locksley—New Mexico, DeWayne Walker—New Mexico State)

Other Minority Hires: 0

Hurricane Hiring Season 2009

Coaching Vacancies: 23 (Akron, Buffalo, Central Michigan, Cincinnati, East Carolina, Florida State, Kansas, Kentucky, Louisiana-Monroe, Louisiana Tech, Louisville, Marshall, Memphis, Notre Dame, San Jose State, South Florida, Tennessee, Texas Tech, UNLV, USC, Vanderbilt, Virginia, Western Kentucky)

African American Hires: 7 (Turner Gill—Kansas, Mike London—Virginia, Ruffin McNeill—East Carolina, Joker Phillips—Kentucky, Larry Porter—Memphis, Charlie Strong—Louisville, Willie Taggart—Western Kentucky)

Other Minority Hires: 0

Hurricane Hiring Season 2010

Coaching Vacancies: 22 (Arkansas State, Ball State, Colorado, Connecticut, Florida, Indiana, Kent State, Louisiana-Lafayette, Maryland, Miami, Miami (Ohio), Michigan, Minnesota, North Texas, Northern Illinois, Pittsburgh (twice), San Diego State, Stanford, Temple, Tulsa, Vanderbilt)

African American Hires: 5 (John Embree – Colorado, Don Treadwell – Miami (Ohio), Pittsburgh – Mike Haywood (Haywood was fired), Kent State – Darrell Hazell, David Shaw – Stanford, James Franklin – Vanderbilt)

Other Minority Hires: 0

So that's the lineup of my personal diary and should you decide to read it, I am certain you find it very interesting and amusing. In recent years, it's true that a greater percentage of African American and minority candidates have been evaluated to be hired. In my view, however, much still needs to change. Maybe you don't see it that way and that's ok. But please take a look at the whole time frame of my diary, from 2006 to 2010. There were 108 job openings and only 20 minorities hired. Also, many of those "openings" closed within mere days—or hours—before new coaches were hired.

Now, put yourself in the position of a young minority coach trying to assess his chances of getting a head coaching job. He sees those 108 job openings with maybe slightly more than a third of them being truly open. But if the black coach shows anger or speaks up about his lack of opportunities, he may not even get a chance for one of the rare interviews when a job is truly open. I suppose you might think that I, too, should shut up. But in my mind that would be like Rosa Parks getting up and moving to the back of the bus. Sorry, I can no longer do that. I hope that after you finish my book, you will understand why. Also, if the United States Congress wants me to testify about all this again, I'm on the next plane. Thanks to Rosa Parks, I will even have the opportunity to sit wherever I want.

CHAPTER EIGHT
WHY ALL FANS SHOULD CARE ABOUT BLACK COACHES

Black football coaches aren't the only people of color who have to deal with the "crackback" effect. William C. Rhoden, the *New York Times* columnist and author, covered the same ground with African American quarterbacks in his excellent book, *Third and a Mile*.

Rhoden's work is an oral history of black quarterbacks in the National Football League. After reading it, I realized that those quarterbacks were definitely subject to being "crackbacked" during the 1970s and '80s. The stress and frustration experienced by African American football players who wanted to play the game's most prominent position during that era was very similar to the experiences that black head football coaches have faced—and are still facing—at many predominantly white colleges and universities in the current era.

It was very common thirty years ago, Rhoden noted, for NFL teams to stymie the dreams of black quarterbacks. Often, they were asked to change position and play wide receiver or defensive back—or else simply ignored in the draft. If the quarterbacks wanted to receive an opportunity in pro football to play their position, it usually meant that they signed with the Canadian Football League and went north. At one time, seven of the CFL's nine quarterbacks were black. Canada was also more welcoming to African Americans in leadership positions, such as head coaches. The Toronto Argonauts hired Willie Woods as head coach in 1980, nine years before the Raiders named Art Shell as the NFL's first African American head coach of the modern era.

Think about this: Warren Moon, an outstanding college quarterback who led the University of Washington to a Rose Bowl victory, initially received no opportunity in the United States to play the position he loved at the professional level. For him, like so many others, the road to the NFL went through Canada. Moon kept his self-esteem intact and took advantage of that opportunity, even if it wasn't what he really wanted or thought that he deserved. I wonder what Moon must have felt when he looked in the mirror every morning.

Leigh Steinberg, Moon's agent, believed that his client should have been drafted as a franchise quarterback. Instead, Moon had to play six seasons in the CFL before he had the chance to throw his first NFL pass—but when he did, he lasted seventeen years in the league, and he accounted for more than three hundred touchdowns by throwing and running. When he finally retired, Moon's 49,325 passing yards were the fourth most in league history. Little wonder that he earned a Pro Football Hall of Fame induction.

And yet, in Rhoden's book, Moon revealed that he was undergoing psychiatric counseling because he still has a lot of anger and frustration over his career. Moon's therapist believes that he hid his pain and didn't deal with the deep wounds that he suffered early in his pro career.

"I tried to keep everything under control, tried to handle things as if everything was all right," Moon admitted. "At a young age you can do that, but as you get older you just don't have patience."

Let me pose a question: Should white people care about how Moon felt and what he endured by having to leave the United States to play pro football?

My closest friend, business partner, and spiritual brother is a man named Steve Snider. I trust him as much any person can trust another person. Steve is also white, so we naturally have had some very deep and intimate conversations about race. I know that Steve cares about me as a human being, not as a black man. That means the world to me. After I resigned as head coach at San Jose State, Steve was the reason I moved to Little Rock from the Bay Area. When I would share my coaching experiences from California with Steve, I knew he could not change anything that had happened. But he always listened with an empathetic ear.

Steve and I have also discussed my studies regarding collegiate football coaches and how their race can restrict employment opportunities. And I have concluded that no matter how much Steve and I love each other, there will always be a disparity in our racial perspectives as it relates to fairness and equality. However, we have learned to disagree in an agreeable way. The best thing about Steve is that he cares about how I feel, even if he might not be on board one hundred percent with my viewpoint. Nevertheless, Steve comprehends that one human being, simply because of skin color, is not inherently better than another. I have discovered that Steve's perspective is not common in older white men—particularly when they think about black men who desire to compete for jobs that have traditionally been filled by white men.

My frustration surfaces, however, when I perceive that Steve discounts the years of research I have given to this topic and begins cross-examining me like the attorney that he was trained to be. Steve will often suggest in an innocent and good-hearted way, "Once black coaches get more experience, I believe they will get more opportunities to be head coaches at predominantly white institutions." My annoyance meter rises to the top and I'll answer, "Brother, you haven't heard anything that I have said."

Steve and I do something that a lot of black and white people in America either can't do or won't do—we are honest with each other when speaking about race. If enough people do the same, things can get better.

Still, if you are a white person, it has probably crossed your mind that I might be making too big a deal about this whole issue. Or that my use of the word *crackback* might be too severe or off center.

Fair enough. Let me address that point.

I admit that some of this is personal. But it's not actually about me, *per se*. I want my children—Destiny, Faith, and Justice—to believe they can achieve anything in our country. And it bothers me that in terms of opportunities for college football coaches, we still have such a long way to go. I want to tell my son that if his dream is to become the head football coach at Tennessee or LSU or Alabama or wherever one day, his dream is a realistic one. Currently, I could not tell him that in good conscience. Too much of my research contradicts that notion.

Regardless of Nick Saban's previous coaching accomplishments, it would be a stretch to think that he would have been selected as the head coach of the University of Alabama following the 2006 football season had he been an African American with the same résumé. In fact, if Saban had been a black man, history suggests that he would have never been given an opportunity to launch his head coaching career at Toledo in 1990. Sad but true. Facts support this hypothesis. Has Toledo ever hired a black head football coach? No.

These thoughts about my own son's potential future—and the futures of so many other African American kids with ambitions to coach—are probably why this issue matters most to me. Yet I am sure that many white people, football fans or otherwise, wonder why they should care. They might ask, "If I am the average Joe fan, sitting in the bleachers at my favorite college stadium or watching the game on television, how on earth does the minority coaching situation affect my enjoyment of football? As I witness another great season of college football unfold, what difference is it to me whether there are three African American head coaches or six or seven—or twenty-five or fifty, for that matter?"

I understand that attitude. Most fans just want to watch the game and see their team win. They want to enjoy the game as a break from the real world, not worry about racial issues from the real world. What's wrong with that? Why should it matter to me?

The answer is simple. Not only is fairness and equality something that should always matter, but college football will be a better and more fun game to watch when it does a better job of embracing diversity among the head coaching ranks. No one argues that college football became a less interesting sport when it embraced diversity among student-athletes. No one thinks that the NFL slipped in quality after 1946 when African American players were again permitted to play pro football after being banned since the game's early days.

In Southeastern Conference lore, the story is often told about the 1970 game between Alabama and the University of Southern California, when USC running back Sam "Bam" Cunningham scored three touchdowns in a 42-21 victory over the Crimson Tide. At the time, Alabama's roster was still 100 percent white, although Coach Bear Bryant had quietly recruited one African American freshman who watched the game from the stands. Cunningham was African American. If Alabama had beaten USC, Coach Bryant would have had a difficult time convincing the boosters that it was time for black players to become part of the Alabama program. And had USC not played Cunningham at running back, it is highly probable that the Tide would have defeated the Trojans. But Cunningham, based on his talent and athletic ability, made the case for Bryant's decision to begin recruiting black athletes and gave the coach plenty of ammunition for university administrators who were still balking. Bryant's famous quote was that Cunningham "did more to integrate Alabama in one afternoon than Martin Luther King had done in years."

I am not the first person to opine that if USC had not given Cunningham his opportunity to beat the Crimson Tide so thoroughly that day, the Alabama football program would never have embraced diversity as enthusiastically as it did. Consequently, I doubt if the Tide would have won their subsequent national championship trophies. Winning attracts the top student-athletes. Along with that often comes an increased revenue stream for the athletics department through corporate sponsorships and private donors.

Today there is no shortage of African American talent on the Alabama roster because university administrators have embraced the concept of recruiting the best talent, regardless of ethnicity. Get my drift? The best talent is often developed when opportunity is the greatest. But this is still a rare concept when it comes to American universities and African American football coaches.

Let me share another story that better describes how black coaches feel when they are denied the prospect of employment for no other reason than the color of their skin. In Rhoden's book, he reports that NFL organizations were well aware of the ability that African American quarterbacks possessed, but certain coaches remained uncomfortable about the idea of making blacks their field generals. The perfect example was Joe Gilliam, who competed with Terry Bradshaw for the starting quarterback position of the Pittsburgh Steelers after Gilliam was drafted out of Tennessee State in 1972. There was never a doubt that Gilliam could play in the NFL. Bill Nunn, a longtime Steelers scout, had ranked Gilliam as high as a fourth-round pick on the team's draft board.

Pittsburgh executives were shocked that when the eleventh round came around, Gilliam still had not been selected. Nunn told Head Coach Chuck Noll that the only thing preventing Gilliam from being accepted in the National Football League was his race, not his ability to play. Noll, wanting to win, replied, "Let's take him." But how do you think Gilliam felt when he heard that story and realized that other quarterbacks had been drafted ahead of him basically because they were white—and he wasn't?

Nunn's statement merely acknowledged the mind-set of white general managers and head coaches in the NFL at the time. In my opinion, this is the mind-set that many college presidents, athletic directors, and boosters currently have when they think about black football coaches. White collegiate administrators and coaches could deal better with racial issues if they would look the truth straight in the eye and call it as Nunn did.

If you are white, I wish for a moment you could put on Joe Gilliam's 1972 shoes and try to walk in them. Let's say that you had been groomed all of your life to be a quarterback, worked many hours to develop your skills and then one day after more than fifteen years of investing your time to improve your talents to play the quarterback position, you were deemed invisible because of skin color. How would you feel?

My contention, as well, is that college football could potentially make more money if there were more diversity in the head coaching ranks. Fifteen years ago, the NFL was the most popular sports league in North America. But ask yourself this: As more black coaches received more chances to lead more teams, did the NFL become more profitable and popular, or less profitable and popular?

College basketball is another good example. Until the mid-70s, there were virtually no black head coaches in the game. Then such pioneers as John Thompson, John Cheney, and Nolan Richardson took over the hoop programs at major schools. They opened the door for other minority head coaches to follow. Since all of this occurred, would you say the NCAA tournament has become more popular or less popular? Check your March Madness office pool. Better yet, check the event's $10.8 billion television contract with CBS and Turner Sports for the rights to telecast the event through 2024. The payout to NCAA schools is $771 million per year.

The NBA's financial profile and revenue certainly haven't suffered with African American head coaches becoming a league fixture. Attendance, television ratings, and endorsement money prove it. In the spring of 2007, the NBA signed a new television deal with ABC, ESPN, and TNT that will pay the league $7.4 billion over eight years, a 22 percent increase over the previous television agreement. The NBA has done a superb job of marketing its product to people of all ethnic groups, but nearly 65 percent of the league's television audience is white.

In each case, the product on the playing field has become more interesting and compelling—and profitable—as the head coaching opportunities have become more minority inclusive.

College football fans are just like those in other sports. They sit around and debate their home team's success—or lack of it. But when college football fans wonder why their favorite team isn't being more creative or is not playing with a more unified effort, I find it interesting that those same fans don't bother to connect the dots. It just might be that the team's lack of creativity or unity is connected to the lack of opportunity for people of all ethnic groups. Just as black athletes have increased the popularity of the sport if given the opportunity, African American coaches might enhance the game of college football if given the same opportunity. But right now, some of the country's most imaginative minds and great motivators are shut out of those college jobs.

Everyone seems to agree that Jerry Rice was the best wide receiver of all time. But did you ever wonder who coached him in college? Rice gained fame in the NFL with the San Francisco 49ers under head coach Bill Walsh. However, Walsh admits he drafted Rice after seeing films of his college days at Mississippi Valley State, where the team ran a wildly innovative offense.

The man who developed that offense was Archie Cooley. Much as Bum Phillips did while coaching the Houston Oilers back in the 1970s, Cooley walked the sidelines wearing a trademark cowboy hat. As an African American coaching at a historically black college, Cooley did not receive much mainstream attention. However, Cooley and his teams put on a show and a half—and won games in the process. His innovation and creativity reminds me of Art Briles, the former University of Houston head coach who was hired by Baylor for $1.8 million annually following the 2007 football season. Briles is white. Cooley never made that type of money because he never received that type of opportunity. We will never know if he was capable of producing at the top level of the college game.

Cooley took pride in keeping Mississippi Valley State's opponents on edge with his unpredictable offensive schemes, such as using a no-huddle scheme to create havoc with opposing defenses. Cooley is often given credit for being the first to implement the no-huddle. Other times, Cooley would stack four receivers on the same side of a formation or draw up a double slot formation and alternate putting his running backs in motion.

Little wonder, then, that Cooley's nickname was "Gunslinger." And in the early 1980s when he had Rice in his holster, the nickname was never more appropriate. Cooley recruited a fluid thrower named Willie Totten at quarterback to connect with Rice and turned them loose. In 1984, Mississippi Valley State averaged a NCAA Division 1AA record 496.8 yards passing per game. The team also averaged 60.9 points and 640.1 total yards per game, also records. One Saturday night, Totten threw nine touchdown passes. Had Cooley been white, even coaching in an all-black conference, I think all of his team's records would have received much more attention. In fact, he would have probably been considered a genius.

Admittedly, Cooley's career trajectory has not been a stellar one since those Totten-Rice teams at Mississippi Valley State. He left there to coach at Arkansas-Pine Bluff, another Division 1AA school, and had a winning record—but was asked to resign because of NCAA academic violations that resulted in a death sentence for the football program. Cooley also was the head coach at Paul Quinn College, an African Methodist Episcopal school in Dallas that recently dropped football.

Cooley said the academic messes occurred because he didn't have the proper clerical support. I find that hard to believe. His alleged improprieties appeared to be blatant, with a total disregard of NCAA rules. With or without clerical support, a coach is still responsible for his program. I wonder what Cooley might have done with a support system that held him accountable and honest. We will never know.

Nevertheless, there are dozens of qualified black men on coaching staffs across America, waiting to be hired as college head coaches. Right now, many of those men are going to the NFL from the college game and never returning. It really bothers me to think about it, because I know what a positive force college football can be for so many young people—of all colors.

In 2003, the Supreme Court ordered the University of Michigan to abandon its affirmative action policy in the admission process. But a lot of people focused on what the court *did* rather than what the court *said*. The court's opinion was that Michigan's affirmative action policy should no longer apply. But in the written opinion, the court actually endorsed the concept of diversity by saying:

> Benefits (of diversity) are not theoretical but real, as major American businesses have made clear that the skills needed in today's increasingly global marketplace can only be developed through exposure to widely diverse people, cultures, ideas, and viewpoints.

The court then cited briefs filed by General Motors executives and high-ranking US military officers. Both expressed the necessity of diversity to create a better automobile company and a better national security force. This is probably why Justice Sandra Day O'Connor wrote: "Effective participation by members of all racial and ethnic groups in the civic life of our nation is essential if the dream of one nation, indivisible, is to be realized."

I am sure that at kickoff time, college football fans are not thinking of Sandra Day O'Connor. But I think they should.

CHAPTER NINE

UNDERSTANDING THE PERSPECTIVE OF WHITE ADMINISTRATORS AND COACHES

When I conducted a confidential survey of white and black assistant coaches as part of my doctoral research, I discovered an amazing fact: many white coaches are just as unhappy as black coaches about the way college football does business in terms of their profession's hiring process.

Specifically, many white coaches believe that black coaches are getting far more breaks and have a much easier time getting good jobs, in spite of overwhelming statistical evidence to the contrary. In response, African American coaches and fans could look at the white coaches and say, "Are you paranoid and in denial?" Or they could take my approach, which is to try and understand the circumstances that have created the white coaches' perception. Because until that happens, there's no way that any meaningful progress can be made toward a buy-in from all parties when it comes to a true level playing field for hiring minority football coaches. Black coaches need to understand—and in some sense respect—why white coaches feel the way they do. Black football fans should also pay attention, because it would probably help them understand the mind-set of some white college football fans, the ones who believe that the sport's lack of African American head coaches is not a major problem for the game.

I can say this much with certainty: the biggest reason for white-coach resentment is the profession itself. College football coaching is a cutthroat business. There are only about twelve hundred jobs available at top-tier Football Bowl Subdivision schools—including head coaches, assistant head coaches, offensive coordinators, defensive coordinators, position coaches, and head strength coaches. Thousands and thousands of men want those jobs. Backbiting and politics are inevitable. Toss in the racial component, and you are brewing a dangerous stew.

So the resentment keeps gurgling and bubbling beneath the surface. My experiences have led me to believe that many white administrators and coaches believe that equality for black coaches' means less equality for white coaches. Following the civil rights movement, integration was tolerated because it was mandated. But in the minds of white people who once supported segregation, integration did not mean that black people could get on the bus, take the front seat and tell the bus driver where to go. Integration, at least in the minds of those white Americans, meant that you can get on the bus and take what's available — not what's mine. I believe that many white coaches and administrators have grown to resent black coaches and administrators when those white coaches and administrators are forced to allow the black coaches into the mainstream, then perceive that black coaches are trying to "take over" by demanding more opportunity and advancement.

I remember what it was like in 1989 when I first brought up the topic of the racial divide in college football during one of my graduate classes at Northwestern State University. My classmates, most of them white, did not even want to engage in any meaningful dialogue. In fact, I sensed that they perceived me to be overly sensitive regarding the subject. They wondered if I had a chip on my shoulder because of the passionate way that I delivered the facts of Dr. Richard Lapchick's article addressing the lack of employment opportunities for black football coaches.

Twenty-plus years later, things are a little better. But it's still difficult for people to honestly express themselves. As you have surely realized by now, I am not shy about speaking up on this issue. In fact, at every opportunity I enjoy spirited debate about it. But whenever I speak about this topic to a mixed-race audience, the most common reaction to my remarks is baffled silence. Some people find the data difficult to believe. Others squirm slightly. But nobody seems eager to open up and share their true feelings.

I discovered that delivering the truth will set you free — but might also get you shut out. After completing and publishing my dissertation and several articles in various journals, whenever asked I have attempted to work closely with the NCAA on this topic. After resigning as the head coach at San Jose State, I decided to present my academic research on this subject at every opportunity to any audience because I had more time to do so. This led to some fascinating experiences for me.

As the twentieth century was coming to a close, the NCAA finally decided to make an active effort in developing the leadership skills of black football coaches—with the idea of better preparing them to become head coaches. Because of my past research on employment opportunities along with my experience as a rare head football coach of color, I was invited to present my findings to two different groups in the program. The first group consisted of young and upcoming minority coaches. The second group consisted of older and more experienced black coaches, who were invited to participate in what was called the "Expert Academy." These older coaches were supposedly already head coaching material, but they needed to be validated and have their sharp edges smoothed over.

I enjoyed seeing many of these black coaches, young and old. I had built relationships with some of the more experienced coaches during my own career on the sidelines. I was also happy to be assisting the NCAA in helping minority coaches recognize the employment barriers and hurdles that I had studied for many years.

However, I didn't believe this type of professional development was necessary for the development of black coaches, just as it was not necessary for white coaches. Nevertheless, I gave the coaches the hard data, and then backed it up with specific stories and personal experiences that had been shared with me or that I had personally witnessed in the profession. I was always given positive reviews. In fact, one NCAA employee told me that my session had received some of the highest evaluations.

I must have been doing a halfway decent job, because the NCAA kept inviting me back each year—until the first of my two scheduled sessions in the summer of 2008. My presentation was the same as it had been in previous years, except with updated statistics. The difference that summer, however, was a new audience member. Charlotte Westerhaus, a black female who at the time was the NCAA's vice president for diversity and inclusion, sat in the room for that summer's first session—the one for younger coaches—and listened to what I had to say.

Westerhaus was not a stranger to me. I had visited with her in February of 2007 in Washington DC, when I testified to Congress on the employment barriers for African American football coaches at predominantly white colleges and universities. After reviewing the transcript of my planned testimony, Westerhaus came over to visit with me in a very professional and cautious way. She was feeling me out as she attempted to make small talk.

As I read her nonverbal cues, I was mildly shocked to hear her indirectly compliment my research by indicating that she thought my testimony was succinct, well written, and factual. She was accompanied to Washington that day by Myles Brand, who before his death in September 2009 served as the NCAA president. He, too, testified before Congress that day and did not question my testimony.

So you can understand why it caught me off guard when, after Westerhaus heard my presentation to the younger coaches in 2008, she had one of her assistants call and tell me that I would not be a part of the "Expert Academy" for the older coaches later that summer. When I asked her assistant what had happened, I was given no explanation but was simply told that Westerhaus had made the change. No further information was provided to me. I have not spoken to Westerhaus since she made that decision. If I had the opportunity, I would ask her if the facts I cited had made her uncomfortable. Rather than being open to the discussion of racial employment issues as a tool to prepare minority coaches for issues of race that lurk beneath the surface of college football, my gut feeling is that Westerhaus basically shut me out and went into denial mode. I must have made both her and the NCAA uncomfortable.

My conclusion: the truth is often painful and perhaps even unbearable for those who propose change but either wittingly or unwittingly thwart the necessary process for change. This is unfortunate. For behind the intrigued silence, I know what lurks: confusion, suspicion, and mistrust. Administrators and head coaches make the situation worse by allowing too many white coaches to keep believing their race is the only reason they did not get hired for a certain position—while allowing too many black coaches to believe that their race is the only reason they *did* get hired.

Whenever I ponder that strange incongruity, I am reminded of a poll that was commissioned by *Newsweek* magazine back in 1993. The poll asked a sampling of diverse males in professional and managerial jobs this question: "Have you ever been a victim of discrimination or reverse discrimination in getting a promotion?" Among white males, 15 percent answered in the affirmative. The same percentage said they had experienced discrimination in "getting a job."

Here's what is so interesting about those answers: In 1993, the same year of the poll, African Americans and Hispanics made up just 10 percent of the total employees in managerial and professional jobs. Meanwhile, white males made up 46 percent of the workforce. You can do the simple math: If one out of every ten white men truly had been held back by a black or Hispanic male for a job, then it means almost half of the blacks and Hispanics in the workforce were receiving promotions they did not deserve—at the expense of white men. But the employment statistics in 1993 didn't reflect that. They showed that on average, African American and Hispanic professionals earned less money and held lower positions than white employees.

Huh? Something didn't compute. If those statistics were true and the minority professionals were making less money and holding down lesser jobs than their white counterparts, then how could half of them be receiving promotions they didn't deserve? And why would 15 percent of the white males in the survey still claim they had been cheated out of a position at the expense of a minority candidate? *Newsweek* editor Ellis Cose addressed this question while citing the same survey in his book, "The Rage of a Privileged Class."

Cose said there were only two possibilities to explain the weird discrepancy between the survey results and the actual facts: First, despite the unfair "advantage" held by African American and Hispanic professionals in getting choice jobs, they were so incompetent that their white counterparts jumped ahead of them on merit. Or second, the white professionals were just way off the mark in their perceptions.

To me, the first explanation is preposterous. And the second explanation is unfortunate but true. I can't tell you for sure how those gross misperceptions by white people develop in other professions—but I definitely know how they develop in football coaching. I've been there.

Obviously, at a major university when an African American or minority coach is hired for a football staff position, the athletic director does not hold a news conference to announce: "Ladies and gentlemen, we chose to hire a minority candidate in order to meet our unofficial quota and maintain our desired percentage of diverse staff members, so I regret to tell the white candidates that they had absolutely no chance to earn this position. However, I can encourage them to apply for the next opening because now the pressure is off and we can hire as many white guys as we want."

No school would be stupid enough to hold such a news conference. However, something just as stupid and just as insidious does happen. In the hallways and parking lots of athletic departments after a minority is hired, someone high up in the administration will whisper on the down low: "Sorry, we had to give a black guy this job—you know how it is." The word spreads through more and more whispering. And the damage is done. In my research and anonymous interviews of coaches, I have come across many examples of these "whispering ruse" campaigns.

What a punch in the gut that must be for the white guys trying to get ahead in the profession. Even if no minority candidate is involved in a job search and White Coach A loses out to White Coach B, it is likely that White Coach A is going to be upset. So what would cause an administrator to give White Coach A an added excuse for not getting the job by telling White Coach A that the opening he wanted "had" to go to a minority coach—and thereby create resentment against all minority coaches, everywhere? My answer: The administrator would rather employ the "whispering ruse" syndrome than tell White Coach A the truth, which is that maybe he wasn't quite good enough to earn the position, regardless of color.

And, yes, it sometimes does happen with black coaching candidates. One who is curious about a job opening will hear from an athletic department insider, often another minority: "Hey, they've got too many black guys on the staff already, so don't bother applying for this one." The "whispering ruse" syndrome does no one any good.

The most common case cited above, the "whispering ruse" syndrome, causes white coaches to feel they've been shut out unfairly from a position. And it causes minority coaches to feel as if they have not earned their jobs on merit. In such a climate, how on earth can we expect any coach *not* to be paranoid? And in the white coaching community, the paranoia is always going to be larger and more dominant—because there are so many more white coaches than black coaches.

But that's not the only reason for white coaches' paranoia. Going back as far as 1954, numerous studies have shown that whites become uncomfortable when they perceive higher concentrations of African Americans in a given situation—whether it is at a restaurant, in a schoolyard, or in a hiring pool. I can remember the first time I saw that paranoia in full bloom—when I was a graduate student at the University of Arkansas. At that time, one of the big sports television personalities was Jimmy "The Greek" Snyder. He was a lumpy character who, the story went, had made millions as a professional gambler. Snyder also supposedly had the inside scoop on pro football and would appear each Sunday on CBS's pregame show to select that day's winners. One evening in the late 1980's, however, Snyder became infamous for another sort of "analysis." A local television crew in Washington DC found him at a restaurant and asked him to comment on the birthday of Dr. Martin Luther King Jr. and reflect on the accomplishments of African Americans in sports.

In the worst way, Snyder didn't hold back. First, he threw out his unproven and untrue theory about why black athletes were becoming so dominant in modern American sports. It had nothing to do with greater opportunity. The true explanation, Snyder said, dated to pre-Civil War times and the days of slavery. "The slave owner would breed his big black with his big woman so that he would have a big black kid," Snyder claimed. "That's where it all started."

That alone was probably enough to get Snyder fired, which is eventually what happened. But for me, the statement of Snyder's that jumped out was the following one from the same interview: "If

I was always ready to call the next play or make a decision based on studying our opponent's tendencies. But for African American head coaches, my studies suggest this is the easy part.

Reaching out to congratulate one of our offensive players after scoring.

One of the highlights of my coaching career was having my son, Justice, join me at practice. My prayer is that if he decides to become a collegiate head football coach, his opportunities will not be restricted by his skin color.

2004 SJSU SPARTAN FOOTBALL
COACHING STAFF

WAYNE SALVATORE
PHOTOGRAPHY

It was this racial demographic of my staff that prompted a San Jose State booster to boldly tell me about a belief among Spartan supporters that our team would have won more games if I had hired fewer black assistants. The booster had failed to recognize that I won more games in my first three years than my previous two white head coaching predecessors, who had employed fewer minority assistants.

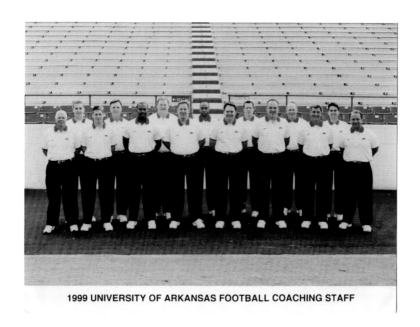

1999 UNIVERSITY OF ARKANSAS FOOTBALL COACHING STAFF

When Houston Nutt became Arkansas' head coach, he embraced diversity and ideas to improve the experience for African American student-athletes in Northwest Arkansas. Nutt also named me the first African American Assistant Head Coach in the history of the Razorback football program. Nutt, was employed at the University of Mississippi from 2008-2011 and employed a diverse staff during his tenure.

Coaching Photo 1993—Danny Ford, Head Coach

The 1993 University of Arkansas football coaching staff. In that era, often the hiring of one African American assistant per staff was the tokenism trend throughout most of college football. Unfortunately, even today, a few coaching staffs continue to define "affirmative action" in this way. Both black and white student-athletes are negatively impacted by staffs not embracing the positive effects of genuine diversity.

The "Fence of Separation." After putting my father to rest in 1983, I noticed this fence, which still divides the graves of black and white people in the cemetery. In 2012, the dead remain segregated in southwest Arkansas.

blacks take over coaching jobs like everybody wants them to, there's not going to be anything left for the white people."

I still recall my surprised reaction when I saw that. I always had suspected some white people thought that way. But it was the first time I realized that such white male paranoia was common enough that a national figure like Snyder would feel comfortable expressing it on camera. The man died in 1998, bless him. But his comment continues to "inspire" me. I think of it every time I hear fans (or coaches) mention that a certain college team's staff is "too heavy" with African American coaches. I confess, I can't argue with Snyder's racial mathematics. If African American men do get more football coaching jobs, then by definition white men will get fewer of them. And in the college game's Football Bowl Subdivision, there are only 120 head coaching jobs available.

However, unless a cabal of African American coaches are meeting in some secret lair to develop a sinister blueprint of world domination, there is no plan for them to "take over" college coaching. They just want a fair shot at every job, like any coach of any color. I don't think it would be a healthy thing or would send a good message if a team had an all-white or all-black coaching staff. But if proper hiring procedures are followed, that would never happen anyway.

Keep this in mind: If every single coach in America were interviewed for a given position, there would be far more white candidates than minority candidates. But some of those minority candidates are going to be better than some of the white candidates, and vice versa. The key is to interview enough of them, rather than "slotting" one job for one particular race.

Make no mistake, however: white coaches still have a major advantage in getting jobs because they usually have more connections. You may know it as the "good old boy" network. From others in the academic community, I have learned that today many white people generally believe that society is now colorblind and point to President Obama or General Colin Powell as proof. But those people often don't dig deeper. If a teenaged African American male with coaching ambitions is forced to attend an inferior public high school with a part-time football coach being paid substandard wages, isn't that African American teenager at a disadvantage over a teenaged white male with coaching ambitions who attends a suburban private high school with a well-paid coach? And that still happens all the time in America.

At what point will the scales be balanced equally so that we don't have to worry about anyone's paranoia? Until then, just as white coaches need to put themselves in the shoes of black coaches who are frustrated at getting head coaching opportunities, black coaches need to put themselves in the shoes of white coaches who are being led by their bosses to believe that race is the prime factor in deciding who gets hired for certain jobs. And black fans need to understand that many white fans are taking their cues from this same "whispering ruse" syndrome. The only way to get past this situation is for coaches and fans of all races to work a little harder—or a lot harder—to understand each other.

Simultaneously, university administrators must become more transparent and less prone to promoting paranoia. It might take a while. The NFL is getting closer and closer to equal opportunity with the success of its Rooney Rule, as I have mentioned, then the university presidents and athletic directors have to also step up and make a play.

CHAPTER TEN

BLACK-ON-BLACK CRIME

When I decided to write this book, I made a promise to myself—a promise to tell the truth and nothing but the truth, so help me God. In keeping my promise, I therefore cannot tiptoe around a sensitive issue. It's one involving extremely dirty laundry that is embarrassing to me.

An examination of history reveals that following the Emancipation Proclamation, black Americans were still required to battle for equality and basic human rights. But I find it sad that so many blacks are no longer concerned or have simply forgotten about the collective sacrifices endured by their ancestors during slavery and the Jim Crow era. From my vantage point, it appears that black America has acquired a self-serving appetite for attempting to acquire the American dream on an individual basis rather than working together so that a rising tide can lift all boats.

According to my family's oral history, my great-great-grandfather was born into slavery around 1828 in Tennessee. His first name was Watson. He was sold as a child to an Arkansas plantation owner. After Watson became a free man, he was befriended by a white person named John Bell Hill. My great-great-grandpa hated the last name he'd been given by his owners and took the liberty of claiming his new friend's last name. That's why my family's name is Hill.

I can't imagine the emotional trauma that my great-great grandfather had to endure on a daily basis as a piece of human property. I also can't imagine how my later ancestors maintained their collective sense of humanity when the Jim Crow laws of their time forced them into segregated restrooms and restaurants and basically told them that their thoughts and concerns didn't matter. The experiences that I described while working as an assistant for Arkansas Head Coach Danny Ford—experiences that nearly broke me down mentally and emotionally—were nothing compared to what my relatives experienced 125 years ago, or even fifty years ago.

However, I do know that my ancestors were engaged in the struggle for equality and were proud people. My grandfather was even given the name "Freeman" as a tribute to that struggle. Therefore, it totally confuses me when the same proud race of brave folks—which once unified its efforts and sacrificed lives by standing together against acts of social injustice—would in today's world so often turn to guns and physical abuse toward each other.

What does this have to do with football coaches? I'll get to that in a few paragraphs. First, let me cite some facts that will make you scratch your head. They just make me sad.

I am using the most recent data I could locate—a study conducted in 2008 by criminologists at Northeastern University in Boston. The study showed that while the overall murder rate in America has decreased since the year 2000, the number of murders among young black males has drastically increased. The numbers include victims as well as the suspects of black-on-black crime. The statistics showed that during the 2007 calendar year, 426 black males between the ages of fourteen and seventeen were murdered, a 40 percent increase from 2000. Furthermore, there was a 38 percent increase in the number of young black males responsible for those murders.

Across all age groups, the federal crime statistics show that between 1976 and 2004, 94 percent of black murder victims were killed by black offenders. And finally, there's this: according to statistics from Tuskegee University, the 2,993 victims of black-on-black homicide in the calendar year 2005 were roughly equal to the total number of black men lynched in America between the years 1882 and 1968.

Obviously, this sends a horrible message about African American culture. But I guess the statistics are no shock to anyone who reads the papers or watches the news. Young black men are killing each other all across the United States. Sadly, there are still hate groups promoting segregation of the races in our country. But the odds of me being lynched by a white supremacist group or even murdered by a white person are statistically less likely than the odds of me being murdered by someone of my own race. I'm not happy to admit that. But it's the truth. This crisis must be addressed internally by African Americans, not the federal, state, or local governments.

The problem of black-on-black crime brings me back to the profession of college coaching. I am forced to admit that a portion of the blame for the lack of opportunities faced by African American college football coaches lies with…other African American college football coaches. Just to be clear, I am not trying to equate that with the act of physically killing another human being. But I believe that the situation stems from similar issues relating to a lack of leadership in black America. I strongly believe that the absence of positive black male role models in the development of too many young black men contributes to black America's leadership void. This is another reason that I support diversifying coaching staffs. The more black coaches we have, the more positive identifiable role models we create for black student-athletes.

However, after studying racial issues for years as a scholar and coach, I have come to believe in a historical effect cited by others: When the United States embarked upon building a multicultural society with the goal of integrating African Americans into the majority (white) culture, the unintended consequence was a quasi-brain drain. Prior to the passing of civil rights laws, black leaders were steadfastly prominent in their own communities—mostly because they were rarely allowed to lead outside of their community boundaries. After the civil rights legislation, many of these same leaders (especially in the professional fields) migrated away from African American neighborhoods. Unfortunately, in numerous cases, this allowed those areas to be controlled and influenced by the worst elements of those communities.

Movies such as *Boyz in the Hood* and *Menace II Society* depict this dysfunctional culture for which no one seems to have a cure. During a visit to Washington DC in early 2010, I attempted to discuss this frustrating situation with a white US Senator. He appeared baffled that I was even attempting to find a solution to black-on-black crime as it specifically related to young black men. He told me: "Good luck—if you succeed, you'll win the Nobel Peace Prize." In many ways, I was offended by his glib and dismissive remark. But on the flip side, I was happy that the senator spoke what he truly felt in his heart about the black-on-black crime issue in America.

Some academics say that in the post-integration age I have described, the system breeds such a cutthroat approach within black neighborhoods—not unlike the plantations of the South during slavery. History tells us that only one or two slaves were permitted to enter the master's house. Those who did often had better living and working conditions than those laboring in the cotton fields. Consequently, those field slaves would scheme against each other for the promotion to the "Big House"—the master's house.

This type of behavior, passed down through generations, has had a negative sociological effect on black men specifically and black people in general. There is a perception that only so many of us are allowed to "rise up" out of our circumstances and succeed in a big way. This can lead to despair, resignation, and a horrible tendency to disdain or harm any member of our community who dares to dream big.

Let me try to explain this by using the Supreme Court as an example. Only two African Americans have ever been appointed to the Supreme Court. Each served as the only African American on the court during their appointment. Nevertheless, numerous African Americans have played a major role in building our country.

Have there been more than two blacks qualified to being appointed to the Supreme Court? Of course!

But for decades, president after president never considered nominating another African American candidate to the court while one was already serving.

I guess you could say it was an unofficial quota system. One black face in the team picture looked good and showed some diversity. Two black faces in the team picture might be a little too diverse for much of the country to accept. So if you were an African American judge who hoped to be that second black face on the Supreme Court, you were eliminated from the prospective pool of nominees, not because of qualification, but because of skin color. This is an example of how race restricts opportunity. Although my knowledge of the judicial profession is minimal, my knowledge of African American culture is fairly extensive. And my hunch is that this unofficial quota structure in the Supreme Court led to some of those potential black nominees vying with each other in vicious ways to get that one precious seat.

Obviously, that's not the most serious kind of black-on-black crime. I really started questioning why we African Americans murder each other at such an alarming rate when I personally witnessed the aftermath of such violence firsthand in December of 2007. And it happened just seven blocks away from the campus of Arkansas Baptist College, where I currently serve as president. It's a historically black college, founded in 1884 by former slaves.

Earlier that summer, I had called in one of my male students for a conference to discuss his classroom underachievement during the spring semester. This same young man's stepdaughter was subsequently murdered during the Christmas holiday season. But the killers' true target was clearly my student. More than sixty bullet holes were found in his home. When I saw it, the place looked like a war zone. I was disgusted. I couldn't believe what I had just seen.

It looked like a scene right out of the movies. But it wasn't. This was real-life stuff.

After speaking with the young black man for whom the bullets were clearly intended, I asked myself, "Where were our black leaders to express outrage?" The perpetrators of this crime were not arrested for a couple of years. When they were found, I don't imagine the investigators—or any other interested folks—were surprised to learn that the guilty parties were young black males.

It seems that acts of black-on-black crime do not unify African Americans. On the other hand, crimes in which blacks are assaulted or mistreated by whites usually result in some sort of formal protest or rally by the black community. I'm baffled why black-on-black crime doesn't unify black people as well. Shouldn't black leaders also lead those sorts of efforts? The black leadership of our country should respond to this black-on-black crisis as we did to the white-on-black racial violence of the 1950s and 1960s. But it hasn't happened. Maybe this is what God has in store for me.

If I say that somebody should do something about it and I don't do anything myself, then I am as much part of the problem as anyone else who's not doing anything. As much as African Americans want someone from outside of our communities to fix this problem, that will never happen. Federal, state and city governments can make laws. But no government can magically transform communities and develop at-risk youth. The "somebody" that we are looking for to help us is each one of us. We are the ones that can stop black-on-black crime in our communities. Or to quote another African American voice: we are the ones we have been waiting for.

Again, this has more to do with black football coaches than you might think. With just a slightly different twist, these same sorts of dynamics show up when black football coaches seek employment at predominantly white colleges and universities, where the evidence demonstrates that only a few positions are open to people of color. It seems to stir up the worst propensities of our African American community—the tendency to savage each other instead of helping each other succeed, plus the tendency for none of our leaders to talk about and soundly criticize what is occurring.

Officially, every college coaching position in America is open to any coach of any race. Unofficially and realistically, that never happens. At most schools, only two or three spots on a football staff are filled by African Americans, because that's the comfort level of most major athletic departments and their major boosters. The situation is certainly better than it was forty years ago, when the average staff had zero minority members—or, at most, one.

Black coaches often scratch and claw to get the few jobs available to them. I realize that white coaches do the same thing for their own jobs. It's a brutal profession when you are trying to climb the ladder and reach the FBS (Division I) level. But the math still works out much less favorably for minority candidates. Here's why: most aspiring college coaches are former college football players. And as statistics show, African Americans are disproportionately over-represented on college rosters.

I had the pleasure of working with Dr. Terry Don Phillips, the current athletics director at Clemson, during my stint as an assistant coach at Arkansas. At that time, Dr. Phillips was serving as the university's senior associate athletics director. He then moved on to become athletics director at Oklahoma State. While there in 1997, Phillips wrote an article in *The NCAA News* that stated: "Minority representation for coaches should approximate the percentage of minorities in the relevant applicant pool." Furthermore, Dr. Phillips noted that qualified coaches should come primarily from those who actually participated in athletics.

If this principle holds true and all of the African American players in college football could be considered part of the job pool, then a huge disparity existed in 1997—and still exists—between the number of African Americans in the coaching profession and the number of individuals available in that pool. And this disparity, which by my assessment is caused by an unofficial ceiling on the number of minority coaches on a given staff, is what provokes the black-on-black employment crime. I've seen it happen way too often.

I can't stress enough how tough it is to land any coaching job at the major college level, be it as a head coach or coordinator or position coach. When some of those spots are unofficially earmarked for one group and others are reserved for a different group based on race, it is easy to understand why black coaches work against each other. It was a phenomenon that I observed almost as soon as I entered the business more than twenty years ago.

Here's how it works: A job will come open. Somehow, on the grapevine, word gets out that it will be a minority hire. Then the negative conversations begin as those minority coaches backbite and plot against each other to get that one precious job offer, spreading rumors and casting aspersions on the other candidate's qualifications. I must confess that I was guilty of participating in this type of behavior myself as a young and ambitious coach—before I looked at myself in the mirror and understood what I was doing.

I am guessing that this sort of thing happens with white coaches as well—downgrading another candidate of his own race in order to gain an edge for a certain job opening. I actually witnessed a white coach doing such a thing when I was assembling my staff at San Jose State. But as a member of a minority race, I guarantee you that my guilt about the situation was much worse. In my opinion, encouraging negativity about people of my own race during my own job hunt is no different than allowing negativity to fester in struggling black neighborhoods. Rather than trying to create a rising tide that lifts all boats, I had succumbed to the "protect your self-interest" syndrome so prevalent in the world today. The malice in my heart caused me, like so many other black coaches, to try and disrupt the chances of other African American coaches in order for my own selfish, personal progress. How sad!

I also want to note an incident that occurred in 2009 at the University of New Mexico involving first-year Head Coach Mike Locksley. Following the 2008 football season, New Mexico's athletic director, Paul Krebs, established a school precedent when he hired an African American to lead the football program. Locksley was one of four African American football coaches hired at Football Bowl Subdivision (FBS) colleges and universities that year.

Early in his first season, Locksley received a verbal reprimand with a follow-up letter placed in his personnel file after an altercation involving one of his staff members. According to the police report, a fight occurred during a "heated" coaches meeting. I was extremely happy for Locksley that he was allowed to continue in his position. When I learned that the coach with whom he fought, J.B. Gerald, was also African American, I said to myself the famous words of Rodney King: "Can't we all get along?"

When the altercation occurred, Locksley's team was 0-4. I knew what he must have been going through, because I started out with an 0-5 record at San Jose State. The stares, glares, and cold shoulders that I received from the boosters and the cruel stuff that was written about me were enough to drive a person insane—and New Mexico football has greater expectations than San Jose State football. The resources are better. So is the fan support. In the San Francisco Bay Area, there are so many other pro sports teams (as well as two other FBS teams in Stanford and Cal) that occupy the media's attention. This certainly isn't the case in Albuquerque, where Lobo sports are number one in fan interest and everything else is in fifth place. So I am certain that the fire was a tad bit hotter for Locksley than it was for me.

The point is, my travails in San Jose could get lost in the clutter, and my face wasn't recognizable unless you were really tuned in to the Spartan football program. A perfect example of this occurred when one of my black assistant coaches actually committed what I call an act of black-on-black football crime. However, it wasn't committed against one of our other coaches; it was committed against one of our black football players.

During the 2003 football season, one in which we should have been playing better, we were all frustrated because of our lack of success. We entered the season with extremely high expectations and didn't come close to meeting them, finishing with a 3-8 record. Following each game, I always encouraged the coaches to go into the locker room and spend time with their players, win or lose. This is where relationships are built and trust is won. However, after one home game in midseason, one of our defensive backs (who was black) said something inappropriate to his position coach (who was also black). As it was reported to me, my assistant coach immediately grabbed the young man around the neck and started choking him.

Needless to say, I was upset. We were already not performing well on the football field, but I thought that at least we could act like men off the field. As I gathered all of the facts and interviewed everyone regarding the incident, I made a swift decision to remove the coach. Remarkably, because the *San Jose Mercury News* did not have a full-time beat writer for San Jose State football, it was nearly three weeks before a story about the coach's dismissal reached the sports page. The reporter covering our team was a little perturbed with me because the university had not released the story and I had not otherwise informed the reporter that I had fired the coach. I told the reporter that this had been a personnel issue and I would not comment on what happened. But I did acknowledge that there had been a locker room incident and that I had dealt with it...case closed.

I doubt if any episode like that one would have flown under the radar at New Mexico. I am quite certain that after Locksley laid his hand on the receiver coach and the coach was not on the practice field the next day, somebody asked some questions. Regardless of the delay in reporting our incident at San Jose State, I was embarrassed that one of my coaches would let himself be provoked into such behavior by a player. And yes, I immediately thought about the potential reaction of white fans and said to myself: "What in the world will they think of me now?" I sensed their emotions even if they weren't uttering them out loud. I envisioned that they would be asking each other: "Is this what we get with a black head coach; a black assistant coach choking a black student-athlete? We don't need any of this. Those people still haven't learned how to behave."

It is never appropriate for a coach to hit anyone. But when I discovered that in the New Mexico incident, Locksley had struck a black assistant coach, I grieved for both of them—not to mention their athletic director, Krebs. I am not sure whether the dispute was over football or if it involved a personal issue between the two men.

The black assistant coach, J.B. Gerald, filed a lawsuit in US District Court against Locksley and the University of New Mexico Board of Regents. The suit was literally filed right before the players were to report for the team's 2010 summer training camp. The lawsuit, as reported by ESPN.com, claimed that Locksley choked Gerald, punched him in the face, and cursed at him in front of peers and athletes. Gerald, the assistant coach, asked the university to pay for physical and emotional pain and suffering, lost wages, and other damages. And that wasn't all. The lawsuit also claimed that the university engaged in racial discrimination against the assistant coach, who is black, by failing to take appropriate action. The lawsuit stated that someone at the University of New Mexico suggested to Gerald "that his career would not benefit if he persisted in complaining of Locksley's behavior."

When the university hired Locksley, the administrators did not have a black-on-black football crime drama in mind, let alone a 2-22 record after two seasons.

Another instance of black-on-black football crime involved a good friend of mine who worked for one of the "Lonely Thirty-Eight" coaches I cited in a previous chapter. Currently, it is not common for a black assistant to have the opportunity to work for a black head coach. The odds are minimal, yet thank God they are improving. In one such situation, race became a factor in a personnel decision even though it should never have happened. A black head coach at one of the Football Bowl Subdivision institutions was hiring an offensive coordinator and quarterbacks coach. There were two black assistants already on the staff. Both felt they were qualified for the promotion to coordinator. However, the black head coach passed over both of them for a white guy who didn't possess any more qualifications or experience than either of those two black candidates on his own staff.

After failing to gain the promotion, one of the assistants left for the National Football League, where he thought he would have better employment opportunities. Before departing the college staff, however, this assistant expressed his disappointment to the head coach. Basically, the assistant was confused about why a black head coach would hire a white man who possessed no more qualifications than the black assistant coaches who had been there with the head coach all along, helping him build the program. The assistant coach told the head coach that he was "killing the fruit," a term that I will define later in this chapter.

The head coach then had a discussion with the other black assistant to get his perspective. The two men were honest with each other and expressed their true feelings: The black assistant coach said he respected the head coach's decision because of his right to hire anyone he wished. However, the assistant coach also felt that he was as qualified, if not more qualified, as the white coach that was brought in to be the offensive coordinator and quarterbacks coach. In fact, the black assistant coach noted that he had served in the exact same capacity at a previous job with success.

At that point, the black head coach finally had to quit hiding his poker hand and own up to the cards he had been dealt. The head coach, in so many words, told the black assistant coach: "You all don't understand. This is not a historical black college. So I can't operate like one."

If the black head coach would have been truly honest with himself, he would have added this: "I wish you guys could trade places with me so you all could understand the social and racial dynamics that I am dealing with. It took them years at this school to decide to hire a black head coach. And now you want me to risk my relationship with the administration and boosters to make one of you happy by giving you a chance to prove your qualifications? I'm sorry. But I am not in the position to do that right now. We have yet to overcome, no matter how it might look. Please be patient. As I prove my decision-making skills to the boosters and administration, I might be able to give you a promotion in the future."

As I mentioned, there are plenty of white coaching candidates who try to undermine other white candidates. But my research indicates that minority candidates experience a far more intense and enhanced version of this syndrome in so many different ways—even with the improved employment opportunities for black coaches.

It comes down to that same math formula that I previously cited. It's not merely about the difficulty black coaching candidates face in trying to earn the few jobs that are unofficially "slotted" for minorities. It's also about the black coaches who are already employed on staffs but hope to reach the next level. They want to break through the even tougher invisible barriers that restrict coaches from moving into staff leadership positions such as offensive and defensive coordinators.

In my research, I have discovered that it is highly unlikely for a minority assistant coach to receive top consideration for a coordinator position unless the white head coach—and at FBS schools, the majority of head coaches are white—has personally witnessed the leadership skills of that same black assistant coach. I believe that this phenomenon is psychological in nature. There is generally no malice intended toward black coaches. It's simply difficult for white coaches, particularly those who grew up in an era where their role models were all white, to perceive that black coaches could be equal to or better coaches than someone that looks more like those role models.

When white coaches at predominantly white institutions took their first baby steps toward diversifying their staffs in the late '70s and early '80s, black coaches were hired at the so-called "non-critical thinking" positions such as receiver, running back, defensive line, and outside linebacker. In the years I have closely studied the makeup of staffs, most black coaches were hired at those positions. And whenever I look at the staff assignments today, I am chagrined to find that's still usually the case.

Position assignment is another reason that so many black coaches are sucked into the dynamic of feeling they must fight with other black coaches for the few opportunities available. The vicious result is a sports version of black-on-black crime—in this case, caused not by racial self-hatred but by the process through which those jobs are filled and the positions available. And the crime has many layers.

Here's another example, based on an experience that I had at San Jose State involving a black university administrator. Immediately upon my hire, this person of color invited me to lunch and welcomed me to the campus. To be honest, my instincts led me to believe this person didn't have my best interest at heart, but I approached the relationship with an open mind thinking that maybe the West Coast was different. I truly didn't understand the significance of my hire in what I had perceived to be a truly multicultural environment. Nor did I think that one of biggest internal enemies at the school would happen to be the same race as me.

Among African Americans at certain institutions and businesses, there is an unspoken pecking order defined as the HNIC, which is an acronym for "Head Negro in Charge." I have never desired to be such a thing. But the "title" of HNIC often comes about when successful black people work within a largely white America. Most black people understand how it works. Organizations governed by a white power structure are usually receptive to one person of color and learn to become comfortable around that one individual. And on the flip side, I have discovered that a black person often clings to the job security in operating as the only person of color in an organization or corporation—because he or she realizes that he or she will always be needed by the organization as an outward show of "equality."

This one black employee is often the organization's "affirmative action baby," and unless another African American is hired, the one black employee will always have a job because, for image's sake, there must always be at least one black person within the organization.

Another form of black-on-black crime is when one black person feels that if another black person invades his or her scene or space, that newer black person has the potential to become a more valuable asset to the organization than the first black person. As a result, the self-preservation instinct kicks in, and black employees actually work against each other rather than working with each other. This is never good—for the two individuals or the group as a whole.

During my time at San Jose State, I experienced something similar to this. The black administrator I mentioned perceived that he was the gatekeeper for African American issues as it related to college administrators and student-athletes on campus. I perceived that he felt his space—and his status as the HNIC—were threatened by my hire. He wasn't a football coach. However, my past research had given me a certain academic status regarding racial issues in college athletics.

In addition, I was blessed with the idea of holding the Literacy Classic football game—bringing Grambling State to San Jose and selling out our stadium while also raising money for the cause of literacy—that brought national attention to San Jose State and raised my national profile. To pull off the game, I needed support from the Bay Area's African American community. The game was a big hit and exceeded all expectations. For that reason, I was named as one of the Bay Area's most influential African Americans in 2003.

However, back on campus, I was told by several folks that my fellow black colleague, the HNIC, was not pleased with these developments because I had not consulted him about the creation of the Literacy Classic. Consequently, this person started doing things to make my job very difficult as it related to the welfare of my student-athletes—such as promising me that all was well with their academics but not performing the necessary checks and paperwork monitoring to make certain this was true. All of this would complicate my efforts to continue improving the program. Ultimately, it was one of the shovels that dug my grave.

Interesting, right? These intra-racial social dynamics are hard to define when relating them to the "outside world." But when they happen to you, it's like a punch in the gut. I have no malice in my heart for the person in question, because when black people treat other black people this way, it often speaks of the insecurities that only the individual can courageously address within himself.

Make no mistake, though. This phenomenon is another form of a "crackback" block. But it's the kind of blindside block where teammates collide with each other, and neither individual reaches the desired goal or objective. And both people end up losing. One man may lose his job or be forced to leave. As for the HNIC, he may have felt threatened that his authority to speak to the white leaders as a definitive voice on black issues would be in jeopardy. But once the HNIC has removed his threat, he resumes his role of tokenism. That isn't winning, either.

I have also discovered that white organizations frequently end up employing unqualified black men—and not because qualified individuals weren't available, but because the white organizations feel more comfortable hiring someone who will have no problem if he is defined as a token. These token-types are usually not secure in themselves. They are less likely to challenge the status quo. In most cases, they are just happy to be employed. And as long as they are receiving a paycheck, they aren't worried about the well-being or development of other minorities who might come along as replacements—because if that happens, the token's value would decrease and they might not be needed.

I want to give you a sense how an African American coach at the college level can go temporarily insane—not only because he is facing the "crackback" effect from forces that are not eager to see a minority coach succeed, but even from his own "teammates." That's how I felt. That is a major reason that I lost forty pounds during the 2003 and 2004 football seasons. It was also recently brought to my attention that a new trend has surfaced in the coaching profession involving minority coaches. It is a trend that I had not initially recognized. But it reminds me that many black coaches are still race conscious about the color line in college football.

When I attended the 2010 American Football Coaches Association conference, I discovered a new phrase being used by black coaches—the phrase I mentioned earlier in relation to the black head coach who didn't promote his own qualified black assistant coaches. Remember? The assistant coach told the head coach that he was "killing the fruit."

At first, I didn't understand the phrase. But then the coach explained it to me. He said, "Fitz, check out the black coordinators that are hired by black head football coaches." I was puzzled. So he related other instances where black head coaches failed to hire qualified black offensive or defensive coordinators. The head coaches were "killing the fruit" on the very tree they had planted. Immediately, I thought back to my time as head coach at San Jose State.

As the first African American head football coach at San Jose State, I was well aware that my every move was being watched and evaluated by the institutional administration and by the program's boosters. For that reason, I am aware of the influences felt by black head coaches who choose to "kill the fruit." Those coaches are looking for approval from the people who are supervising and evaluating them. In many collegiate football programs where an African

American head coach is hired for the first time, the hiring of a black coach as an offensive or defensive coordinator will also most likely to be a first.

And because most of the African Americans hired as head coaches will not have prior experience at that job, athletic directors (most of whom are white) will logically suggest and even recommend to inexperienced black head coaches that they should seek and employ a staff with experience at the coordinator positions. Athletic directors might even go as far as suggesting that the pool of experienced minority coordinators is extremely shallow.

I recall when Oregon State interviewed me for the head coaching vacancy following the 2002 season. I was told that I had impressed the three member hiring committee that had flown into San Jose to interview me and that I needed to prepare as if I was going to be the next head coach. In a follow-up conversation with the athletic director, I was instructed to identify the prospective coaching staff members that I would attempt to hire and be prepared to share those names with him in 48 hours. Although race was never discussed, my experiences as the first African American head football coach at San Jose State, which I would have also been the first at Oregon State gave me great insight into his unspoken concerns.

Black collegiate head football coaches at predominantly white institutions understand the spotlight and overt identification that comes from being the first of their race in a given job. I liken it to a white man playing tailback in the National Football League today. Everyone is watching to see his skill level to see how he actually won the starting job.

After taking over at San Jose State, I hired a black defensive coordinator and a white offensive coordinator. Their skin color didn't matter to me. I felt they were the best men I could hire for our program. Both were excellent coaches.

Sadly, as a staff, we developed some issues of cohesion. I didn't do an effective job of managing my coaches. I accept responsibility for that. I was naïve. I figured that all the coaches would work together because it was best for our team. But during my entire time at San Jose State, we struggled defensively. After taking the time to step back and objectively assess what occurred, I can see that our inability to effectively work together defensively kept us in the cellar statistically year after year.

Realizing that situation, I worked myself into exhaustion in my job at San Jose State, which detrimentally affected my ability to lead my staff. I understood that if I did well there, I would hit the lottery by earning a huge contract from a larger and richer program. However, if I did not succeed, I would almost certainly be out of the head coaching game forever, and the odds of the institution hiring another African American would be greatly diminished. As we all know, I missed my target. I am the one to blame for it. Not the administration, boosters, assistant coaches, or anyone else.

I understood even more the negative lingering effects of my lack of wins while visiting with the interim San Jose State president, Don Kassing, in November of 2004. As we sat in his office, working out my resignation settlement, I explained to Kassing that I hoped that my lack of success would not keep him from seeking other qualified African Americans as potential candidates to replace me. I remember vividly his innocent response.

"Do you think there is someone out there that we should consider?" he frankly asked me.

Frustrated, I replied by pointing out that his mind-set—the perception that there might not be very many qualified black head coaches—was exactly the problem that stymied so many African Americans in the profession.

In a twisted fashion, this perception also affects the decisions of African American head coaches when they have to make those critical hires of offensive and defensive coordinators. If an African American head coach realizes that his school's administrators question the number of qualified minority candidates, it can affect the

African American coach's own hiring process. He will put his one opportunity to win in the hands of offensive and defensive coordinators that will cause athletic directors and boosters to nod and say: "Good choice."

Black coaches, like white coaches, prefer to complete their contracts and receive their total financial compensation. Hiring white coordinators can buy black head coaches more time from the people who make the choices to hire or fire. But for minority assistant coaches seeking a promotion, this becomes the definition of "killing the fruit"—and another example of black-on-black crime.

My content analysis of the thirteen black head football coaches who led major college programs entering the 2010 season revealed that 23 percent of the coordinator positions at those schools were staffed with African Americans. It would have been great for all involved if that number would have been closer to 50 percent. There were certainly enough qualified black coaches to fill those jobs. And if the black head coaches would have stepped up and hired more African American coordinators, it would have helped make up for the lack of minority coordinators at the 107 major colleges led by white head coaches. Instead, those thirteen black head coaches filled just *six* of their twenty-six available coordinator positions with African American coaches—and two of those six were at the University of Houston, where Kevin Sumlin employed black offensive and defensive coordinators. If you eliminate Sumlin and Houston from the picture, that 23 percent figure quickly drops to 16 percent.

It might seem odd that coaches who have waited and waited for the opportunity to lead their own programs would not reward similarly ambitious minority coaches, just to keep the fruit ripe and sprouting. But that is not happening. Does it surprise me? Not after being a head coach at a predominantly white institution and experiencing the social and racial dynamics that take place on college campuses and at booster club meetings. I completely understand the rationale behind this hiring phenomenon.

Unfortunately, when my own black defensive coordinator at San Joe State failed to produce impressive results during our first two seasons, it did not reflect well for other black assistant coaches who wished to become defensive coordinators at their own schools. You probably think I am obsessive on this point, and you are correct. But if you learn nothing else from reading this book, I hope you understand that unlike white coaches, black coaches are too often evaluated collectively. So when black football coaches and black leaders in general are put in spotlight positions, those individuals have a much smaller margin of error. If they fumble their opportunity, it always carries negative connotations for other blacks to be hired in that same position.

I totally comprehend why my losing record at San Jose State will for several generations have a lingering negative effect in terms of another black head coach ever being hired at the school. The job has since been filled twice, and to my knowledge, no African Americans were serious candidates. If SJS doesn't drop football in the future, I hope I live to witness the day that the institution hires its second African American head football coach.

Should President Barrack Obama's job performance as president speak for all black Americans, specifically black men? Maybe it shouldn't. But quite frankly, it does. If President Obama is deemed to be a disappointment and is voted out after one term the way President Jimmy Carter or President George H.W. Bush were, it will probably be much tougher for another black candidate to win the nomination of either major party. Obviously, that wasn't the case for white candidates in the wake of President Carter or the first President Bush.

This is why, for every African American in college sports, perfection is almost mandatory. One person's mistake can have a ripple effect on all of us. Which brings me to another unfortunate such example.

In June of 2010, I attended the National Association of Collegiate Directors of Athletics conference in Anaheim, California, for the induction of Chuck Bell into the NACDA Hall of Fame. Bell of course, had hired me at San Jose State back in 2001. I was in Anaheim to celebrate his induction with his family. This was the first time I had ever attended the NACDA conference. I recognized several athletic directors that I had met during my coaching career. One of them particularly stood out to me—Damon Evans at the University of Georgia. Evans was the first black AD to be hired in the Southeastern Conference.

I felt a special connection to Evans. I had met him in the early '90s at the University of Arkansas. Frank Broyles, the athletic director at the time, had attempted to hire Evans, who at that time was employed at the NCAA headquarters in an executive capacity. During his visit to Fayetteville, my wife and I hosted Evans and his wife. Ultimately, Evans turned down the Arkansas offer and remained with the NCAA but later did accept an associate AD position at Georgia, his alma mater. He was obviously gifted and very talented. In 2004, at the tender age of thirty-six, the school selected him to run the entire athletic department.

Evans's hiring was a monumental one for blacks who aspired to become athletic directors in the SEC, a league where "booster-itus" runs rampant and can greatly influence the personnel decisions in athletics departments. For six years it was said that Evans performed admirably at Georgia. He was awarded a new five-year contract that was scheduled to kick in on July 1, 2010. The deal guaranteed him $550,000 annually with a $20,000 raise each year. But the night before the contract was supposed to take effect, Evans made a huge mistake. While visiting Atlanta, which is seventy miles from the Georgia campus in Athens, Evans was arrested for driving while under the influence of alcohol. To top it off, it was late at night, and he had a lady in his car who wasn't his wife. This was a bad mistake for any man but a huge mistake for a black man.

When I saw the story, I remembered how proud and happy I had been a few weeks earlier when I'd seen Evans in the lobby at the Marriott Hotel in Anaheim. I had thought to myself, *See? We can lead programs when given the right opportunity to do so.*

Because Evans had been the face of the athletic program in Georgia, the school had used him strategically to show how progressive it was. With that in mind, I thought Evans could survive the DUI even though he was featured in a public service video announcement on the scoreboard before every home Georgia game saying, "If you drink and drive, you lose." But once the details came out, I knew immediately that he didn't stand a chance of surviving. Why? He crossed the line. Evans was busted with a twenty-eight-year-old female in his car, and the police report said that he had red panties between his legs. The arresting officer said that Evans had attempted to exert influence by asking that no charges be filed because of his status as the Georgia athletic director.

Evans claimed that the woman was just a friend. This story fell apart after she told police they had being seeing each other for about a week. After reading the facts, I concluded that Evans must have forgotten that he was a black man. All of his fastidious efforts to dress right, speak right, act right, and do all the many right things for many years exploded like a bomb, with shrapnel hitting all black men throughout the state of Georgia—and throughout athletic departments from coast to coast.

Once the police report details were made public, Evans offered his resignation. His arrest and scandalous departure from Georgia was an immense blow to all African Americans because it, too, was effectively a crime against them. I am certain that it made things more difficult for other minority candidates for athletic directorships across the country – because, as I have indicated, at too many schools, African Americans are still judged collectively. Georgia moved quickly and in less than six weeks hired George McGarity, who had been employed at the University of Florida, where he served as senior executive assistant to the athletic director. McGarity, like Evans, was a Georgia alumnus. His hiring was well received by the Bulldog nation. McGarity is white.

In my opinion, it will be a long time before another African American leads the Bulldog program. Truth be known, I would assume that the University of Georgia's president Dr. Michael Adams, took some heat for hiring Evans in 2004. So you have to applaud Dr. Adams for his initial courage.

In the days after Evans's arrest, blogs and internet chatters were comparing him to Tiger Woods. It might be done consciously or unconsciously. In studying those blogs and chats, I noticed that no one compared Evans to Roger Clemens or John Edwards or other famous white philanderers. This is why I refer to the Evans incident as black-on-black sports crime—because while the consequences were not calculated, the effect is the same: African American candidates for jobs in athletic departments get hit without seeing it coming. I don't know when black men and black coaches will be looked at in the same light as white men and white coaches at every single university in America. But I know we aren't there yet.

Could this situation change? Currently, the Black Coaches Association is the recognized "voice" for promoting minority progress in the profession. Founded in 1988, the BCA's mission statement is straightforward. The organization wants to address significant issues regarding the employment of minority coaches and assist the aspirations of those minorities.

But the "voice" has not always been a steady and united one. At the last BCA conference that I attended in 2003, there were fewer black football coaches in the room than in the early 1990s. I think the participation of the football coaches has decreased due to the fact that the BCA lacks a defined structure and a specific way to execute its original mission. It is a national body headquartered in Indianapolis with no regional branches or components. This makes it difficult for the BCA to be effective in all corners of the country.

Things have improved in the last couple of years with the slight increase in the hiring of more African American head coaches. But imagine how rapidly progress would take place if there were regional branches of the organization keeping a stronger eye on the landscape in the various conferences.

I give credit to the BCA's executive director, Floyd Keith, for bringing a sinking ship back to water level. But he is only one man. How can he have a complete handle on the minority coaching dynamics in Florida and, say, Idaho or Montana? And beyond that, how could he possibly monitor any "killing the fruit" situations and institute some sort of program or initiative to make it less of a problem? How would Keith ever find the time to do that?

I believe that if the BCA wants to develop the most influential voice possible for employment equity, the organization must mimic the model established by the National Association for the Advancement of Colored People (NAACP). Perhaps the BCA could even become a subsidiary of the NAACP—and change its name to something like the NAAMFC, the National Association for the Advancement of Minority Football Coaches. However, a name shouldn't matter. The mission should.

I am certainly aware that the NAACP has its own critics. But over the years, it has accomplished much in terms of raising awareness and bringing needed change to our society. It does so with local, state, and regional chapters and more than one person out front, trying to cover all the bases.

Similarly, the BCA needs to empower leadership throughout the states and all of the football conferences. That way, coaches in these various regions can serve as both monitors and spokesmen for the group. Again, this is no insult to Floyd Keith. He is simply spread too thin. I think we're kidding ourselves if we think Keith can play "BCA cop" for the entire organization coast to coast. In fact, under the current structure, I don't even know how the BCA can evaluate its own effectiveness—which, quite candidly, is already in question.

Bottom line: Keith and the BCA still lack genuine nationwide support.

And his job has been incrementally more difficult since 2004, when a new piece of NCAA legislation eliminated the BCA Football Classic. This was an early-season game between two marquee teams with the proceeds used to fund the BCA office. Now, those funds must be raised through other resources. That's proven to be a difficult chore.

Finally, and most troubling of all, the BCA has not successfully mobilized support from African American professional athletes or African American civic leaders in cities around the country—at least not in the numbers necessary to exert significant influence. Those athletes could also contribute their financial resources to implement the sort of regional plan I've suggested.

Don't get me wrong. I support the BCA and its mission and will always assist in moving the organization forward if asked. After I suggested that the organization change its name to be more inclusive of other minorities—say, to the Minority Coaches' Association, I was told that my idea was considered seriously. But it was ultimately rejected. Change is difficult to embrace when staying the same is what you truly desire. The BCA is open to coaches of any color. But it's still called the BCA. With a name change to Minority Coaches' Association or some such variant, coaches of Latino or Asian heritage could feel more comfortable about joining—which in my opinion is absolutely what needs to happen.

Navy's head football coach, Ken Niumatalolo, is the second person of Polynesian descent to be named head coach of a Football Bowl Subdivision football program and the first Samoan collegiate head coach on any level. He should feel embraced by the BCA, not begrudgingly admitted. I remember Norm Chow, the head coach at Hawaii, asking me about this exact subject. Coach Chow, whose heritage is Asian American, asked me if he could become a member of the BCA. I told him of course he could—and wondered why he didn't think it was possible. He told me that because he wasn't black, he did not think that he would be accepted. That gave me a bad feeling.

I have that same feeling too many other times, whenever I hear another story like that about my minority coaching brothers acting like anything but brothers toward each other. Until we see the meaningful changes that I have mentioned to remedy the situation, it is highly likely that we will continue to see black-on-black crime in the college coaching profession. And that makes me sick.

Perhaps there will never be a strategic plan within the BCA organization to mobilize coaches from coast to coast within each conference which could lift all the boats. But in the absence of that, I can certainly say this to minority coaches everywhere: See all those boats filled with potential equality? Please help lift them…keep them afloat. Don't help sink them.

CHAPTER ELEVEN

MY SPARTAN LESSONS AND RAZORBACK EDUCATION

Someone once said that experience is what you get when you don't get what you want. That defines my four years at San Jose State.

I never wanted this book to be solely about my own experiences. I still don't. But I believe my story can be instructive to the larger issue of how African American and minority coaches are forced to navigate the storm-tossed waters of college football—in such a different way. Historically, most head coaching positions offered to African Americans are at programs on the fringes, where you're always paddling upstream against a ridiculously difficult current.

That more or less describes San Jose State. I continue to believe that I was blessed in being selected to lead the Spartans football program starting with the 2001 season. But in retrospect, I shake my head at the many challenges and barriers I faced on a daily basis. Initially, I thought things would improve over my four seasons there. But I would soon learn that the many daily obstacles that I faced would actually become standard operating procedures on my Silicon Valley campus.

When I began my collegiate coaching career as a graduate assistant at Northwestern State University in Natchitoches, Louisiana, it wasn't long before I envisioned myself as a head coach at a major college. I always thought that I could turn a bad program into a good one if I ever received the opportunity to be the head man in charge. My recruiting success at my other stops led me to believe that I could convince the best student-athletes to join my efforts,

247

regardless of any given football program's profile. All I needed was the chance to outwork my competition.

There were times when I questioned if my dream of being a head coach would come true. In 1994, I had applied for the head coaching position at Yale, and I got a phone interview but nothing materialized. On top of that, the research regarding black coaches that I started collecting in 1989 was not encouraging. As a young assistant coach, I had seen so many talented African American men become invisible when it came time to move into football leadership positions at major college football programs. If I was going to be invisible, at least I wanted to do it in a field with more secure employment.

So to stay sane and feel as though I wasn't chasing a ghost, I cut a deal with myself. I decided that I would quit the coaching profession when I turned forty years old if I had not been hired to lead my own program. Getting out of the business at that age would still give me about twenty-five years to establish myself in another profession.

Interestingly enough, both of those things would happen, but not in the way I envisioned. I was selected to be the head coach at San Jose State at age thirty-six yet still left the profession at age forty. But the lessons I learned during my "tour of duty" at San Jose State, both personally and professionally, forever changed the way I viewed life.

It all began in early December of 2000 at the University of Arkansas, where I was serving as the football program's assistant head coach, recruiting coordinator and receivers' coach. Our staff was busy preparing to play in the Las Vegas Bowl against the University of Nevada-Las Vegas. We had just finished what was considered a disappointing season for Arkansas. At one point, our won-loss record was 3-6 and our bowl hopes were very slim. But somehow we rallied to win our last three SEC games and became bowl eligible. We had defied the odds and reached our third consecutive bowl game, making it three-for-three for my boss, head coach Houston Nutt, who had been hired in 1998.

As we practiced in preparation for our Vegas trip, I was also busy outlining the recruiting execution plan for my fellow coaches. We'd assembled two strong classes after playing in New Year's Day bowl games following the 1998 and 1999 seasons. I knew we needed another strong recruiting effort to make certain that we didn't endure another disappointing season such as the one we had just experienced. I understood that the Las Vegas Bowl was better than no bowl at all. But I also knew that none of us would stay employed at Arkansas very long by merely qualifying for such a second-tier (or third-tier) bowl game.

Right about that time, San Jose State University called. For the previous nine years, I had been dealing with the racial dynamics of recruiting top football talent to northwest Arkansas, an area not known for diversity. Therefore, I was more than enthusiastic to go west and lead the Spartans as their first African American football coach. However, I didn't know much about the program itself. During my brief tenure as an assistant coach at Utah State in the winter of 1992, I had gained some basic knowledge about my future employer. At the time, San Jose State was a member of the Big West Conference that competed against Utah State. Because the Bay area was my assigned recruiting area, I spent a lot of time in the Spartans' backyard trying to convince student-athletes they should spend their college years in Logan, Utah. At the time, Logan and Fayetteville had a lot in common.

This explains why, as I considered the recruiting advantages of being in California, I thought if I came to San Jose State and signed up some "bona fide ballers," we could win our league within a few years—even though the Spartans had moved up from the Big West to the tougher Western Athletic Conference. I was sure that recruiting would be the key. I've always subscribed to the old coaching bromide—the Xs and Os don't matter nearly as much as the skill level of the Johnnies and the Joes.

Fortunately, during my tenure at Arkansas, I had been around a few skilled recruiters. I learned the most from Jack Crowe, who was fired as head coach the day after The Citadel beat us in 1992. Often walking right up to the edge in terms of violating the rules, Crowe was very strategic in his recruiting tactics. I was impressed with how, as a white man, he was able to put black families at ease and establish trust in a very unique way.

I witnessed this first hand when he convinced Henry Ford, one of the best high school defensive tackles in the nation, to leave his home in Fort Worth, Texas, and play for the Razorbacks. Henry would go on to be drafted by the Houston Oilers and spend ten seasons in the NFL. It was because of the relationship that Crowe established with Ford's mother that Henry ended up at Arkansas. I remember Crowe telling me to call Henry every day just to say hello. Today, it's illegal under NCAA rules to contact recruits by phone that often.

Danny Ford, who would eventually succeed Crowe as Arkansas's head coach, was also knowledgeable about the recruiting trail. Crowe had worked for Ford at Clemson, where at the tender age of thirty-four Ford had coached Clemson to the 1981 national championship and consistently had very talented teams that produced NFL players. However, after Ford took over as the head football coach of Arkansas, I often worried about taking him into the homes of middle-class African American families, because I was scared of what he might say.

He could, for example, have a slip of the tongue and say "boy" without understanding the negative connotations of his words—especially given the racial history of Arkansas. Ford's good ol' boy persona turned off several middle-class African American families on recruiting visits. On the flip side, when we made a visit to a black family in Carrolton, Georgia, where the prospect lived with his elderly grandmother, the Ford persona paid off in a surprising way. Ford was doing his best to make the family feel comfortable, which apparently worked, because the grandmother offered to share her chewing tobacco with him. Ford refused but told her that he had his own and reached inside his dress jacket pocket, pulled out his pouch, and joined in the chewing festivities. We signed the recruit.

This was in stark contrast to Houston Nutt, who followed Ford at Arkansas. I actually felt empowered taking Nutt into the homes of African American families. Being raised by his parents in a multi-cultural educational setting, Nutt had a unique upbringing in Little Rock. His father was a teacher and coach at Arkansas School for the Deaf, where students learn to work together, regardless of skin color. Nutt also explained to me how on many occasions he found himself in the minority among his many black friends. Consequently, when it came down to recruiting black athletes, Nutt was a smooth operator.

In fact, Nutt even understood the importance of having Black Entertainment Television (BET) on the University of Arkansas cable systems as a tool to recruit black student-athletes to the school. Coach Ford didn't seem to understand why this kind of thing made any difference. I did not believe there would be any such issues as I moved to the multicultural Bay Area, particularly when the San Jose State campus was just a thirty-minute drive from Oakland, the hub of Northern California's African American community.

The chain of events that led to my taking over the Spartan football program began when the late Keli McGregor, who was serving as president of the Colorado Rockies baseball team, put me on alert that I would likely receive a phone call from Chuck Bell, the athletic director at San Jose State. I had worked for McGregor in the early 1990s at Arkansas when I was a dormitory counselor while serving as a volunteer football coach for the Razorbacks.

At that time, McGregor was the school's assistant athletic director for student-athlete support services. McGregor then left Arkansas for a position with the Rockies. But in late autumn of 2000, Bell called McGregor to inquire about any prospects McGregor might have for the head coaching position at San Jose State, should it become vacant. Bell and McGregor had become acquainted when Bell was employed at Colorado State and had dealings with the Rockies in Denver.

Although McGregor wanted to recommend me, he first called Dean Weber, the University of Arkansas director of sports medicine, to see if Weber believed I was ready for such a position. Weber had seen many assistant coaches leave Arkansas and become successful head coaches. Based on these past experiences, he usually had an idea about who was ready for such a move and who wasn't. Weber gave me the green light. McGregor then told Bell that I was his guy if he could persuade me to leave Arkansas—something I had no plans of doing in the immediate future. Although I was eager to become a head coach, things were going well for me at Arkansas. I figured that I could be patient for a few more years.

Then I received the phone call from Bell. He wanted to fly down and visit with me in Arkansas. I should have known something was strange about the situation since he didn't invite me to San Jose for an interview. But I told Bell that I was wrapped up in recruiting, preparing to take a Florida recruiting trip. Our team was also preparing for the Las Vegas Bowl. I informed Bell that I would love to talk to him upon returning from Florida. Bell flew into nearby Bentonville. I met him at his Holiday Inn suite in Springdale.

I had done a little research on San Jose State and the surrounding area. But my heart's deepest desire was to recruit a national championship team at Arkansas. I thought I had one of the best jobs in America, working as an assistant head coach at the Frank Broyles Athletic Complex for Houston Nutt. I really had no reason to even think about leaving. But all of that would change after I had the chance to meet Bell.

As I walked in his suite, he was very friendly and open. I can't remember the exact words, but Bell said something to this effect: "I've been searching across the country for our next head football coach, and God has brought me to visit with you about being that guy." My ears perked up. Was this a calling on my life? Or did I just want to be a head coach so badly that I would travel nearly to the Pacific Ocean to fulfill that goal?

I never sent in an application for the position. Nor would I ever have applied for the opportunity to replace the current coach, Dave Baldwin, who had just finished up the first winning season at San Jose State since 1992. I discovered later that Baldwin and Bell had fallen out and that Baldwin's agent had refused the athletic department's initial offer to extend his contract, which was expiring after the 2000 season. In response, Bell withdrew any offer and did something unprecedented—he hired the first African American football coach in the history of the San Jose State program.

Bell left me a contract to review and told me that I was his first choice. He expressed to me that I came highly recommended by everyone he had contacted. He said he would be in touch early the following week. My heart started beating fast. It hit me that I was going to accomplish a lifelong dream to become a head football coach at major college football program. I started thinking about which people I could hire for my staff, plus about all the other stuff that I had been going over inside my brain over the previous twelve years.

What didn't register in my mind, not even for a second, was that my energy and persistent dedication to build the Spartan program would not be enough to make it work, or that resources for the football program were so scarce. Nor did I realize that in many ways, I was being set up for failure, just like many other ambitious minority coaches who want to be a head coach so badly that they will eagerly take over programs that have very little chance to be successful.

When I was contemplating whether I should stay at Arkansas, I read an article in *USA Today's* sports section that addressed the lack of black collegiate football coaches at predominantly white colleges and universities. An athletic director was quoted in the story, saying that one reason for the lack of black coaches in the top tier of college football was the lack of head coaching experience among black coaches as a group. With that in mind, I knew that I could elevate myself into the small pool of African Americans with head coaching experience. That way, when a job at a bigger school opened up, athletic directors around the country would have me on their radar. Finally, I thought it could well be this opportunity or no opportunity.

And so, after I began leaning toward taking the San Jose State position, I visited with Houston Nutt. When he asked why the job appealed to me, I told him it really didn't on one level, but then explained my theory about being able to recruit well enough to be competitive and win enough games to land that big job with a rich contract. I was a realist. I knew that as an assistant coach at Arkansas, it would be very difficult for me to get a head coaching job at, say, Oklahoma or Missouri. But one of those schools might call if I succeeded at San Jose State. My point was that as an African American who played his college football at an NAIA institution without a professional playing career on my résumé, I probably wouldn't be getting very many opportunities to say no. Nutt asked me to go see Frank Broyles, the legendary former Arkansas football coach who was then the school's athletic director. Nutt said I should show the San Jose State contract to Broyles before making any decision.

After walking upstairs to visit with Broyles, I was highly disappointed with his response. It's important for me to note how supportive Broyles had been of me and my family during my twelve years at Arkansas. His kindness and assistance to my wife while I served my country in Desert Shield and Desert Storm is something I will always be grateful for. Broyles loves winning. He was on your side, win or tie. But he didn't like defeat and wouldn't tolerate it. When the Arkansas football team was losing, the entire climate of the Broyles Complex, named after him, was unpleasant.

Nevertheless, as a former head coach, I knew that Broyles valued my recruiting skills and the way I coached the school's wide receivers. He realized how my players performed for Arkansas at a winning level. In addition, I had recorded a very high graduation rate among my position players. He knew that I brought added value to the athletic program and the university as a whole.

However, I guess that Broyles had grown tired of colleges trying to hire me away from Arkansas—although I had never applied for any of those jobs. Two years earlier, I had been offered the head coaching position at my alma mater, Ouachita Baptist University, in my hometown of Arkadelphia. To keep me in Fayetteville, Nutt had asked Broyles to give me a nice salary increase and a three-year contract. At that time, in the late 1990s, contracts were rare for assistant football coaches at the Broyles Complex. The following year, Texas Tech Head Coach Mike Leach asked me to take over recruiting for the Red Raiders' football program. Leach's job offer was very attractive, and Gerald Myers, the Tech athletic director, added job security by giving me an option to become an administrator after a minimum of three years on the football field.

Once more, Nutt requested another contract extension for me along with a salary increase that would at the time make me the highest paid recruiting coordinator in the Southeastern Conference. Broyles granted me both, so I was content. I felt that my services were valued. It also meant something to be employed in my home state.

But this time, with San Jose State calling, I knew the situation was different—even before I visited with Broyles. At San Jose State, I would have a chance to lead the entire program. It was a challenge that I had to think hard about refusing, although my salary would be about the same as I was making in Fayetteville after factoring in the cost of living in Silicon Valley. Even so, I don't think that I would have left if Broyles had countered by making a similar offer he had made to our Arkansas defensive coordinator, Keith Burns, two years earlier.

After the 1998 football season, Louisiana Tech had dangled its head coaching job to Burns, who was a hot commodity after his defense had played extremely well during our 9-3 season en route to the SEC West co-championship. We had also received an invitation to the Florida Citrus Bowl, where we faced Michigan.

After Louisiana Tech sought Burns to take over its football program, he wrestled with the idea of leaving Fayetteville. According to Burns, Broyles subsequently worked out a financial incentive by giving Burns an instant cash bonus to stay. We were all excited about his choice. I thought we were building something special and with Burns' defensive achievements and that he deserved his reward. But it was evident that Broyles did not value my talents as much as he did the talents of Burns.

I understand that being in charge of a defense in the SEC is a major responsibility. But recruiting top talent is just as important, if not more so. In the SEC, you have no chance to win unless you combine top talent with the best possible coaching. A perfect example is Vanderbilt University. Vanderbilt always has great coaches, but they never have the best players. Check their winning percentage. I think it validates my point.

I knew that Nutt didn't want me to leave Arkansas. He realized that I was struggling with my decision because we were having so much fun. But as I showed Broyles my contract and discussed the options, Broyles did not ask me to stay or make me a counter-offer as he had done for Burns. After about two minutes, Broyles said, "If you don't take the job, you can always tell people that you turned down an opportunity to be a major college head coach."

At that moment, any thoughts I had of staying at Arkansas evaporated. I realized that although I held the title of assistant head coach, Broyles didn't value me as much as I had previously believed. Consequently, I felt that I needed to strike out on my own and build my head coaching résumé. I always respected Broyles, because I was always able to go to him when I saw race-related problems at Arkansas, and he'd always acted in the best interests of winning and improving the situation. That's why I was so confused when he seemed so ambivalent about me staying at Arkansas.

After moving to the Bay area, the honeymoon of being a head coach was really special. At thirty-six years old, I was feeling pretty good about myself. I had always wanted to live in a city, and every night when I drove home, it tickled my heart that the Highway 101 sign read "San Francisco" going north and "Los Angeles" going south. I was living a dream.

Then I woke up.

My family was staying back in Arkansas as I was getting things off the ground in San Jose. But after assembling my coaching staff, all of us had to stay in a two-bedroom apartment because of budgetary restrictions—or at least that is what the athletic administrators told me. So we bought air mattresses and slept three to a room. I didn't have a large salary pool to distribute among my coaches. Therefore, I hired just eight full-time assistants my first year, giving me a smaller staff than other head coaches. I decided to fill the gap by working with our receivers myself, aided by a graduate assistant. Not the ideal picture, but I didn't focus on the negatives. I was just trying to figure out how to improve the program.

During my first spring practice, we didn't have caps for our coaches to wear. So I drove to the school bookstore and bought caps with my own money. Little things like that didn't really bother me. But I failed to realize that this stuff was just the tip of the iceberg. We had no apparel contract with Nike or Adidas, so all of our equipment and uniform needs were bid out each summer for the cheapest price that the athletic program could find. Consequently, when I arrived we had to use worn coaching apparel from the previous staff because new gear wouldn't be ordered until the following summer. When you have limited resources such as we had at San Jose State, you don't order extras. You order just what you need to get by.

Bell, my new athletic director, had said that he wanted me to put my own stamp on the program, including designing new uniforms and helmets. After talking to a few companies, I realized that Nike and Adidas didn't want us. So I decided to do something creative. I didn't have anything to lose and thought that I could find respectable quality uniforms at a competitive price from a new company that wanted to build a brand and grow with us. I was that daring.

That was the first big mistake I made.

I went with an unproven apparel company from Dallas that featured investors who were players from the NFL Cowboys. I thought the middle-aged African American woman who headed the company had more financial backing, but she was in way over her head.

This company was named 4-Players Only. I thought that had a nice recruiting ring to it. And when I showed the uniform design to the student-athletes, they all responded favorably. I knew that uniforms were a huge aspect of recruiting, and I was looking for anything to give us an edge. I understood that if we wanted to be better, we would have to be different. We couldn't take over the Bay Area trying to duplicate Stanford or Cal-Berkeley. We didn't have the money or resources.

The problem was, 4-Players Only couldn't deliver. I was so happy that San Jose State had given me my chance, and I wanted to give someone else the same sort of opportunity. I helped this woman land a story on ESPN.com about her company with the angle that our team was going against the grain of traditional college apparel. Everything went as planned—except the quality of the uniforms. They didn't fit right. They kept falling apart. It was an awful experience, one that caused me unnecessary stress as I prepared for my first game as head coach.

I fired that company immediately after the season and went with Adidas for the rest of my head coaching career. But that was just one of the many problems I would face in my inaugural year. It left a bitter taste in my mouth. In a sense, I felt this was an act of black-on-black crime. It's companies like this one that hurt other black-owned businesses. Not only are black coaches judged collectively, but so are black businesses. Sad but true.

In my mind, the Spartan boosters and alumni are mostly great people. For the most part, they treated me professionally. However, many of them were in denial because they wanted to be the athletic equal of Stanford, the Pac 12 school located about twenty miles north of San Jose State. The two universities have played football against each other since 1900. When I was hired, someone told me, "The alums don't care who else you beat as long as you beat Stanford."

However, I went to San Jose State with the idea of winning the WAC championship and becoming bowl eligible. I wanted to build a program, and if we happened to beat Stanford in the process, great. But I wasn't going to let winning or losing to Stanford in September—the game was always played early—be the reason for our season. Now, a victory over Fresno State was different. Fresno State was a WAC rival and in our path toward a championship. We had an opportunity to beat Fresno State two out of the four times that we played them when I was the Spartans' head coach. But we could never get it done.

Pat Hill, the Fresno State coach, gave our team a nice compliment after our two teams met in 2002, when the winner of the game was guaranteed an invitation to play Georgia Tech in the Silicon Valley Classic Bowl game. After our team lost, Pat sought me out in the locker room, where I sat dejectedly. One of our receivers had dropped a touchdown pass that would have given us the victory. Pat said it was the best San Jose State team he had ever faced up to that point. I appreciated that and thanked him. But it still felt as if somebody close to me had died. We had the game and let it slip through our fingers.

During that 2002 season, we did turn a few heads. After being picked last in the conference, we put together a remarkable string of victories. And the funny thing is, because of my ignorance, I didn't even realize what we had accomplished. I thought we were supposed to do what we were doing. But I wound up getting an education in the real handicaps faced by lower-tier programs such as San Jose State. I think it's instructive to examine that season, just to show the travails faced by coaches at that level—many of them minorities, because the San Jose State-type programs are ones that African Americans are the most likely to lead. It is why, when I see what Turner Gill did at someplace like Buffalo, I am nearly in awe.

At San Jose State before my second season, I worked out an arrangement with the city leaders of Little Rock to pay us $150,000 to visit the city and play a game against Arkansas State, which was coached by my college teammate, Steve Roberts. I pursued that deal because Bell had told me that every time we played at Spartan Stadium, we lost about $50,000. Our home attendance was so lousy—with ten thousand to fifteen thousand showing up for games—that it could not cover our expenses. But I wanted some new equipment for our players and wanted to upgrade our facilities. So I asked Bell this question: If I arranged that game in Arkansas, could we spend any of the proceeds on specific improvements? I figured it would be better than the negative $50,000 we would bring to our budget by playing a home game against Sacramento State.

Bell agreed with me. So we worked it out, got a victory, and got paid. After expenses, I think we netted about $60,000 for the trip to Little Rock. As I was learning the economics of college athletics, it started making sense to me when, in the midst of that 2002 season, we were featured in the *USA Today* sports section as the college program with the most frequent flyer miles. We played thirteen consecutive weeks and traveled nearly thirty thousand aeronautical miles. Of our thirteen games, only four were played at Spartan Stadium.

I was so naïve that it didn't dawn on me that I had no real chance to be successful because Bell had been instructed by San Jose State's administration to do whatever it took to balance the athletic budget, which had been running annual deficits of nearly $1 million prior to his arrival. Consequently, Bell followed the direction of his bosses without strategically positioning the team for success.

In addition to our other challenges, we had just sixty scholarship student-athletes as opposed to the full limit of eighty-five scholarship players allowed by the NCAA. This situation was the result of a decision made by the previous coaching staff to offer a majority of scholarships to community college players. Most of them would be at San Jose State for only two years. This caused a problem.

The NCAA permits a limited number of new scholarship offers per year—up to twenty-five, depending on the number of seniors graduating. Thus, we were always playing catch-up in getting to the maximum eighty-five scholarships. It's a simple math formula. If twelve of the twenty-five scholarships each year go to community college players, those players will be gone after two years and that "recruiting class" will only consist of thirteen players in its third and fourth years. So the most scholarship players you will ever have is seventy-six (with twenty-five in year one, twenty-five year two, thirteen in year three, and thirteen in year four). And that doesn't account for the few scholarship players who may leave every season for academic or personal reasons.

As near as I could determine, there had never been a strategic plan to field a San Jose State football team with eighty-five student-athletes on scholarship. Every head coach wanted to win now, not later. And that meant using the scholarships for community college talent. When I began recruiting more high school seniors, I was taking a risk that we'd be caught short in mature talent but figured it would pay off in the long term.

In retrospect, that was a bad choice. During the 2002 season, it created a double whammy. The travel sapped us. And the lack of scholarship players meant we had little depth, so we couldn't substitute as much. No surprise, then, that those early season games followed a pattern. After the trip to Arkansas State, we went to Seattle and led the University of Washington 10-0 at the end of the first half but faded and lost 34-10. The following week, the same pattern repeated itself against Stanford, with us running out of steam in the second half. We were now 1-2.

I was pleased with our effort. However, I knew that we had to do something different or we would falter after halftime every week and finish 1-12. In a staff meeting, I made a decision to cut practice time back to only ninety minutes on Tuesday and Wednesday rather than the standard two hours we had been doing every day. We were going to need every bit of energy that we could muster for our trip to play Illinois, the 2001 Big 10 defending champion Illini.

We entered the game as thirty-five-point underdogs. But I again believed we were poised for an upset because on film, it appeared that we had more team speed than the Illini. I didn't think they could stop us from scoring. I was correct. The trouble was, we couldn't stop their offense either. With the game tied 35-35 and less than two minutes remaining on the clock, we got the ball back on about our own thirty-yard line. All we needed was a field goal for the victory. We executed the drive perfectly and successfully kicked a thirty-seven-yard field goal to win, 38-35. This was a huge confidence builder for our program.

But again, reality would soon rise up and smack us in the face. It happened when we arrived back in San Jose to unpack the bus after we had picked up both a victory and a precious $500,000 paycheck for our program. There was a problem. The local Major League Soccer team, the San Jose Earthquakes, had scheduled a game that same night in our stadium. The facility was not managed by our athletic department but instead was controlled by Spartan

Shops, an independent university agency. Spartan Shops' mission was to do anything and everything to bring more revenue to the school. As such, the agency leased the stadium to the Earthquakes and permitted them to have total control of the facility on soccer game nights.

Thus, as we approached "our" stadium and "our" adjoining Simpson Complex where "our" locker room was located, we were told that we could not pull our charter bus onto the stadium grounds and park in our usual spot. We had to park the bus two blocks away and haul all of our equipment into the building. I felt so sorry for my guys. They were tired and had given their all on the football field for the school, scoring an amazing upset of a Big 10 team on the road. I took a lot of calls from the press asking about the victory. But I knew that we needed to get focused on our conference opener against the University of Texas El Paso.

We approached the UTEP game with a lot of confidence and a 2-2 record, knowing that a lot was at stake. We wanted to be bowl eligible—which meant winning seven of our thirteen games—and we could see that the Miners were one of the needed victories on our brutal schedule. We were happy to be playing our first home game, although we again couldn't draw fifteen thousand people to the game, resulting in another net financial loss for the athletic department. We had an awesome offensive game plan and won 56-24. Momentum was building; time for another plane ride.

We were eager to visit Texas and play a struggling Southern Methodist team. The southern heat and humidity is always a concern for a West Coast team, but we rallied in the second half to get another road victory, making us 4-2 overall and 2-0 in the conference. This was surprising to everyone but me. We were receiving a lot of ink about our success—but looming ahead was the game I had most feared during the preseason of 2002. We were next scheduled to visit Ohio State. In hindsight, this was the first nail in my coaching coffin at San Jose State.

And it could have been prevented.

Back in January of 2002, I studied our schedule and saw the game in Columbus. I brought it to Bell's attention. I sensed that he was ashamed to have assembled such a brutal schedule for our program, but he explained that it was necessary to balance the athletic budget. I told him we should really try to get out of the Ohio State contract and instead have one open week or play an opponent at home so that we could have at least five home games. Bell told me that if I could arrange to get out of the contract, he would grant my request.

At that point, I started to realize that I was not merely the head football coach; I was also a part-time administrator. But deep inside, I was disappointed. Why couldn't Bell make the phone calls to Ohio State? I learned that former Ohio State running back Archie Griffin, the Heisman Trophy winner, was the athletic department administrator responsible for the football scheduling. I put in a call to him.

After getting Griffin on the phone and having some small talk, I attempted to explain our scheduling dilemma and asked if he would consider finding another opponent and letting us out of the contract. I told Griffin that I really needed his support. Thirteen games in thirteen consecutive weeks, nine of them on the road, were more than I felt we could handle. The Ohio State game was scheduled in the seventh week, the perfect time for us to take a break before we ventured into the second half of our season. After listening to my awful situation, I think Griffin sympathized with me. He promised to try and fulfill my request.

My prayers were not answered, however. Griffin contacted me as spring approached in 2002 and said that he could not find an opponent to replace us. Griffin said he was sorry. I understood his plight, though. Every time Ohio State plays at home, the Buckeyes draw more than one hundred thousand fans and produce millions of dollars.

The expected result occurred on our trip to Ohio. The Buckeyes were big, fast, and strong. I knew that their coach, Jim Tressel, would line up and run the ball right down our throats and pound us into submission. I was mostly worried that the traditional Big 10 physical approach to football would beat us up for the rest of the season. Believe it or not, before kickoff, I pondered starting our backups at every position as a semi-protest against our schedule, with the idea that our starters would play in the second half when Ohio State would put its reserve players in the game. I just didn't have enough cowardice in me to do so—although I later realized that it would have been the best thing for our team and my coaching career. We took a whipping both physically and emotionally, losing by a score of 50-7 to the eventual 2003 national champions. The game destroyed our confidence and inflicted painful wear and tear on the limited bodies that we fielded.

We were now 4-3 and next had to make yet another trip, this one to Reno for a game against the University of Nevada. Same old story. After leading in the first half, we sagged in the thin air that comes with high altitude and lost the game. We were in a downward spiral and lost our next two games as well. After starting out 4-2, we now had a 4-6 record and appeared to be headed toward a 4-9 finish.

I knew that we were a fragile team. I had been very careful in how I spoke to the players after the four straight losses. Nevertheless, the next week against Louisiana Tech when we made a bunch of mental mistakes in the first half, I couldn't take it anymore. I exploded in the locker room at halftime. I said in a very direct way that we were imposters wearing football costumes and were basically "trick or treating" by asking the Bulldogs for candy, rather than playing the game of football with passion and purpose. It worked. We came from behind and beat Louisiana Tech to end our end our losing streak and to keep our slim bowl hopes alive.

Back to the airport. The next week, we traveled to Oklahoma and faced the University of Tulsa, coached by my old friend, Keith Burns. Fortunately for us, Tulsa was struggling and not playing well and we won the game—but lost our first and second team running backs in the process. That gave us a 6-6 record with Fresno State coming to Spartan Stadium. We had defied the odds and put ourselves in position for the first bowl invitation in twelve years for the Spartan football program. I felt confident that we would beat the Bulldogs in spite of our running back injuries. In fact, I took our team to the middle of Spartan Stadium after our Thursday practice and did a walkthrough of accepting the bowl bid in the middle of the field. I wanted them to sleep on it and replay it over and over in their minds.

There was a lot of hype in the game's buildup, and I was expecting a packed house. When I walked in the stadium for pregame warm up and saw it less than half full, I couldn't believe it. I was extremely disappointed. After twelve games, including those nine exhausting road trips, we had a chance to reach a bowl, and there was no support from the third largest city in California. I was especially disturbed by this because the NCAA had recently passed legislation that required an average home attendance of fifteen thousand for teams to remain in Division 1A. And we didn't have fifteen thousand for our biggest home game of the season. I thought that I had done my part, and it was painfully obvious to me that the marketing department had not done theirs.

Nevertheless, we took the lead at halftime before letting it slip away. Fresno State beat us 16-13, and the Bulldogs accepted the bowl invitation. I was crushed. We were building a football program, but during the time away from my family in the foreign land of California I had become emotionally disconnected from my wife and three kids. I was carrying the weight of trying to be a successful black head football coach so that, in turn, I could be a voice who could advocate for more black coaches to be hired. Unfortunately, being a successful head football coach had become more important that being an All-American husband and dad.

Still, I had tasted a little head coaching success, and my name was being mentioned for a few openings around the country. I was interviewed for the head coaching position at Oregon State and made the list of three finalists before I withdrew my name when Bell was able to get me a two-year contract extension through 2006. I also received a housing allowance increase that I so badly needed to help pay my monthly $3,200 rent. I should mention that I was proud of the accolades that the team received for our herculean effort in 2002. In addition to other honors that I had received for the performance of my players, I was acknowledged as the African American Hall of Fame Coach of the Year. My head was swelling and my ego was enlarged.

With all that, I hoped things would get better in 2003, my third season with the Spartans. They actually got worse. Finding a way to average fifteen thousand people was going to be a major challenge. If a Fresno State game with a bowl bid on the line didn't attract a good crowd, I knew that we needed to do something to boost the attendance or we would be legislated out of Division 1A under NCAA rules at the time. What I had in mind would require more time away from my family, but that didn't seem to bother me. I would soon discover that my two young daughters were scared of me, because I was always so tense and not much fun to be around because of my short fuse.

Primarily, I knew that we needed to bring some big-time recruits to our campus if we were to reach the next level. As a result, I became involved heavily in the recruiting process, which put me on the road as if I were an assistant coach. I also was involved in a plan to schedule a home game against Grambling State University, the historically black school that has many fans in African American communities from coast to coast. Grambling almost never plays on the West Coast. I felt that we would be able to pack the stadium and skew our season average fan attendance for the 2003 season. Again, I was forced to become more than a head coach, this time getting into the marketing game.

The event would be called the Literacy Classic. We would tie it into the grand opening of our school's new state-of-the-art Dr. Martin Luther King Library. When I presented the idea to San Jose city leaders and Bell, initially they didn't get the vision and were not very supportive of the plan. They didn't think the game would draw enough fans to guarantee a payment of $275,000 to Grambling. In Bell's mind, if we were losing $50,000 for each normal home game, it was suicide to commit that much money to an opponent. He initially refused to support the Literacy Classic concept. I understood his rational reasons. So I asked him if it would be all right for me to seek support from the African American community. He agreed.

I began pounding the San Jose pavement. I found two individuals, Tommy Fulcher and Andre Chapman, who came to my rescue. Without these two community leaders, the game would have never happened. Fulcher and Chapman guaranteed the payout for the Grambling football team and band. With that type of support for my vision, I felt obligated to make sure that we pulled off the event. Thus, when I should have been spending time with my family and leading my football team, I was out trying to promote this game, which was captivating the Bay Area by storm. Given our mandate to average fifteen thousand fans, I believed that I had no other option. I didn't realize that I was nearing burnout. Late one night, I nearly killed myself when I drove off the road on Monterey Highway when I fell asleep driving home from my office to our home in the town of Morgan Hill, about twenty miles south of San Jose. Thank God for His angels.

The Grambling game, televised nationally on ESPN2, was a huge success. It drew a crowd of 31,681, still a football attendance record for Spartan Stadium. The marching band from Grambling wowed the crowd. And we won the game, 29-0. I was excited about the 2003 season. We were picked to finish in the upper half of the WAC. I believed that our roster was the best I'd assembled in my three years at San Jose State. I was enthused about us being good enough to claim that bowl trip that had slipped through our hands the previous November.

However, after the Grambling triumph, we once again had a national powerhouse on our schedule—Florida. It was a road game, of course, for a huge payday. The previous spring, I had called the athletic director at Florida to see if the school would allow us out of the game. I knew that going to "The Swamp" in September and playing in a sweltering stadium would not be an excellent experience for our team.

The trip pushed us into a downward slide. Our athletic department business manager, John Twining, had asked if we could travel from San Jose to Gainesville by departing on a Friday morning rather than on Thursday, as I had originally been promised. Twining and the department wanted to pocket more of the large payout from Florida and leaving a day later would save thousands of dollars. Why I agreed to this, I still don't know. Just call me stupid. Traveling across the country and changing time zones is not easy on the body. Throw in a hostile environment, a talented opponent, plus the oppressive heat, and your chances are even more miniscule. We actually led the game early, 3-0, before Florida rolled up the next sixty-five points. And that was the final score, 65-3.

The next week, we lost to Stanford and then prepared to play Nevada in a Thursday night televised game. At this point, I was dealing with eligibility issues and didn't have my starting center. I thought the situation was becoming political, and my support from the administration was waning with each loss. Very few people appeared willing to help me improve the situation. I knew we needed more people on the academic support side of our equation. I was starting to wear down physically and, frankly, beginning to experience some serious family problems. But my decision was still to grind away at my job.

The Nevada game featured the stirring return of Neal Parry, one of the most inspirational young men I've ever been around. During a game in 2000, before my arrival at San Jose State, Parry had sustained a devastating injury that resulted in the amputation of his right leg. He had it replaced with prosthesis and vowed to play again. I promised him he could if he won a position fair and square. Neal earned a spot on our punt return team. His first play was an emotional moment, but we lost the game, 42-30. Then we went to Houston and were defeated by Rice in the final two minutes.

As I sat down in the locker room following that loss, I felt as if my world was caving in on me. My brother, Shawn Hill, had driven down from Dallas to support me. He could tell that I was hurting. I didn't understand what was going on with our team. Entering the 2003 season, I had thought we could win at least eight games. Now we were staring at 1-4. We did beat Southern Methodist in the next game but then flew to Idaho and were humiliated by Boise State, 77-14.

That game nearly destroyed us from within. My players thought that I didn't believe in them, because when reporters asked me to explain such a lopsided loss, I responded that we must coach better, recruit better, and play better as a team. That statement offended several guys, and they brought out their feelings in our weekly team meeting.

We split the next two games against Hawaii and Texas El Paso before Fresno State punched us in the chin, 41-7. We lost our last game to Tulsa, 34-32, to close out an unsatisfactory 3-8 season. We lost three of the games by a total of nine points, giving up the lead in all of them during the final two minutes. That can lead a man to drink.

I started to feel the wrath of alums. I knew that I had to do better. But the season had taken a toll on my body. My weight had been around 220 before the season started, but I was now around 189 pounds. The losing record and family problems had taken away my appetite. During the season, I had seen a doctor because I couldn't sleep at night. I was basically given tranquilizers for bedtime use and still felt drugged the following morning.

We lost some very good players due to graduation, so I knew that we needed to get out and find replacements. I convinced my old friend, Keith Burns, who'd been fired at Tulsa, to come in and take over our defense. I thought that Keith's experience would be invaluable to us during the 2004 season. What I didn't know was that it would be my last season as the Spartan head coach, although I had two years remaining on my contract. I guess that I should have seen it coming.

When I appeared at a Quarterback Club meeting the week before a home game in November, I knew that the alumni wanted me gone in the worst way. I felt the temperature drop several degrees when I walked in the room. I also felt almost invisible, but I understood why. I was identified as a losing black football coach in a room filled entirely with white boosters. There is no way I could blend in, and to be honest, at that point I didn't care to do so.

I mentioned earlier that in October of 2004, Bell had visited my office to inform me that a group of boosters had decided that they wanted both of us fired. A month later, Bell told me that he was resigning effective at the end of December. After several conversations, I finally pulled the truth out of him: the university president, Don Kassing, had fired Bell and decided to let him go out with a little dignity by allowing him to tell people that he had resigned.

Subsequently, we won just two games in 2004. Following the Boise State game that we lost in three overtimes, Kassing called me into his office and told me that he felt the program needed a change. He first requested that I work in his office as an administrator—but I told him that whether I was fired or resigned, I was heading back south. My children missed Arkansas. Also, California in so many ways had taken a toll on me. I told Kassing that I would think about my future and come back to see him after we played Tulsa the following week. If we couldn't agree on a separation package, he could fire me and send me on my way. The administration was very concerned about my relationship with a multimillionaire booster, Charles "Chuck" Davidson, but he told the administration that as long as the school treated me fairly, he would create no problems. I will forever be grateful to Mr. Davidson for his unwavering support.

We lost to Tulsa, and the next day I signed an agreement to resign effective December 31. In the agreement, I received the two years left on my contract as severance, along with moving expenses back to Arkansas. I also had to agree that I would never attempt to work at San Jose State or file a discrimination lawsuit against the school.

Following my meeting with Kassing, I went in to see my staff as I normally would do on a Sunday. I instructed them that I was resigning and that our upcoming game against Fresno State would be our last together. I had negotiated a three-month severance package for the coaches. That wasn't a lot. But considering the history of SJSU, it was generous.

Our sports information director, Lawrence Fan, planned a Monday afternoon press conference, and I announced that I would be leaving at season's end and working with Dr. Lapchick as visiting scholar and research associate at the Institute for Diversity and Ethics in Sport at Central Florida. I also knew that I wanted to write this book.

Six days after my resignation announcement, Fresno State came to town and spanked us. I took my whipping with dignity and started preparing to leave the program that I had started building four years earlier. We had made a lot of progress but did not record enough wins to warrant saving my job. I accepted that. I truly was burned out on coaching and decided that I had had all I wanted. Quite frankly, San Jose State destroyed my appetite for coaching.

I didn't succeed in what I'd wanted to accomplish in Silicon Valley—win a Western Athletic Championship. By worldly standards, I failed. However, I had put a strong infrastructure in place for the program to be competitive by planning strategically and recruiting effectively. The proof was in the pudding. In 2006, San Jose State recorded a 9-5 record and won the New Mexico Bowl under their new coach, Dick Tomey. I was so happy for the student-athletes because my staff recruited nineteen of the twenty-two Spartan start-ers in that game.

Before I left town, the *San Jose Mercury News* ran an editorial headlined: "Fitz Hill leaves San Jose State. Available: one stand-up coach." I left San Jose with a 14-33 record, but I returned to Arkan-sas with my dignity and the desire to serve my godly purpose.

There are ten things that I learned as the result of being the assistant head coach of the Razorbacks and head coach at San Jose State. I think all of them apply in a broader sense across all of college football—and life in general:

1. When addressing issues of diversity and race-related em-ployment opportunities, it is necessary to do so with wis-dom, tact, and facts. Anything that can be measured can be improved. Personal feelings that promote self-interest must be avoided. Experience has taught me that if a person is perceived trying to promote and bring attention to himself, nobody in the target audience really wants to examine the larger problem. All they can see are your personal motives. So they will rarely examine the value and benefits of diver-sity to their organization or program.

2. Define diversity. The best way to do this is by pointing to a successful model that works while addressing these issues. It's far easier to sell a non-diverse organization on diversity's benefits in a positive way, rather than focusing on the prob-lems that result when a multicultural climate is not created. A picture is worth a thousand words when trying to explain why diversity works.

3. Make sure that diversity is bringing added value to the bottom line. If college football boosters and college admin-istrations understand that diversity is an asset and not a liability, they will buy into the new paradigm. If winning

is truly important and diversity gives football programs the best opportunity to recruit, manage, and retain the necessary talent to your campus or organization, the only people who will fight that diversity are people who do not want to win.

4. Before accepting a job, always visit the place and people with whom you will be working. I was so eager to become a head coach at the college level, I signed on for the job at San Jose State without seeing the school or getting to know the people who would determine my future by the support they would provide—or not provide. By the time I showed up on campus, I had already agreed to accept the head coaching job with no understanding of the land mines and booby traps that awaited the school's head football coach.

5. Hire the most experienced and competent people that you can find to help you do the job that you were hired to do. A head coach must be effective in delegating. But you can't delegate when the people on your staff can't do the jobs they were hired to do.

6. As a head coach at a school such as San Jose State, the athletic director must agree to let you play a major role in scheduling games. I am now convinced that winning more games, rather than going on the road and prostituting a team for big money, is the best way to strategically build a program. It is far easier to raise money after you have gone to a bowl game than to be sitting at home during the bowl season because of a brutal schedule in September in an effort to balance the budget.

7. Check the commitment to winning by examining the recruiting budget. At San Jose State, we needed to turn over

rocks and stones to find great recruits that most people overlooked. So it was imperative that, during the twenty-day spring recruiting period, we maxed out our chances to evaluate talent. But because of budget cuts and a lack of resources, we were not able to get all that we needed out of spring recruiting.

8. Visit with the compliance director and make sure everyone is on the same page in regard to serving the student-athlete. That was never the case during my tenure at SJSU. It wasn't that the administration didn't try; it was just that the administration didn't know what constituted effective support for student-athletes. Ignorance is expensive in college athletics. San Jose State would eventually pay the price when, after my departure, the NCAA issued punishments for the school's inability to have players progress satisfactorily toward a degree. The situation improved only when the school administration beefed up the budget for academic support.

9. Never forget that race matters—even when people say it doesn't or can't comprehend its effects. It is true that race can work in the favor of a minority coach in the right situation. But every situation is different, and cultural differences can be barriers to understanding the total dynamics of race. Winning makes African American coaches more tolerable at predominantly white colleges and universities. Losing makes them even less tolerable than losing white coaches.

10. Keep God first, family second, and job third. This is scripture. Seek first the kingdom of God, and all else will be added. If I would have done that at every step of my career, all would have been well. Unfortunately, at both San Jose

State and Arkansas, I too often tried to do it all by myself. God allowed for me to learn some important lessons from my experiences, and I am a better person because of it.

CHAPTER TWELVE
-DIVISIONAL PARITY-
IN A BAD WAY

Let's say that an athletic director from a Football Bowl Subdivision school truly wants to do the right thing. Let's say that this athletic director wants to interview some good minority candidates as part of a wide-ranging search to hire the right head coach.

Or let's go further. Let's say that—knowing that the current head football coach is white—the athletic director wants to be pro-active and encourage the head coach to interview some minority candidates when hiring his next offensive or defensive coordinator.

Assuming all that happens, where do those athletic directors go to look for qualified minority candidates?

One place, of course, would be their current staffs. Another would be on the current staffs of other Football Bowl Subdivision schools. But by definition, that's a limited pool.

It stands to reason, then, that the athletic directors would want to expand the search by going to the same places they find so many worthy white candidates—the football programs at the five hundred or so smaller colleges who play the game at a lower level. Those lower levels used to be called Division 1AA, Division II, and Division III. Today, the 1AA schools are known as the Football Championship Subdivision. The others are still called Division II and Division III. But whatever you call them, these programs are breeding grounds for coaches to excel and show they are ready to coach at the top level.

Just look around college football today. You can find plenty of examples. Jim Tressel coached at 1AA Youngstown State before being hired at Ohio State. Mack Brown's first head coaching job was at 1AA Appalachian State before he eventually moved on to win a national championship at Texas. Rich Rodriguez, former head coach of Michigan, obtained his first head coaching job at Glenville State College. In 2008 and 2009, Cincinnati won the Big East title after hiring Brian Kelly from Central Michigan in 2006. Central Michigan plucked him from Grand Valley State, where he won NCAA Division II national championships in the 2002 and 2003 football seasons.

Kelly is an outstanding football coach who, of course, has since moved on from Cincinnati to Notre Dame. All he needed was an opportunity to step up. Thank God nothing blocked that opportunity for him, because Kelly most definitely earned and deserved it. It is safe to assume that the without the opportunity he received at Grand Valley State, he wouldn't have been hired at Cincinnati or at Notre Dame.

There are several quality Division II football programs that are the equal of Grand Valley State. Two that come to mind are Glenville State College and the University of North Alabama. But there are many others. So, when an athletic director at a top-tier Football Bowl Subdivision program is looking for a new head coach, why not interview the best minority candidates at those Division II schools?

I'll tell you why: because those minority candidates barely exist. The numbers show that there are fewer African American head coaches in the NCAA's smaller divisions than there are at the top level Football Bowl Subdivision—and the disparity is even more striking if you exclude historically black colleges and universities, which until fairly recent times were the only programs where minority coaches could even find jobs.

I know what you're thinking: Here come the numbers again. And you're right. The numbers are so darn powerful. During the 2008 football season, there were 122 schools playing in the NCAA Football Championship Subdivision, the former 1AA. Of those 122 jobs, excluding the nineteen African American coaches at HBCU schools, only six were held by minority coaches.

And moving down the ladder:

In Division II, there was just one African American head coach out of 120 programs. In Division III, there were 229 schools playing football. Only four had minority head coaches.

Which gives us the final tote board: Of all the schools playing football below the top-tier Football Bowl Subdivision during the 2008 season, only 6 percent of those teams (thirty of 471) had head coaches who were minorities—and that's including the African American coaches at historically black colleges. If you do not include those nineteen men and those nineteen jobs, the percentage drops to 2 percent (eleven out of 452).

The situation is especially striking at Division III schools, where just 0.2 percent of the football head coaches—one fifth of one percent—were African American in 2008. And don't try to rationalize that fact by saying that those schools seldom hire minorities to coach other sports as well. It simply is not true. At those very same Division III schools, 4.2 percent of the women's teams were coached by African Americans.

Know what that means? At the time the data were collected, a Division III female athlete is twenty-one times more likely to play for an African American coach than a Division III football player is.

And why does this situation exist? For the answer, you have to drop down another level—to the high schools. That's generally where the smaller colleges find their football coaches. But at the high schools, the same invisible barriers to hiring African American coaches also seem to exist.

I'll admit, I have done no in-depth research on this part of the equation. But going strictly on observations and my experience of dealing with high schools as both a football coach and college administrator, I feel very confident in making this statement: there are a lot of parallels between certain types of high schools and the way college football is stratified in America.

For example, inner-city high schools are very similar to historically black colleges and universities. They frequently operate in their own specific communities with an enrollment skewed heavily toward minorities. Their football coaching staffs are made up primarily of African Americans. A few years ago the *Dallas Morning News* did a story documenting this fact, finding that the overwhelming numbers of African American coaches in the city were employed at inner city schools.

This can lead to some funny incidents. Once, when I was recruiting for the University of Arkansas, I vividly remember visiting with Reginald Samples, who was then the head football coach at Dallas Lincoln High School, which was always a hotbed for talented student-athletes. As we sat in the weight room, an assistant coach from the University of Iowa entered and interrupted our conversation. The coach from Iowa was white. But he attempted to be hip and fit in by using a "soul shake" when he introduced himself to the Lincoln High head football coach, who was black. I saw the smirk come across Samples' face, and I chuckled because the white coach was doing his best to try and make an uncomfortable situation more comfortable.

The school demographics are much different in the integrated, football-crazy suburbs of the South and Southern California. I also worked those campuses during my time at Arkansas and San Jose State. I noted that those schools often displayed the same dynamics as the top-tier Football Bowl Subdivision programs. There might be one or two black assistant coaches per staff but not very many black head coaches. In fact, think about this: many high schools in our country have still never been visited by a collegiate black head football coach. White high school coaches and high school administrators seldom see one.

I was reminded of that when, as San Jose State's head coach, I traveled to Southern California with one of my assistant coaches for a spring recruiting visit. We were greeted at a high school by the head football coach, a white guy. My assistant introduced me as the San Jose State head coach. But apparently this did not register with the high school coach, whose brain must have been filled with the preconception that all college head coaches are white. He must have assumed that I was San Jose State's primary "recruiting coach," who was coming to recruit the black athlete.

Why do I say that? Because when we were preparing to leave the school after our visit, the high school coach asked us, "Now, who did you say that your head coach was?" My assistant pointed at me and said, "This is him." The high school coach was very apologetic for not showing me more respect—at least that's what he said. But the fact is, there were and are so few black college head coaches at the college level, it is hardly common for high school coaches to come face-to-face with a minority member of that collegiate head coaching fraternity.

I was reminded of this when I saw a story in the *Minneapolis Star-Tribune* about a man named Don Hudson. Back in 1971, he became the first African American head football coach at a predominantly white college when he accepted the job at Division III Macalester College in Minnesota. This was eight full years before Willie Jeffries of Wichita State became the first black head coach at a Division I school.

Hudson was promoted to the head coaching position at integrated Central High in 1968. Upon his appointment, all of the white assistant coaches quit. Hudson left there for an assistant coaching position at Macalester, a famously progressive institution located in St. Paul. When the head coach quit one season later, administrators promoted Hudson.

Often, Hudson would tell stories about how he would go on the recruiting trail to the all-white communities in northern Minnesota, introducing himself as a college head coach. When he walked in the door, many of the high school coaches would drop their jaws. Hudson eventually learned that he should do most of his recruiting in the larger and more diverse Twin Cities. He left Macalester after only four seasons. But even today, almost forty years later, I wonder if Hudson is still the only African American college head coach to visit some of those northern Minnesota communities.

Minority college head coaches at the Division II and Division III levels are virtually invisible. Imagine how invisible the relatively few African American or other minority high school coaches are to Division II and Division III college administrators. It's probably the biggest reason those administrators do not see minority high school coaches as potential candidates to fill football jobs. Heck, those administrators seldom see any minority high school coaches, period. There aren't very many of them outside of large urban inner-city schools.

And if very few minority coaching candidates are hired at Division III or Division II schools, they obviously don't get the chance to show their talent for the bigger schools in the Football Bowl Subdivision. It's a trickle-down (or trickle-up) issue.

Ohio State fans knew that Jim Tressel, the Buckeyes' head coach from 2001 to 2011, came to the school after his very successful run at Youngstown State, a Division 1AA program. But what if Tressel had never been given the opportunity to even coach at Youngstown State? Tressel was hired there after doing a successful job as a high school coach in the area. But odds suggest if he had been born black and coached at an inner-city high school, Tressel would never have made the jump to Youngstown State—and then would never have been the head coach at Ohio State.

My guess, however, is that you may have never before contemplated this particular part of the minority-coaching equation. The football programs in Division II and Division III are not in the limelight nationally or often even regionally. Thus, the lack of employment opportunities for minority coaches at those levels is largely ignored by both the media and the American university community.

And you know the old saying: "Out of sight, out of mind." If nobody had ever pointed out the dismal hiring record for minority coaches at Football Bowl Subdivision institutions—the big guys of college football—what do you think the population of African American football coaches at that level would be today? It was only after many years of pointed commentary and criticism that the FBS schools, following the 2009 season, finally seemed to be getting the message. They made enough minority hires to raise the percentage of African American coaches at that level to 10.8 percent of the programs—which was roughly the same percentage they had reached in the mid 1990s. That's why I am tentatively optimistic about whether universities have really turned the corner on this issue. We have been here before, only to see the progressive hiring practices slam into reverse to the point where, in 2002, there were only four African American coaches employed at FBS institutions.

The NCAA is supposed to represent schools and athletic programs of all sizes. So it must take notice of the current situation in Division II and Division III. One of the best ways to create a great group of minority candidates for openings at FBS schools is to tap the talent pool in the other NCAA divisions. But first, there must be candidates at that level who can be tapped.

Wait, you say. What about those coaches at the historically black colleges? In 2008, there were nineteen of them. They should be fine candidates for jobs at the higher level, right? Wrong. They rarely, if ever, receive offers from predominantly white institutions. Remember how Eddie Robinson, the legendary Grambling State coach, was never given a job by a bigger school? One prominent white NFL assistant coach told a friend of mine, who at the time was employed at a Southwestern Athletic Conference (SWAC) university, that if he wanted to be considered for a job in the pros, my friend "needed to get out of the 'Chitlin' League' and get into some real coaching."

Instead, the same trend of ignoring this highly qualified talent pool continues year after year—with a recent new depressing twist.

Frequently, if a minority coach from the NCAA lower levels does, in fact, move up to the staff of a Football Bowl Subdivision school, the coach's first stop is usually as a graduate assistant. There are two of them at each school. The jobs are created for young coaches to break in at the big-school level. The grad assistant positions usually pay very little money. They are quasi-internships and require the person to enroll at the school and take classes. But it's a good way for a young coach—of any color—to break in and learn the ropes.

Or at least, it used to be. Lately, the grad assistant positions have been used in another way entirely. Some head coaches are giving those jobs to veteran coaches who have been fired at other places but still have a year or two left on their contracts, which means they are still getting paid. Or on some occasions, the grad assistants are simply older coaches who are out of work and willing to forego a real salary.

Thus, at Auburn University before the 2009 season, Coach Gene Chizik hired his former recruiting coordinator at Iowa State as a "grad assistant." At Tennessee, before moving to Southern California, Lane Kiffin brought aboard former Syracuse offensive coordinator Mitch Browning as a "grad assistant." And at Alabama, Coach Nick Saban hired former Virginia offensive coordinator Mike Groh as a "grad assistant."

None of this was—or is—against NCAA rules. But it's clearly not what the organization intended for those grad assistantship positions. To improve the diversity of the coaching profession at the graduate assistant level in the Football Bowl Subdivision, I have been a proponent of allowing each team to employ three graduate assistants instead of the current two—as long as one of those three graduate assistants is a minority. This idea has never gained steam. But I still think it is the right thing to do.

Instead, we have Chizik and Kiffin and Saban using those two graduate assistant positions to hire old pals. This effectively shuts out spots for promising young minority coaches as well as negatively impacting the advancement of potential candidates to fill these positions from Division II and Division III schools. Why do athletic directors put up with this stuff? I guess because too many of them don't want to fight their head coaches over it. All of these practices make me wonder how many athletic directors really do want to do the right thing—at any NCAA level.

No one can argue with the statement that lower division NCAA schools could be employing more minority head coaches today. It would just take a little more effort on the part of those schools and their administrations to recruit coaches from either the inner city high schools or the ranks of minority assistant coaches at other levels. But I don't see that happening. Instead, in terms of minority hiring, I see too much parity across all divisions. And it's the wrong kind of parity.

CHAPTER THIRTEEN
WHY SOME RED FLAGS ARE MORE EQUAL THAN OTHERS

I want to believe that every official at every football game is honest and trying to do the best possible job. I want to believe the officials make every call with no undue influence from the crowd or other factors. But what I have learned over the years is what every sophisticated fan already knows:

Zebras aren't robots.

By that, I mean that referees and officials are flesh and blood. They aren't robots. They aren't perfect. They can make mistakes. Most college fans accept that. They hate it when a blown call goes against their team. But they understand the human factor. Goofs happen. That's why conferences have spent major dollars on video replay units and procedures in recent years. The conferences want to keep the goofs to a minimum. From my personal experiences on the college football sidelines, I am a huge supporter of video replay to right a wrong. Still, there are many judgment calls where the "human factor" cannot be avoided.

But there's one part of the "human factor" that is seldom considered: football officials, like all people living in today's world, are not immune to the forces of society that can lead to a difficult and (in my view) troubling dynamic on Saturday afternoons if one of the head coaches happens to be an African American.

First here are the facts. To my knowledge, no one had ever done a survey to see what proportion of game officials in the various Football Bowl Subdivision (FBS) conferences are minorities—African

American, Asian American, or Latinos. So I did some research. The conferences had no problem sharing the information. During the 2009 football season, here were the relevant figures:

Conference	Total Officials	Total Minority	Percentage
Big East	43	3	7%
Big 10, MAC*	150	18	12%
Big 12	74	18	24%
Conf-USA, Mtn. West, WAC *	105	25	24%
Pac 10	43	8	19%
SEC	78	14	18%
Sun Belt	66	12	18%
OVERALL TOTALS	596	82	14%

*These conferences share an officiating pool.

My reaction to the numbers: If they have not already done so, I hope in the immediate future the Big East will recruit more minority officials...plain and simple. And it's very difficult to believe that in all of those Midwestern states represented by the Big 10 and Mid-American Conference schools, there are only eighteen qualified minority referees to work major college games. Still, overall, the conferences seem to be giving fair opportunities when hiring officials—particularly when you compare the percentages in the above chart to head coaching opportunities.

However, even in the conferences where there are a decent number of minority referees, they of course are spread among the different crews. With six to ten games involving conference schools on a given weekend (especially during non-league play), it is a common occurrence to find just one African American official on the field. Usually, there are two at the most. If you happen to be an African American head coach, this situation can throw a whole different twist into the referee-coach relationship. My personal experiences attest to that.

Example: I remember once at San Jose State during warm-ups before a game, I began a conversation with a black official. From my memory, he was riding solo that day on the Western Athletic Conference (WAC) crew as the only African American wearing a striped shirt. But like most officials of any race, he was polite and said hello. We exchanged quick pleasantries.

But then the black official said something else. As I tried to strike up a longer and warmer conversation, the official told me that he had to keep moving because it would look too much like "clustering"—as if the two black guys were concocting a plan to benefit each other. I was blown away by his statement. As this was happening, of course, a few of the white officials were having a lengthy discussion with my coaching counterparts, who were also white. Obviously, on that side of the field, "clustering" wasn't an issue.

The black official, of course, meant me no harm. I suppose it was just a natural survival instinct that is triggered when you stand out like one black dot on an 8.5x11-inch white sheet of paper—or in our case, a black officiating dot and one black head coaching dot.

I've spoken with other black head coaches who've had similar experiences. Like me, they are certain that race has influenced bad calls by certain officials. I know that's really hard to prove categorically. It sounds like something out of a movie like *Remember The Titans*, when the black high school coach was dramatically discriminated against by game officials.

All I can go by is what has happened to me and some other coaches. I kept notes, mental and otherwise. I can tell you—as well as show you game film of our San Jose State game against Hawaii in 2004 when a correct call by a lone black official was overruled after the ruling was questioned by a white referee. The flag was subsequently picked up for no penalty. It affected the momentum of the game. Unfortunately for me, the effect was negative.

After my resignation as head coach at San Jose State, this same white referee must have felt sorry for me. A few days after my announcement, I coached my final game with the Spartans. About seventy-five minutes before the kickoff, my coaches and I were in our dressing room when the officials came in to go over routine game procedures. I saw the same official who had overruled the call of the black official in the game against Hawaii without ever offering me an explanation. Now, weeks later, he was apologizing for his error in judgment. The official admitted that he never should have questioned or overruled the call. But the white referee partially blamed the black official for the incident, saying that the black official didn't "stand up" for his call the way he should have.

Huh? My reaction was, "So what?" The original call was correct. Why should the black official's ability to "stand up" for the call even matter? In my view, this white official was basically labeling the black official as a token. A token does not have to be black; it's merely someone who has a face but no voice and is there just to occupy space. I do not know how the racial dynamics work within refereeing crews. Most of them seem to get along very well. But I wonder if, because of their minority status and fear of being labeled troublemakers and/or losing their jobs, black officials are less likely to be as vociferous as white officials.

My athletic director at San Jose State, Chuck Bell, eventually noticed this phenomenon as well. After one game, he asked me, "Do you ever feel as if you're getting the short end of the stick by officials because you're black?" My answer was, "You said that, Chuck. I didn't. But I have to admit that I'm growing suspicious."

I wasn't the only coach who, over the years, had grown suspicious. A colleague of mine, who has coached in the Big 10, Big East, and Conference USA, says that as an African American coach on the sidelines, he has noticed how white officials favor white coaches when tight decisions are made.

"If it's a close call," this colleague of mine says, "they're going to protect their own." Of course, you can never be sure exactly what's going on in the heads of officials, white or black. But once you have lived the experience and dealt with biased behaviors and attitudes on a regular basis, it is not difficult to identify the dynamics that are taking place. And you never improve the situation if you don't question the behavior. An African American head coach formerly employed at a BCS institution told me personally how one head official had talked down to him "as if I were a child" during the traditional pregame meeting between the head coaches and officiating crews that takes place in the locker room before kickoff. The head coach was offended but was very professional and reported the official to the conference headquarters. On another occasion when an African American head coach was struggling and his job was on the line, a white official made the remark during a protested call that it really didn't matter because the coach was going to be fired any way.

I think more of officials' integrity than to charge any conspiracy. So here's the conclusion I have reached: certain white officials seem to show a tendency toward making calls that are unfair to black coaches—even though those white officials might not be intending to do so. My experience also shows that black officials are frequently not willing to "stand up" or "speak up" for their calls because they are fearful of being singled out as "difficult." Those black officials realize that they are small in number. On the average officiating crew, they may fill just one or two spots. They won't complain about the status quo. They understand that there is stiff competition for those rare positions to open up. They want to keep pleasing their supervisors. So in most cases they are willing to keep their mouths shut and speak only when spoken to.

So what does this have to do with number of black football coaches? Let me see if I can make some sense of this for you. Once a black coach is given the opportunity to lead a major college football program, other obstacles can impede progress which, in turn, affects the employment opportunities for aspiring black coaching candidates. Although I never believed that any official had it in for me because of the color of my skin, I must admit that the calls that went against my team often left me very suspicious if in fact the calls were color coded. Any type of racism that isn't blatant can be hard to prove. But research has revealed some "things that make you want to go hmmmmmmm."

The mind-set at work in the WAC's case became evident to me at one meeting between our league's head coaches and the supervisor of officials. When I tried to address the issue of diversity in our officiating crews, the supervisor told me as humbly as possible that he did not look at color when he hired officials. He said that he did not hire black officials or white officials, just the most qualified. This was the same "logic" that I heard used for years and years when it came to hiring minority coaches.

The "logic" was flawed, because even though the supervisor of officials was obviously on record for supporting equal opportunities for African American officials, the statistics in terms of actual minority officials on the field did not jibe with his policy. And little progress was being made, from what I could see with my own eyes. I didn't press the issue with him, however. Experience has taught me that that managers and educational administrators become defensive when it is suggested that their organizations or institutions have not provided access to equal employment opportunities.

Here's my feeling: until college administrators and managers—including officiating supervisors—are able to view African American officials in much the same light as they perceive themselves, they will remain racially insensitive to promoting equal opportunity in the profession.

This doesn't happen naturally. Blacks and whites often will not openly discuss their true feelings concerning race-related issues, especially in a work context, because they fear possible reprisals or harm to their careers. This lack of genuine, open, and honest dialogue on the topic contributes to a stale and stagnant employment situation.

It's not just me saying so, either. Using well-accepted scholastic findings regarding the interaction of races, social scientists would suggest that a large number of blacks on an officiating crew can significantly affect the character of inter-group relations between black and white officials. The larger the number of American American officials, the more likely that whites in the group will perceive the African Americans as threatening and deny them access to employment opportunities. This is why the number of black officials hired by conferences to referee college football games at FBS institutions is frequently limited. Has there ever been an officiating crew at a major college game where the majority of game officials were not white? Not yet, from what I've witnessed.

It sounds fine to say, "We want to hire the very best official, regardless of color." But too often I've found that used as a justification for an officiating supervisor to pick a candidate with which he's familiar—and usually, that guy is white. It's the same "principal" that athletic directors use when hiring head football coaches—and we have seen how that's worked out over the years. It is unfortunate that studies, even recent ones, indicate that many white managers and educational administrators do not accept the observation that competence and leadership traits are not naturally associated with African Americans. Those who possess these traits are thought to be the very rare exception instead of having an ingrained quality for a candidate who has reached the level of consideration for a head coaching job.

How does that situation affect the people who are assessing candidates for officiating jobs? The hiring supervisors may not perceive African American candidates as men capable of making the quick decisions needed on the gridiron at critical moments. Or, to put it in Al Campanis's terms, the African American candidates may not have "the necessities." It's going to take the same conscious effort on the part of the conferences to diversify the pool of officials as it will take for white educational administrators to hire more African American head football coaches.

Here lies the problem. I believe that many institutional leaders and people in athletic management positions have lost interest in this issue. They don't want to perform the self-analysis that's needed to unmask covert forms of employment bias on their campuses—or in their conference offices. Too often, white administrators still assume that current hiring practices operate independently of race and that the playing field is already level in terms of employing officials. Yes, even in the Big East—where the 2009 data shows that only seven percent of game officials are minorities.

That's what makes my gut squirm. I hear what these administrators say. Then I see what they do. And it doesn't match and it hasn't matched in terms of hiring minority head coaches or, even more significantly, conference commissioners. As we approached the 2011 football season, there were 11 conference commissioners in the Football Bowl Subdivision. Each position was filled by a white male. Do you know who hires the commissioners? Presidents of the member institutions make these hiring decisions. I am sure that if you asked them about the lack of minority representation at the commissioner level, the presidents' rationale would be a familiar one ... namely, that there aren't any qualified minority candidates to lead the conferences. My suggestion is to go find them, just as we do with the student-athletes.

It takes a concerted effort to achieve proper diversity. That's why the NFL implemented the Rooney Rule. I hope some conference, somewhere, has machinery in place to identify and recruit minority officials and commissioners. Does the WAC? Sounds as if that officiating supervisor doesn't even think it's worth discussing.

I have to confess that I originally wondered if black coaches were just overly paranoid about an officiating bias against them. But over successive years, I began studying the dynamic more deeply. So did some other people, apparently, as they watched other sports. In 2007, a University of Texas economist named Daniel Hamermesh released a study along with two other professors, one from McGill University and one from Auburn University. This fascinating study suggested that major league baseball umpires hold a slight, inherent bias toward pitchers who share their race or ethnicity.

"I am absolutely sure it's unconscious," Hamermesh told the Associated Press about his claim. "It's not that the umpire goes, 'Gee, it's a white guy, I'm going to help him out,' or 'It's a black guy, I'm going to screw him.' In this society, people subconsciously prefer people like themselves."

The study was quickly pooh-poohed by those in baseball. But I knew exactly what Hamermesh was saying. I remembered what my coaching colleague had said about football officials "protecting their own" on close calls. And when I examined Hamermesh's data—he scientifically charted that white umpires called strikes on 32.06 percent of pitches from white pitchers but only 30.61 from black pitchers—I was even more convinced that the professor was onto something, although the two figures are not statistically significant. The even more intriguing result of his study was that black and Hispanic umpires had similar favorable "strike" percentages toward people of their own races.

And here was an even more telling statistic: In games when either starting pitcher or neither starting pitcher matched the plate umpire's race, the home team won 53.8 percent of the time. But when the home team starting pitcher's race matched the umpire's race, the home team won 55.6 percent of the games. I know, not a huge difference. But if all else is equal when two evenly matched teams play each other, this could be the statistic to help you decide on which team to place your bet.

If that phenomenon is true in baseball for starting pitchers, why isn't it possible that it could be true in college football for head coaches? As long as I live, I won't forget what happened in San Jose State's 2003 home contest against Hawaii.

Here was the deal: Entering the final minute of the game, we were trailing 13-10, but I felt very good about our chances to win. With twenty seconds remaining, we had the ball at Hawaii's five-yard line after a first down running play, giving us a second-and-goal situation. We called our last timeout of the game to make sure everyone was on the same page for what we wanted to do next. I figured with that amount of time, we had two shots at the end zone even if the clock didn't stop after the first play.

And I was right. On second down, we completed a pass to our tight end, and he was tackled on the goal line. Some of my San Jose State players signaled touchdown. One of the Hawaii players knocked the ball away from the linesman, who had ruled the play as no touchdown but was trying to spot the ball. At that point, the clock should have been stopped by the referee or a penalty for delay of game should have been called against Hawaii.

But neither of those things happened. The linesman recovered the ball and ran it back to the hashmark. We had no timeouts. The clock was running. But my team was aware of the situation and quickly lined up in a legal formation on third and goal. Our quarterback took the snap, stepped back, and spiked the football. The scoreboard clock stopped with 0:01 showing. I had decided to go for a touchdown to win the game rather than kick a field goal to tie. We needed a win and were just inches away.

But wait. The referee was waving his hands. He conferred with the back judge and declared that the game was over. The referee then ran off the field without ever talking to me, in spite of the one second showing on the scoreboard. The officials were keeping time on the field, and one said his clock showed 0:00. For the record, there had been no problems with the scoreboard clock the entire game. We were never using the field clock as the official time.

But none of that mattered. We had lost. I couldn't believe it. Hawaii's players started rejoicing. Our team was upset and angry. I tried to plead my case, but as I mentioned, the crew chief had run off the field like a scolded dog. During our postgame handshake, Hawaii's head coach, June Jones, apologized to me for the horrible officiating.

The next day, I became even angrier when I reviewed the video-tape of the game telecast—from the University of Hawaii's network. It was all there, just as I thought. You could even hear the whistles blowing with 0:01 left on the clock. But the referee still messed up and called the game over. If you want to see the whole mess for yourself, you can go to YouTube and check it out. Just type in the key words "closing seconds," "San Jose State," "Hawaii," and "2003."

We appealed the result to the Western Athletic Conference office, based on several objections. One, if there was a discrepancy between the scoreboard clock and the time being kept on the field, it should have been corrected when we took our last timeout with twenty seconds remaining. That never happened. We were under the impression that the scoreboard clock was accurate, because no official told us otherwise. Also, the person running the scoreboard clock clearly did not hit his toggle switch until the whistles blew with 0:01 showing.

This, of course, could actually mean there was just three-tenths of a second left. Scoreboard clocks in football don't break down fractions of a second. The point is, after we spiked the ball, there was some time remaining. Yet we were denied the opportunity to run a fourth-down play.

Guess what? The league reviewed our protest and ruled that we were correct in every detail. The officiating crew was sanctioned and suspended for the following week—although the crew chief was hired by the Big 12 the following season.

Right about here, I should mention that this crew chief was a white guy. Do I think he had it in for me because I'm black? Not necessarily. Do I think this might have been one of those two percent subconscious cases where a referee reacted differently to me because I was not of his same race? Yes. Do I also believe that this kind of thing happens in several college games across the country every autumn? Absolutely.

To be honest, I think about that one incident quite a bit. In my mind, it was a case of extreme unfairness—not a blown call, as often happens because we are all human. The WAC office agreed with me. But the outcome of the game didn't change. Unfortunately, in 2003 we did not have an instant replay official in the booth to review the blatant missed call. But it definitely worked differently in December 2009 when I was watching the Big 12 championship game.

Texas and Nebraska were battling for the Big 12 title. It felt a little like déjà vu for me, in some sense. Colt McCoy, the Longhorn quarterback, scrambled around toward his right sideline as time was running down before he finally tossed the football out of bounds. Too late, it seemed. The scoreboard clock—thought to be official—showed no time left. Nebraska head coach Bo Pelini began walking across the field to meet Texas head coach Mack Brown after what appeared to be a stunning upset. The result would certainly screw up the BCS bowl pairings and negate the much-anticipated national title game between Alabama and Texas.

But then the officials said, hey, wait a second. And it turned out to be the second that I didn't get in October of 2003.

As the Nebraska and Texas players were told to cool their heels, game officials automatically deferred the decision to the instant replay booth. Because there was so much at stake, tension grew. Finally, the instant replay official overruled the official game clock, put one second back on the clock, and gave Texas the opportunity to kick a game-winning field goal—which the Longhorns did.

That's when I had a 2003 flashback of the game official running off the field at San Jose State—without ever giving me his rationale for such an action. Although this was a different game situation, it was still a subjective decision, even as the video was being reviewed. By rule, the clock was supposed to stop when the ball hit a solid object beyond the sidelines. In this case, the ball thrown by McCoy first made contact with a solid object at the railing of a luxury box on the field level of the new Dallas Cowboys' stadium. Because the video replay wasn't in 3-D, no one could truly tell the exact instant when the ball made contact with that railing. The replay official had to make his best guess, depending on the ball's movement. It was still a judgment decision, one that worked in favor of Texas and against Nebraska.

I hope that you understand that this is not about me. I am trying to explain this principle: experiences shape our perceptions. And those perceptions become reality when we don't have anyone questioning what we perceive to be real. The divergent perceptions and life experiences between black and white people have resulted in the development of two different definitions of racial and employment discrimination. Those different definitions have a tendency to structure our personal perceptions, resulting in black and white people perceiving their employment realities differently.

And that's what I am asking you to do here. Take a moment and change your lenses to look at race issues from a different perspective. You might not be comfortable doing this. But to grow as a person—and as a sports fan—you must get out of your comfort zone.

I have no anger or malice in my heart for the decision made by the head WAC official, although it was at a pivotal time in my coaching career. I let go of that stuff a long time ago. After all, even if our San Jose State team had been given that one extra second, we still might not have been able to push the ball the one inch we needed to reach the end zone. But our team deserved the opportunity to try.

According to social scientists, there are biological reasons that govern how humans respond to people from different races. A powerful part of our brains, the amygdala, desires that the world run on a routine cycle rather than one of change. The amygdala is located within the limbic system, an area of the mind that deals with the way we perceive and respond to the world. Relentlessly, the amygdala urges us to favor the familiar—in this case, the sight of members of our own race, if that's the skin color of the people we grew up trusting and loving in our own families.

I realize this is tricky stuff and a controversial claim. Even when you look a man directly in the eye as you communicate with him, it's impossible to always realize what is in his soul. We will never know if, had I been a white coach, the crew chief in that Hawaii game would have been more open to hearing my appeal that afternoon and leaving one second on the clock to give us a chance to win or tie the game. And we'll never know if, had the referee been black, he would have stayed on the field to hear my objections. But it's not as if I am going that far out on a limb by raising these questions. I simply don't believe that people, when considering these issues, connect all of the dots. Remember, I'm an academic. I see research all the time about all sorts of stuff—some of which backs up my gut feelings. One piece of research involves an analogy using lima beans.

In 2007, two social psychologists released a study revealing that four out of five people harbor unconscious negative biases toward members of other racial groups. The research by Professor Robert Livingston of Northwestern University involved showing subjects positive and negative images and pairing them with racial surrogates.

Livingston's experiment was based on the theory that evolution has predisposed people to distrust "the other." Also, that racial prejudice is a symptom of the human brain's natural tendency to categorize and form emotional associations with objects. This is especially the case when the objects are perceived as negative objects.

Professor Livingston and his research partner, Professor Brian Drwecki of the University of Wisconsin, also discovered that most people are powerless to totally overcome any negative feelings toward a different race—even when reason tells them they should. That's where the lima beans come in. People can be told that lima beans are one of the healthiest foods they can eat. But that will never cause people who hate lima beans to suddenly think they're delicious. "The individual can certainly control whether he or she will eat lima beans, but has almost no control over whether he or she will like the taste of lima beans," Professor Livingston said in a university publication about his study.

Personally, I think this is what happens to certain white game officials. They tend to feel uneasy about "the other"—the rare African American coach the referees encounter working college games—and this subconscious feeling overrides the white official's sincere attempts to be colorblind and totally neutral. Meanwhile, the black official will not "stand up" to overrule his white crew members in such situations, because the black official does not want to rock the boat and jeopardize his job. For African American college coaches, it creates a double whammy. And it's real.

Do I think this situation can change? Yes, in time. Maybe one day we can solve all this by having robots officiate college football games. Until then...well, at least the replay machines are colorblind.

CHAPTER FOURTEEN
BASKETBALL'S FASTER BREAK

The question gets put to me so often I can almost hear it coming before the actual phrase is uttered. Whenever I start talking how the opportunities for African American college football coaches have been so slim, the most frequent and fastest retort is:

"Yes, but why is it so different in basketball?"

I understand why people ask. So let me devote one chapter—albeit a somewhat brief one—to explain the answer. Then we'll get back to football.

College basketball is indeed much further along in the quest for racial coaching equality, if that's the phrase you want to use. In fact, college basketball is almost on a different planet in that regard. In recent years, the percentage of African American men's basketball head coaches has wavered between 25 percent and 30 percent. In the 2008-09 season, the percentage was 28.5 percent.

The statistics back up what the average fan sees when he or she tunes into games; it seems as if every week, in every big game between top college hoop teams, at least one of the head coaches is a minority. Fans are used to seeing their faces. No one thinks it's strange to see a black man leading a prominent team at a prominent school. It's not even a big deal any more. Makes you wonder how we got to that situation, huh?

The answer to that question is the name of one person. John Thompson.

In 1971, Thompson was a former college and pro basketball player who had established himself as a great high school coach in the Washington DC area. Saddled with a lousy 3-23 basketball team, the administration at nearby Georgetown University was impressed with Thompson. With nothing to lose, university honchos fired their coach and offered the position to Thompson.

On a comparative timeline, this was seven years before Willie Jefferies became the first African American major college football coach at Wichita State. In 1972, hiring an African American basketball coach at any prominent school was considered a radical idea.

"In those days, if you were a black coach, the top programs didn't come calling," Thompson told *Sports Illustrated* in an interview. "So you had to turn your program into a top program." I should note that it is much easier to do this with a basketball program than a football program because fewer athletes and resources are involved.

Thompson didn't have an easy time of it at Georgetown. He was 12-14 in his first season with the Hoyas. But three years later, he went 21-7 and reached the NCAA Tournament. He recruited players traditionally out of the Georgetown orbit, including several African American kids from the most urban neighborhoods in the major eastern cities.

Thompson was a hard-nosed disciplinarian, and the media generally perceived him to be unfriendly. His attitude, along with his policy of sequestering players on road trips, gave rise to the phrase "Hoya Paranoia" in referring to his program. Reporters and broadcasters didn't always embrace Thompson's approach. But they couldn't criticize his winning record. He guided the Hoyas to three Final Fours and won a national championship in 1984. Thompson was also an outspoken advocate for his players. In 1989, he walked off the court before one game and skipped another as a protest against Proposition 42, a piece of NCAA legislation that mandated more severe eligibility restrictions.

That walkout was emblematic of Thompson's principles. In his view, the Proposition 42 eligibility standards were unfair because they were based on a minimum SAT or ACT score. Thompson strongly believed that such tests were biased against members of minority groups and underprivileged youth. In 1990, the NCAA rescinded Proposition 42 and eventually created a different eligibility formula.

All of that was significant and important. But who's kidding whom? The only reason anyone in college sports listened to Thompson in that case—or listened to his opinion about anything—was that he had won championships. Given my lousy winning percentage at San Jose State, imagine how stupid I would have looked if I had decided to protest the Academic Progress Rate (APR) legislation by walking off the football field during a game. I would have been fired or at the very least severely reprimanded.

Thompson was not the first African American basketball head coach at a Division I school. That honor fell to Will Robinson, who in 1970 was hired at Illinois State. And in 1972, the same year that Thompson was hired at Georgetown, black coaches George Raveling and Fred Snowden were hired by Washington State and Arizona, respectively.

All three of those men had their share of winning teams. But none were as spectacularly triumphant as Thompson. That's what made him such an important figure for African American basketball coaches. When athletic directors saw a black man walking the sidelines and succeeding at such a high level, they became less reluctant to hire a minority coach for their own teams.

Just one good example: In 1982 when Temple University had an opening for a head coach, the school offered the position to John Chaney, a black coach with an excellent record at a Division II program, Cheyney University. By then, Thompson had been labeled a big success at Georgetown, so it was easier for Temple officials to make the Chaney hire and sell it to the Owl alums. Within one season, Chaney had his Temple team in the NCAA Tournament—and by his sixth season, he had the Owls ranked number one in the wire service polls before taking them to within one victory of the Final Four. By the time he retired in 2006, he had won 516 games at Temple. At that time, Syracuse coach Jim Boeheim was asked to place Chaney's career in perspective.

"John Chaney and John Thompson made it possible for the black coach to get in the college game," Boeheim told *USA Today*. "Administrators need to win to keep their jobs. So when Chaney and Thompson won games, that's how black coaches got hired."

This is a precise explanation of how, regardless of the sport, black coaches are evaluated collectively. The difference is that in basketball, it has worked to the benefit of black coaches because of Thompson and Chaney's success.

But I believe another factor was at work in their success: Thompson and Chaney thrived at schools that were not major college football powers. Georgetown and Temple did not have huge athletic department budgets before they arrived. That lessened the influence of athletic boosters, who are relied upon to finance the big-time programs. This, in turn, allowed the athletic directors to make the bold move of hiring a minority.

Likewise, when the athletic directors of big-time football schools subsequently began seeking out African American basketball coaches, the athletic boosters almost never raised objections because they cared far more about football, anyway, and the achievements of Thompson and Chaney had proved that a minority basketball coach could lead a school to the NCAA promised land.

This effect then fed on itself with sort of a tag team hiring process. In 1985, one year after Thompson won a national championship at Georgetown, Arkansas hired Nolan Richardson, an African American coach who'd won conference championships at the University of Tulsa. It was no smooth ride for Richardson at Arkansas. I know. I was on the school's football coaching staff while Richardson was there. But he waded through a lot of distractions—the death of his young daughter, university politics, and what he perceived as racial tension toward his approach of leading the basketball program to the Final Four in 1990. He won the national title four years later and returned to the championship game the following year.

All of that winning didn't magically turn Richardson into a white coach in the eyes of white basketball fans—but it did make the notion of a black college basketball coach more acceptable. The same held true at the University of Georgia, which hired African American coach Tubby Smith in 1995, one year after Richardson won the NCAA championship at Arkansas. After Smith won forty-five games during his first two seasons at Georgia, he was hired away by the University of Kentucky, another Southeastern Conference school. Smith promptly guided the Wildcats to a national championship in his first season.

Of course, at both Arkansas and Kentucky, expectations were raised by the massive success. But when Richardson and Smith failed to deliver Final Four teams every year, they were criticized in spite of consistent winning records, which happens to all coaches regardless of color. Richardson was fired at Arkansas in 2002 after a bitter dispute with Athletic Director Frank Broyles, and Smith resigned under heavy pressure following the 2007 season.

In the case of Richardson, I won't go into all the details that led to his termination at Arkansas. You can track that down in other books if you want. However, upon Richardson's exit, Arkansas administrators replaced him with another African American coach, Stan Heath. To many black observers, the move was a cynical one, made strictly to combat Richardson's claims that racism had played a part in his treatment by the Arkansas administration. Heath did compile a winning record before he, too, was dismissed by Arkansas after failing to take the Razorbacks beyond the first round of the NCAA Tournament. I will say this: even if the Razorback administration was operating in a cynical fashion—and I have no evidence one way or the other—it was at least an affirmative move image-wise to replace Richardson with Heath. And it was a sign of how much progress has been made in the sport of basketball. Following the completion of the 2010-11 collegiate basketball season, Arkansas hired its third African American basketball coach when the administration brought back Richardson's former top assistant, Mike Anderson.

The tally to this point, then, shows that three African American basketball coaches have won Division I national championships. But in football, the total is zero. Obviously, there has not been an equality of opportunity. But I wonder: Would we have the same situation in basketball if John Thompson had not become such a dominant winner at Georgetown almost thirty years ago? He framed a picture in the minds of administrators and fans alike. Suddenly, when their brains envisioned what a national championship coach looked like, a black man appeared in the photo.

That has yet to happen in football. In fact, entering the 2011 football season, Tyrone Willingham remains the only African American coach who has taken a team to a BCS bowl game—the Rose Bowl at Stanford and the Fiesta Bowl at Notre Dame. He lost both games. And Willingham is now at least temporarily out of the game after being dismissed at both Notre Dame and Washington.

As a result of all this, when administrators and fans envision a national championship coach, they picture someone who looks like Pete Carroll or Urban Meyer or Nick Saban. There has yet to be a comparable John Thompson figure as a college football coach…or a Nolan Richardson…or a Tubby Smith. There has not even been a John Chaney figure, a black coach who didn't reach the national championship game but was always knocking at the door.

In my opinion, when the first African American football coach wins a BCS national championship, it will provoke a sea of change. Suddenly, that photo in people's minds will change. It changed in the NFL, for example, when in 2007 Tony Dungy became the first

African American head coach to win a Super Bowl—and did so by defeating another African American head coach, Lovie Smith of the Chicago Bears.

Two weeks earlier, one day after that Super Bowl match up was set between two black coaches, the Pittsburgh Steelers filled their head coaching opening by hiring Mike Tomlin, a young African American assistant coach from the Minnesota Vikings. Personally, I don't think it was a coincidence. The Steelers might have offered the job to Tomlin anyway. But the fact that Dungy and Smith were about to face off in the Super Bowl certainly brought acceptance to Pittsburgh's decision at all levels. Tomlin then justified the decision by leading the Steelers to the Super Bowl title in 2009 and posing with the Vince Lombardi Trophy. He also led the Steelers back to the Super Bowl in 2011.

I strongly believe that the same thing needs to happen in college football. An African American coach must reach the pinnacle. He must pose for that imaginary photo inside alums' heads of the "ideal" coach. Of the current black coaches, I believe Charlie Strong at Louisville and David Shaw at Stanford may have the best chance at a national championship.

I don't want to lay those heavy burdens entirely on Strong's and Shaw's shoulders. But in my opinion, there are only a few African American college football head coaches at programs who have the necessary institutional resources and commitment to win a national championship. Currently, the other two black coaches are Turner Gill at Kansas and Joker Phillips at Kentucky. Both are heading up programs where institutional support should not be an issue. But the odds of Kansas out-recruiting such Big 12 conference rivals such as Texas and Oklahoma—as well as beating those opponents consistently—are not promising. But it can happen, and that's why we play the game.

At Kentucky, I am hoping administrators will support Phillips in what I think can be a very challenging situation for him as the first African American to lead the Wildcat football program. But his situation is much like Kansas in that nobody expects Kentucky to win a SEC championship or a national championship in football. Gill and Phillips will help the perception of black football coaches if they post consistent winning percentages as black head coaches in their leagues—barring any changes that conference expansions and mergers might bring.

Maybe African American head football coaches should reach out to John Thompson for advice and inspiration. I also hope that at some point, an African American football coach will have something else in common with Coach Thompson—a national championship ring. Nothing would do more for African American college football coaches.

CHAPTER FIFTEEN

SIX-POINT PLAN
(WITH TWO EXTRA POINTS)

In February of 2007, the Super Bowl was played at Dolphin Stadium in Florida. As the hype machine hummed before the game, the most popular story angle was the unprecedented historic achievement of both teams being led by African American head coaches. Tony Dungy was on the sidelines for the Indianapolis Colts. The Chicago Bears were Lovie Smith's team.

The two men deserved every bit of that hype. And not just because of their skin color. They are both great coaches. I imagine that if you spoke with Colts and Bears fans, they'd be quite happy that the NFL has become more diverse in hiring head coaches.

But as I read all the stories, I also keep asking myself this question: How long will it be until college football has a national championship game where both head coaches are African American?

That time may unfortunately be many years away. Pray that I am wrong.

How could I say otherwise? The odds are just too great against it, considering the rate at which minorities are hired as college head coaches. Those odds won't improve until Division I universities implement significant changes in their hiring policies. In the five BCS games following the 2010 season, the ten head coaches were white. In this book, I have tried to make my case about the coaching inequities with no sniveling or wailing. I've just laid out the facts, told you the stories, and given you the evidence.

However, everyone hates a person who hashes over problems without offering a solution. I have solutions.

In fact, it is scary how simple it would be to correct the inequities that I have outlined in the previous chapters. It would not really involve much heavy lifting—or even any truly controversial moves. It would mostly involve common sense. It would also involve college administrators bringing the same sort of hiring policy perspectives to football that they use in other areas of their universities. How could that be controversial?

I want to believe that even the most ardent critics of affirmative action do, at heart, want there to be fairness when it comes to hiring someone for a job in any profession. So that's the main focus of my six-point proposal (with two extra points) that could be implemented immediately.

As a bonus, my plan would also help colleges pick better coaches—of all colors. And every coach of every race would receive the best shot to pursue his dreams.

POINT ONE:
Stop the Secrecy

Deception is good on the field in college football. People are still talking about all of those "gimmick plays" that Boise State pulled off while defeating Oklahoma in the 2007 Fiesta Bowl.

When deception is used that way, it can be fun. But deception is not good when it comes to hiring football coaches—particularly at public universities. Yet so many institutions sanction it, either knowingly or unknowingly. Some colleges practically embrace it.

I've seen how the whole deal works, plenty of times. A school fires a coach. The school needs to hire a new one. Candidates are found. But some of those candidates are head coaches—or top assistants—at other schools.

Often, those candidates don't want their bosses at those other schools to know they are interested in leaving to go somewhere else. So they give their agents permission to inquire about potential employment and ask that their interviews be kept confidential.

Schools are usually happy to go along with the request—and not just because those schools are eager to make candidates happy. Many times, the schools want to keep one candidate's name secret from another candidate anyway. So interviews are conducted in clandestine locations—either away from the athletic department on campus or sometimes in another city entirely. An athletic director might fly into town, obtain a hotel room, and invite the candidate up for a room service dinner so nobody sees the two of them together.

The same thing happens in the NFL. In fact, when Miami Dolphins owner Wayne Huizenga was looking for a new head coach in January of 2007, he flew his private plane to Costa Rica where he was intending to meet secretly with USC Head Coach Pete Carroll.

Well, it was supposed to be secret. The meeting's cover was blown when some Internet bloggers obtained the tail number of Huizenga's jet. They consulted a website that charted commercial and private flights, figured out that Carroll was also in Costa Rica, and then put two and two together.

But if you remember, the reason Huizenga needed a new coach was that his former Dolphin coach, Nick Saban, had played his own game of deception. Toward the end of the 2006 NFL season, rumors surfaced that Saban was interested in leaving the Dolphins to become head coach at the University of Alabama, which had fired Mike Shula.

Saban told reporters that this speculation was ridiculous. He swore to Dolphin fans that the rumors weren't true. Saban said he had not talked to Alabama and was planning to stay in Miami indefinitely. Saban might have been technically correct in that he had not personally spoken with Alabama officials. But it appears his agent had the university on speed dial.

News reports later revealed that while Saban was denying those "rumors," there had not only already been contact between Saban's interests and Alabama, he and his representative were secretly negotiating contract terms. Those same Internet bloggers used the same website to track an Alabama booster's plane, which had flown to Miami to pick up Saban and bring him to Tuscaloosa—a trip that Alabama officials wanted to keep quiet. Then, suddenly, surprise! Saban was announced as the new head coach.

The Dolphins are a private enterprise. You can make the case they have the right to conduct a coaching search like some sort of James Bond spy novel. But the University of Alabama is a public institution. It is supported by the state's taxpayers. Doesn't the university have an obligation to keep hiring practices transparent? An institution would never hire a provost or a dean using similar methods. Why is it permissible to hire a football coach this way?

If a school wants to confine the search solely to a buddy of the athletic director—or to the favored candidate of a booster who contributes the most money to the football program—the school can do exactly that. There is no accountability and no way to tell if every good candidate is even being considered. Current employment trends create doubt and question if all candidates are being held to the same standards.

Is it any wonder so many minority coaches believe there might be a covert conspiracy to deny them an opportunity for job interviews? Is it any wonder that so many coaches—of all races—feel they aren't getting a fair shake when it comes to hiring?

The remedy is easy: drop the veil of secrecy. Require all interviews of all head coaching candidates to take place in an open atmosphere. Make sure every candidate is made public so that the school's football fans know that the university is making a broad effort to hire the best person for the job.

And what if a prime candidate has a job elsewhere and says he does not want to have his name made public as a job seeker? Tell the guy thanks, but if that's the case, then he is no longer a candidate. In recruiting a high school kid, if a college has to cheat, then that college will also probably be cheating the kid eventually. Likewise, if a coaching candidate will deceive his current employer surreptitiously to interview for a job at a new school, he will probably do the same thing at the new school eventually. After all, if the institution is public and funded using state financial resources, the process should be open and no gimmicks or games played. If the president of a college gets hired through a completely wide open search process, shouldn't the football coach as well? How would the alumni and supporters of the college or university like to wake up one morning and find out that their new president was a person that just slipped into town without anyone knowing except the few who made the decision?

What I recommend is making the hiring process an open book. This would do wonders for the morale of all coaches. It would eliminate any—well, most—conspiracy theories. And if a school is comfortable going through two or three cycles of hiring without once talking to a minority candidate, people can draw their own conclusions.

POINT TWO:
Cool the Jets

Rush, rush, rush. Nothing moves faster than the hiring process for a Division 1A football coach. To hear athletic directors and school presidents tell it, they have no time to conduct a measured, methodical review of coaching candidates. It simply isn't possible. There is recruiting to do! Players might decide to transfer! Continuity must prevail! We can't wait around!

In 2004 when the University of Illinois fired its head football coach, Ron Turner, the school allegedly conducted a wide-open search for Turner's successor. Illinois announced it was taking applications from any interested candidates, who were supposed to submit their résumés and names by 5 p.m. on December 6.

Guess what happened? Less than twenty-four hours after that deadline, Illinois announced that Ron Zook was the school's new head coach. Sixty-two former Illinois players composed a letter to Athletic Director Ron Guenther expressing concerns about the way things went down. One of those players was former Illini running back Howard Griffith. He noted that two minority candidates were interviewed for the opening in the final hours of the "search" but believed it was only as an afterthought. Word was out among alums that Zook, who had been ousted at Florida, had agreed to take the deal several days before the deadline, which fell on a Monday.

"We know the offer didn't come until one minute after 5 p.m. that day, officially," Griffith told Associated Press. "But you know a hand was shaken probably (the previous) Tuesday or Wednesday. That's what reasonable people would think."

Reasonable people don't just think such stuff. They know it to be true. Lou Holtz was out the door at South Carolina for about five minutes in 2004 before Steve Spurrier was hired to replace him. In 2001, Notre Dame took only slightly longer to hire George O'Leary after Bob Davie exited South Bend. And so on.

The excuse that schools inevitably use is that, with recruiting commitments hanging in the balance, filling the head coaching position quickly is mandatory. Also, if a school does not act in making an offer to a top candidate, he might go somewhere else.

At best, these are rationalizations. At worst, they are devious cover stories. There is no demonstrable proof that hiring a head coach quickly results in a better won-loss record. After the 2000 season at Ohio State, the school administration dithered for weeks and weeks until finally hiring its third or fourth preferred candidate, Jim Tressel of Youngstown State. Tressel coached the Buckeyes to a national championship in his second season and went on to win seven Big 10 championships. He resigned amidst a strange memorabilia-for-tattoos scandal following the 2010 season. But his success on the field shows that hiring fast doesn't necessarily mean making the best choice.

It would benefit the process if the NCAA would orchestrate a gentlemen's agreement of a two-week "cooling off" period between the time a coach is fired or quits and the time when a new coach is hired. This would allow all coaching candidates to receive a fair look and would prevent schools from rushing to hire a new head coach before half the candidates even know the job is open. It would allow schools to take a deep breath and do some due diligence before making the hire. It would certainly give minority candidates a better chance to put themselves in play for a job.

Heck, if this rule had been in effect several years ago, Notre Dame might never have suffered the embarrassment of hiring O'Leary, who was fired a few days later. With a mandatory "cooling off" period, there would have been ample time to vet O'Leary's résumé and discover how he had misled employers by falsely claiming he had earned a master's degree at New York University and that he had played three years of college football at the University of New Hampshire.

It is quite possible that schools would still make up their minds prematurely about who they want to hire then simply hold off on the announcement for two or three weeks. But that's where the rest of my proposals would come into play. If this policy were enacted, an institution would be forced to use the two-week period as intelligently as possible.

POINT THREE:
Diversity on Both Sides of the Interview

Right now, at too many schools the "hiring committee" for a new football coach basically consists of two people—the athletic director and school president. Sometimes, it consists of only one person. If so, it is usually the athletic director. The president then usually rubber-stamps the choice.

Again, in professional football, that concept might fly. A team owner is operating his own business. But college football has no single "owner." College football has a diverse pool of stakeholders—administrators, trustees, faculty members, students, alumni, and boosters. And if the school is a public institution, you can throw in the taxpayers too.

If you eliminate those diverse stakeholders from the coach-selection process, how can you ever expect to see a diverse field of candidates? You can't. Oh, it might happen, if the athletic director has an open mind and does a lot of homework. More often, an athletic director carries around a short list—in his pocket or in his head—of potential replacements for his current head coach. And when that coach quits or is fired, the athletic director makes one or two phone calls to get his man. This leads to accusations of the "good old boy" network.

The NCAA could correct this process with one swift piece of legislation. Schools could be required to form an advisory committee for head coach openings. As we all know, colleges can become bogged down in bureaucracy. So the committee would have to be set up wisely, with an ability to be efficient and nimble. I would suggest that it be appointed by the school president, who could set up the committee as a year-round athletic advisory board that would already be in place when an opening occurs. The committee would consist of five or six people representing all of the stakeholders mentioned above.

Would this committee do the actual hiring? No. But it would be in position to suggest names of candidates, to interview those candidates when they come to the campus, and to file strenuous objections if the athletic director appears to be making a radical or nonsensical move. It would also provide greater transparency on the hiring process and make the candidates confident that they are not victims of the "good old boy" syndrome.

Would this process lead to hiring better people? I would like to think so. In the NFL, opening the door wider in terms of coaching searches and extending their reach has paid huge dividends, which brings me to my next proposal.

POINT FOUR:
Follow the Leader

During the 2002 football season, the NFL recognized it had a significant problem with racial inequity. Of the thirty-two head coaches in the league, only two were black—Dungy of the Colts and Herm Edwards of the New York Jets. This was of great concern to the NFL Players' Union, because 67 percent of its membership was African American. Some of the union members and some former NFL players began lobbying owners to make some changes in their hiring philosophies. The situation had been festering since at least 1997 when there were eleven head coaching openings in the league. When those eleven jobs were eventually filled, none of the new coaches were African Americans.

No surprise there. Few minorities were even being interviewed for the openings despite of their qualifications. They were feeling the same frustration felt by Tony Dungy in 1993, when he was the Minnesota Vikings' defensive coordinator and six head coaching jobs opened up.

"We were coming off a playoff season with the number one defense in the league—and I never even got a phone call," Dungy would later tell *Sports Illustrated*.

With persistence, Dungy finally did get his first head coaching job in Tampa Bay, before being dismissed there and moving on to Indianapolis. But most other minority candidates were experiencing the same chill that Dungy did whenever a head coaching position became available. Things really began to heat up when civil rights activist Jesse Jackson and attorney Johnnie Cochran joined the cause. They threatened legal action if the NFL did not do something.

Dan Rooney, the Pittsburgh Steelers' owner, answered the bell. He proposed a radical idea, at least for sports. Rooney wanted to require every NFL team with a head coaching vacancy to interview at least one minority candidate before filling the job. A team that failed to follow this guideline would be subject to severe fines. After the 2002 season, owners passed the measure—which became known as the Rooney Rule.

The rule's intention was threefold. First, it would give more minority candidates the chance to audition for head coaching positions. Second, even if those minority coaches did not earn a head position, the experience of going through the interview process would make them better in their next interview. And third, the names of the minority coaches who interviewed for the positions would be circulated in the media and around the league, putting them on a list of likely candidates for coordinator positions as well as the next head coaching positions.

How dramatically has the Rooney rule affected the NFL? By the 2004 season, there were a record fourteen minority offensive and defensive coordinators. There were also 173 minority assistant coaches, another record. At the start of the 2006 season, there were seven African American head coaches in the NFL.

And, oh yes. There were those two African American head coaches in Super Bowl XLI. Most observers agree that Lovie Smith would never have been hired by the Bears without the Rooney Rule. When the team brought him in for an interview, he was not the top candidate. But when he was put on a level playing field with the other interviewees, Smith wowed the Chicago team officials and earned the job.

But in college football, there is no Rooney Rule. Why not? Because the school presidents and athletic directors who make up the NCAA feel that one isn't needed. At the organization's annual convention in January of 2007, the late NCAA president Myles Brand scolded Division 1A schools in his opening speech for failing to offer more head coaching opportunities to minorities, declaring, "We're not anywhere close to where we need to be." However, Brand did not propose any new NCAA legislation.

But I will. You can call the new legislation the Eddie Robinson Rule if you want, honoring the great Grambling coach. The Rooney Rule can be used as a template. Before any Division 1A university hires a football coach, it must give a serious interview to at least one minority candidate. A school could interview as many other candidates as it wished—candidates of any color. But one would have to be a minority.

One difference: instead of a university simply being fined if it failed to follow the Eddie Robinson Rule, the school could potentially lose scholarships and be barred from going to a bowl game for a season or more.

Frankly, such a rule should have been implemented in the NCAA years ago. Why should the allegedly enlightened academic community allow the crass and money-grubbing NFL to seize the higher moral ground on this issue?

POINT FIVE:
Put Your Diploma Where Your Whistle Is

As I have mentioned, when it comes to hiring football coaches at Division 1A universities, pretty much anything goes. Athletic directors—and even some school presidents—act more like cowboys rather than academics when it comes to football. It's almost as if there are no laws and no scruples, just like in the Wild West.

I am thinking particularly here about what happened during the 2004 football season at Auburn University. Two days before Auburn played Alabama in November of that year, Auburn president William Walker and athletic director David Housel were off ridin' and ropin' up a storm. Without head coach Tommy Tuberville's knowledge, they were secretly interviewing Louisville coach Bobby Petrino and asking if he would be interested in replacing Tuberville. Slight problem: Tuberville had not been fired. He didn't even know his job was in jeopardy.

When word leaked out about Walker and Housel's actions, the you-know-what hit the fan. The Alabama governor was outraged, and Walker ended up resigning. Tuberville stayed. Granted, this is an extreme case. But as a case study, it's a perfect example of how universities that otherwise follow strict standards and practices in other areas throw out the rule book for football.

Know who suffers? Minority candidates suffer. Here's why: if a school does not have specific hiring criteria when it is searching for a new head football coach, it leads to all sorts of confusion. Candidates have no idea what to put on a résumé. When you're trying to break through a glass ceiling, the best ammunition is to remove any doubts that you are qualified for the job. But if there are no clearly defined or stated qualifications for the job, how can anyone know what it will take to become "qualified"?

Combine that dilemma with the fact that athletic administrators have shown a tendency to be extremely subjective when evaluating football coaching candidates, and you can see why so many minority coaches believe in those conspiracy theories.

You might be shocked to know that in many cases more academic preparation is required to coach at the high school level than is necessary to be employed as a coach at a Division 1A institution. Because of the teaching and faculty needs, many small colleges will require coaches to have a master's degree. Major college football jobs don't require one. I have personally witnessed an assistant coach being hired without a college degree.

Unfortunately, a resume does not seem to mean much—at least not an official résumé. While doing my doctoral thesis, I interviewed dozens of Division 1A assistant coaches. One of the most intriguing responses to my questionnaire about how coaches are hired was this piece of information from a director of football operations at a Southeastern Conference school:

> The main criteria for hiring is and always will be marriage, children, legal record, personal vices. Married fathers with no criminal record and total abstinence from liquor and tobacco are hard to find in any racial or socioeconomic group.

No doubt. But is it fair to people applying for head coaching jobs to keep them guessing about the "criteria" required? I think not, but this frequently happens to coaches because the institution, in its official job posting, does not list the above-mentioned "criteria" and qualifications as job requirements. And whether you agree or not that these requirements are fair, they should have been made public. It would have saved a lot of coaches a lot of wasted time.

Right now there are a lot of job-seeking coaches who waste a lot of time seeking head coaching vacancies that they have absolutely zero chance of obtaining. They are operating strictly on guesswork. Is previous full-time college coaching experience in Division II or Division III preferred instead of graduate assistant experience at the

Division 1A level? Does head coaching experience at the community college level mean more to potential employers than experience
as a lower-level assistant at a four-year school? If a coach knows, he
can attempt to get that experience before he applies for a Division
1A job.

Many times the following happens: A minority coach applies
for a job and is simply told, "You are not qualified." But no one tells
the minority coach what that means. And when that coach sees a
school hire a white coach with less experience or less education, the
phrase seems to mean that the black coach was not part of the "good
old boy" network.

During my research, a black coach employed in the Mid-American Conference underscored this very point by telling me, "I do
not believe, or I would not like to think, that school administrators
are outwardly racist. Unfortunately, in this profession, employment
is generally based on who you know. I sincerely wish résumés were
taken a lot more seriously in our profession so that a person can get
hired or interviewed based on his credentials and accomplishments."

Once more, setting things right should not be complicated.
Uniform standards should be set. At a minimum, for example, every
head coach of a Division 1A school should possess a master's degree
or be required to pursue one after being employed by the hiring
institution.

Colleges should also be required to publicly state the level of
experience or expertise necessary for a job—and adopt a policy of
never hiring a coach who does not meet those requirements over a
coach who does. That way, when a job candidate is trying to prepare
himself in the early years of his career, he can pull out the list of
requirements. He can check them off as he completes them. And
when he completes those requirements, he will know it really means
something.

And what happens if two coaches, one minority and one white,
both meet the same requirements and the white coach is hired? So

be it. Administrators are entitled to do as they wish. But with a more standardized list of prerequisites and qualifications, the conspiracy theories and the resentment will be more easily deflated. As an extra added attraction, the players should receive the benefit of more competent and proficient coaching.

POINT SIX:
More Opportunities, Painlessly

As we have learned in previous chapters, one excuse that administrators use when trying to explain why they don't hire more black coaches is the small pool of candidates. The good news: it shouldn't be that hard to dig out a bigger pool.

At the Division 1A level, most coaching aspirants begin their careers as graduate assistants. These jobs are low paying and are stepping-stones to a full-time job. Currently, the NCAA allows Division 1A schools to employ two grad assistants. As you can imagine, the competition for those two jobs is fierce. There are always many more applicants than positions available.

My suggestion, then, would be for the NCAA to work with member institutions to create and approve an extra graduate assistant position to be filled by a minority at all 120 Division 1A schools. The expense would not be onerous, given the small stipend that grad assistants are given. But the 120 extra jobs could be financed by tapping the diversity program fund that already exists. Either that or the NCAA could tap the enormous profits generated by the BCS bowls. Or perhaps the NFL and NFL Players Association could combine to donate the money.

Who could argue against this proposal? By adding the extra position, no jobs would be taken away from white graduate assistants—or any current grad assistants, for that matter. Individual schools would not have to come up with extra dough for the extra position because it would be paid for by outside money. More young coaching talent would be exposed to Division 1A football. And long term, it would produce more qualified minority candidates for full-time college positions.

Two-Point Conversion

1

The next two are quick ones. In recent years, schools have tried to gain more control over the actions of their most rabid athletic boosters. In some cases, these boosters are urged to attend an educational seminar at which NCAA rules about improper benefits and illegal support are outlined. Why couldn't boosters also be asked to undergo an educational program about diversity? This program would explain why diversity makes the college game better. It could also foster candid dialogue on the issue—so that when the hurricane hiring season begins in the late autumn, boosters would understand why the hiring practices outlined above are in place.

2

Keep the next Tony Dungy or Lovie Smith from leaving college football.

Can this be done? Or will the African American football "brain drain" to the NFL keep happening? Will minority assistant coaches continue to leave the college game for the pros because that's where they believe they have the best opportunity to become head coaches?

The answer to these questions is entirely up to college football and the changes it can choose to make. I am praying that the establishment will do the right thing.

CHAPTER SIXTEEN

REMOVING THE CHIP
FROM MY SHOULDER

I know this book is about football coaches. But it is also about the way society deals with football coaches—and how football coaches fit into that society. I know this book is about sports. But it is also about how sports can teach us so many lessons about life in general.

That means right now, I am going to talk about God a little bit. I know it's probably not why you opened the cover. But my Christian faith is a part of my life and, I would suspect, the lives of many people reading these words. If I didn't mention my faith, I would be running from who I am—and from the purpose that I believe I was destined to fulfill. My faith and belief in God actually provided the courage for me to write this book.

Fortunately for me, God has always been a large part of my life. I was raised in the church, and I thought that I was a committed Christian. I was far from perfect, but I did try to live up to the Christian virtues that my parents tried to instill in me.

But doing right for God's sake was often a chore for me. I preferred to do what made me feel good—the normal temptations to which teenagers often succumb—and not always what was right. Yet even as I found success in academics and in sports, it is unfortunate that I evaluated my Christian commitment on the curve by worldly standards and not biblical principles.

It took a 14-33 record during my head coaching career at San Jose State for me to realize that my priorities were grossly out of order before I moved from a religious regimen of worship to a genuine relationship with Jesus. Prior to that, instead of seeking that relationship, it was far more important to me that I could possibly become the first African American coach to win a Bowl Championship Series (BCS) game or national football championship. I had always acknowledged Christ as my personal savior, but I was not seeking Christ first, maybe not even second. In all honesty, I really didn't know what that even meant. I didn't have a model of what that commitment looked like when I was growing up.

While serving as head college football coach at the largest public education institution in the Silicon Valley, I was challenged on numerous occasions about the way I spoke out about my faith.

There are many stories in the Bible that reveal the tests that God often puts his children through when they seek a genuine relationship with Him. I was convinced God called me to the Silicon Valley to lead the San Jose State Spartans football team. How could I know that my four years in northern California would, in some ways, be like Moses's forty years in the desert? I didn't produce a lot of fruit. We never had a winning football season. My marriage, which had never been great prior to moving to California, was critically challenged. My desire to be perceived as an effective coach and a great recruiter—just to land that eventual multimillion dollar contract at a bigger school and buy more stuff to make to make my family "happy"—was what motivated me.

I didn't realize that having me around was what my wife and children truly desired. God works in mysterious ways. He can get your attention to find out if you really want to be blessed by Him rather than trying to bless yourself.

I am thankful that, at age forty, I painfully discovered that money really doesn't raise kids. Parents do. As outlined in earlier chapters, I decided to make a career change and follow God's purpose, not mine. I'm not saying it has been a piece of cake. But today, even though many of my personal experiences at San Jose State were not pleasant, I count all of those trials and tribulations as a joy. The documented terrible calls by the WAC and Pac 10 officials, which potentially cost us as many as three victories at pivotal moments of the season? I count it all as joy. The demeaning and ugly letters and remarks by fans and alumni that I received? I count it all as joy. The personal attacks on me and my family over the years? I thank God for his saving grace that my family remains together.

I also thank God for giving me the courage to tell this story regarding the effects of race in the hiring of college football coaches and to not worry about how I will be perceived. I no longer worry about the consequences of telling the truth. Many people, black and white, do not understand how black coaches often feel like emotional prisoners when they work in predominantly white athletic departments. I am also certain that there are black and white coaches who disagree with my assessments. That's fine, especially if they personally haven't experienced it.

However, if those coaches are in denial, I hope this book will make them rethink their attitudes and ignite them into speaking the truth about racial issues as they relate to black football coaches on college campuses. There's no question in my mind that some predominantly white institutions are trying to do the right things in terms of creating a positive environment for black student-athletes and increasing diversity in those schools' athletic departments. Yet after reading this book, I would hope you agree that if you examine the minority representation on a broader national scale, minimal progress has actually been made in this area.

Improving the numbers of minority coaches was supposedly a major initiative of NCAA President Myles Brand before he died in September of 2009. Brand, however, placed the blame for the lack of minority hirings on NCAA member institutions rather than accepting responsibility for it.

It still boggles my mind that member institutions of the NCAA are eager to enforce legislation as it relates to governing everything else, from eligibility, recruiting, to academics—but when the issue of employment opportunities for black coaches arises, the issue suddenly becomes "the prerogative of each institution." If that is the case, why shouldn't each school also be able to enforce its own admission standards for athletes rather than follow the NCAA's clearing house guidelines?

It is unfortunate that open, forthright discussion concerning racial issues does not occur frequently enough in higher education, especially in the sport of football. It is also sad that black coaches have been extremely reluctant to own up to their honest feelings regarding employment opportunities at predominantly white colleges and universities. That is why I felt that I had to write this book. I am out of the game now. I can comment without fear that it will come back to haunt me in a job interview.

Other black coaches can't do that—or won't do it. Through discussions with some of them, I've learned that they refuse to speak out because they worry about reprisal from white athletic directors and coaches whose support and goodwill is essential to securing employment and keeping a coaching job. This reluctance of African American football coaches to speak openly about their perceived unequal treatment should not be confused with complacency. It is better understood as a painful adaptation to a society that seems to have lost interest in the evaluation and critical analysis necessary to unmask covert forms of employment bias and discrimination on mostly white campuses. It's as if by electing the first black president, people of every color don't think they are allowed to scream when something goes off track racially in America.

In the case of African Americans, it might be a simple means of survival. That's what Alvin Poussaint, an associate professor of psychiatry at Harvard Medical School, would suggest. He once said, "It's always a risk for a black person in a predominantly white corporation to express individual anger." The reason in this case? White athletic administrators and coaches often do not understand why such anger exists. As a result, they are likely to dismiss the complainer as a chronic malcontent or maladjusted person who perhaps needs to be eased out of the department. And what is this called? Being "blackballed."

My research, both statistically and anecdotally, has shown that many African American football coaches believe that if it were not for the color of their skin they would have had more opportunity for advancement in the coaching profession at the college level. They see white coaches with less ability progress much further than black coaches. And while those black coaches point to the color of their skin as a restricting factor, they can never be sure if that's true—partly because the institutions they work for never acknowledge any such bias.

This book is not an attempt to spark or agitate African American football coaches into being more vocal about employment inequities. Nor is it meant to alienate or provoke reprisals from the many white athletic administrators or coaches who have been instrumental in increasing opportunities for African American coaches. In fact, many white coaches paved the way for my development and assisted in my coaching career. Among those, I would include Sam Goodwin, Norman Joseph, Donnie Cox, John Thompson, Ken Hatfield, Jack Crowe, Charlie Weatherbie, Joe Kines, Greg Davis, Larry VanDerHeyden, Joe Pate, Charlie North, Mike Bender, Rocky Felker, Louis Campbell, Harold Horton, Joe Ferguson, Kay Stephenson and Houston Nutt. Without their collective support, I would have never been a head football coach at the major college level.

Over the last few hundred pages, I simply wanted to provide an in-depth analysis and explanation of how race affects and impacts the careers of African American football coaches at the college level—no matter how subtle and unplanned that discrimination has been.

For me, sharing the collective experiences of both black and white coaches has been a liberating experience. This book contains more than twenty years of research on this subject. I put my personal efforts into these studies while coaching and recruiting in hopes of creating greater access and opportunities for black coaches aspiring to be head football coaches. When I began this research as a young graduate student, I remember feeling as if I were going to change the world by bringing the injustices to light. I ignorantly assumed that everyone would want the data so that institutions could move forward properly and correct a wrong in much the same way that many white and black people did during the civil rights movement.

Thankfully, I didn't know what I know today—that most college administrators simply do not want to actively address the situation. If I had known that, I probably would have stopped collecting this research material a long time ago. The NFL has made excellent strides at creating more minority coaching opportunities in professional football. But the problem remains painful at the college level.

I return to the claim made by Southeastern Conference Commissioner Roy Kramer in his *Washington Post* quote from November of 1997—which, despite the quote's age, is a reflection of past and current problems within the profession. I was shocked when such an obviously smart man said that institutions were making a full commitment to hire black coaches across the board. When he said those words, no black head football coach had ever been hired in the Southeastern Conference.

A dozen years later, three black coaches have since been hired in the the conference. As we look to the second decade of the twenty-first century two of the twelve SEC football programs are led by African Americans, in a region of our country where African Americans make up a more sizable portion of the population— and a more sizeable portion of football fans, football coaches, and football players. Although it has been minimal, the SEC has made some improvements. The Big 10 Conference, however, can't stake similar claims. As current as the 2011 football season, they are the only major football conference that doesn't have at least one African American coach leading a team. Hopefully change is coming.

As I write these words, I feel in a sense as if I have lost a football game—and it wasn't even a close one. From my many discussions with black football coaches, I know so many of them think they have been confined to the bench before the season even begins, with no opportunity to even compete for a starting position. These coaches believe that they have done everything necessary to prove they are deserving of a chance to lead a big-time football program. But those opportunities are elusive—which results in all but a few black coaches becoming invisible at the college level.

I try to be self-aware. At times, I do wonder if my feelings are real or just perceived. But through these studies, I have learned that perception can become reality. I believe that many black coaches who aspire to become head coaches at the college level have been and will continue to be cheated unless the process to select those positions is changed. Although some crackback blocks are legal in the game of football, this invisible *crackback* in hiring practices is not. It's a blindside block in the back. But nobody has the guts to make the call.

My intent with this book is to speak about the issue in non-academic terms so it will help enlighten a diverse audience of collegiate football fans—and let them know how it actually affects them every Saturday during the football season. But it is also my hope that this book will end up on the desks of NCAA leaders, college presidents, university boards of trustees, and athletic administrators who are involved in creating policies that could finally create a level playing field for prospective black head coaches.

I am afraid if this doesn't happen, there will be minimal progress for years to come. In America, it is obvious to me that at certain times, doing the right thing is something that people must be forced to do. Why? It's very simple. For more black coaches to get more good jobs, more white coaches will have to get fewer good jobs. That creates a natural blowback from white coaches—and certain members of the white college community.

I'm so glad that I didn't finish this book five or six years ago when I began writing it. I am sure I would have come across as the stereotypical Angry Black Man and many people would have immediately tuned me out. I thank God that I have reached a point in my life where I am no longer incensed or upset on a daily basis that institutional leaders at predominantly white colleges and universities apparently do not see black coaches in the same light as they do white coaches.

With this book, I have done all that I can for this cause. I'll leave the rest to providence and God. I have been called to a new ministry at my college. It is an outreach mission to tackle the crisis of African American young men who currently are dropping out of high school at more than a 50 percent rate—which often leads them to becoming domestic terrorists in their own communities and going to prison. I feel certain that this mission is one of the reasons I was appointed to serve at Arkansas Baptist College.

The school was founded in 1884 to educate former slaves and their sons and daughters. I believe that if we can get young men back on track, in Little Rock and elsewhere, we can take back our African American communities in every city and make our nation safer. That's the vision God has given me, and I am committed to tackling this problem by any means necessary. It will be a major challenge that requires the same laser focus our communities utilized to overcome Jim Crow and other injustices.

What does this have to do with football? The lessons I learned as an athlete and coach—and while pursuing the truth about minority hiring practices for college coaches—will always serve me well. Through football, I learned perseverance. I learned how to analyze and make decisions. I learned that it's not always the best team that wins, it is the team that plays the best. I learned that in a team sport, an individual player can't have a personal agenda if the team wants to succeed.

I saw how on a football field a person can do much more than he thinks he can if encouraged and motivated by the right coach for the right reasons. I saw plenty of coaches who could do that. But many of them were African Americans who did not—and maybe never will—get the chance to provide such encouragement and motivation as head coaches because of an archaic hiring framework that has been carried forward into the twenty-first century.

For all of that, I think if college administrators ponder the information in this book, some of it will sink in the next time one of them goes through a coaching search. That's the fundamental reason for this book. And that's why I was burdened by the heavy chip on my shoulder until I figured out a way to shift that weight into something more constructive – the book you have just read. I have delivered the truth and I have been set free. It's in God's hands now. But I am also rooting very hard for people to heed their inner conscience and do what is right for other human beings. Not just for college football, but for the country and world where I want my grandchildren and great-grandchildren to live. It will make the game day kickoffs of the future just that much sweeter. I can't wait.

SELECTED BIBLIOGRAPHY

Books

Cose, Ellis, "The Rage Of A Privileged Class," Harper Perennial 1993

Groves, Roger M, "Innocence In The Red Zone: The Adversity And Opportunity Of Bobby Williams—The Story Of An African American Coach In Big Time College Football," BookSurge LLC 2005

Hurd, Michael, "Black College Football," The Donning Company, 1998

Rhoden, William C., "Third And A Mile: From Fritz Pollard to Michael Vick—an Oral History of the Trials, Tears and Triumphs of the Black Quarterback," Random House Publishing Group 2007.

Ross, Charles K, "Outside The Lines: African Americans And the Integration Of The National Football League," New York University Press, 1999

"San Jose State University Football Media Guides 2001-2009," Lawrence Fan, Editor

Woodward, C. Vann, "The Strange Career Of Jim Crow," Oxford University Press 1966

Magazine And Newspaper Articles

"A Call To Civil Rights Action In College Football," by Dr. Richard Lapchick, ESPN.com, Dec. 8, 2008

"Basketball's 40-Year Dash," by John Akers, Basketball Times, February 2008

"Bear Bryant's Biggest Score," by Allen Barra, *American Legacy Magazine*, Winter 2006

"Black Coaches Sidelined" by Ivan Maisel, Dallas Morning News, May 31, 1992

"Book Review: Forty Minutes Of Hell; An Interview With Author Rus Bradburd," by Pardeep Toor, It's Just Sports, mlive.com blog, January 2010

"Brand Calls For Hiring Of More Black Football Coaches," by Associated Press, Jan. 6, 2007

"Coaches: In Black And White," by Austin Porter, Arkansas Times, Dec. 13, 2007

"Ex-Players Concerned How 'Open' Search Was," by Associated Press, Dec. 15, 2004

"Few FBS Offers For Black Coaches," by Pat Forde, espn.com, Jan. 19, 2009

"Football: Another Season Of Black and White," by Dr. Richard Lapchick, Sports Business Journal, Sept. 11, 2006

"Getting Ahead By Staying In Place," by Phil Taylor, SI.com, Dec. 24, 2008

"The Importance Of Good Coaching In Football" by Ron Dickerson, TheSportDigest.com and The United States Sports Academy 2002

"Keith Has Clear Goal: Equality," by Malcolm Moran, USA Today, Oct. 11, 2002

"Legal Action Could Be Required to Force Change," by Rod Gilmore, espn.com, Nov. 16, 2005

"Macalester's Hudson: The First, But Forgotten Until Now," by Jay Weiner, ESPN.com, February 13, 2008

"Man Guilty Of Threatening Ex-Irish Coach Willingham," Associated Press, July 6, 2006

"Minority Coach Hiring Should Be Priority For Big Ten," by Adam Rittenberg, espn.com, May 2009

"NCAA reaches 14-year deal with CBS/Turner for men's basketball tournament, USA Today, April 22, 2010

"NCAA Shameful In Minority Hiring Record," by Johnette Howard, Newsday, Jan. 28, 2007

"NFL Leads Colleges In Promoting Minority Coaches," by Pat Forde, espn.com, Feb. 16, 2007

"Oregon Hears The Call To Action," By Richard Lapchick, Special to ESPN.com, May 22, 2009

"Panel: Minority Coaches Bypassed; At King Library, Avenues Suggested," by Brandon M. Bickerstaff, San Jose Mercury News, Aug. 23, 2003

"Prince Joins Short List Of African American Coaches," by Rebekah Dryden, KWCH 12 Eyewitness News, Dec. 5, 2005

"The Program," by L. Jon Wertheim with special reporting by Andrew Lawrence, Sports Illustrated, March 5 2007

"Recruits' Choices Could Turn Tide In College Football Minority Hiring," by Christian Ewell, Baltimore Sun, Jan. 25, 2005

"Some Scholars Look At Racism By Studying Advantages Whites Enjoy," by Jayne Noble Suhler, Dallas Morning News, Sept. 13, 1998

"Willingham Wants Change To Declining Number of Minority Coaches In College," Associated Press, Nov. 13, 2008

Legal Documents and Research Papers

"Affirmative Action In Higher Education: A Retrospective And Prospective Look At Race-Based Preferences" by John W. Murry Jr. and James J. Van Patten, presentation to the National Organization On Legal Problems Of Education, 1995

"Constitution And Bylaws Of The Association Of Black Collegiate Football Coaches."

"Contrasting Perceptions of Employment Opportunities Among Collegiate Football Coaches," Research Paper by Dr. Fitzgerald Hill, 2001

"Effects Of Percent Black On Blacks' Perceptions Of Relative Power And Social Distance," by Arthur S. Evans Jr. and Michael W. Giles, Journal of Black Studies, September 1986

"Head Football Coaching Qualities Sought By NCAA Division 1A Athletic Directors" Research Paper by Curtis Blackwell II, Walter Abercombie and Dr. Frank B. Wyatt, 2001

"The Impact Of Race As It Relates To Employment Opportunities For Collegiate Football Coaches," Research Paper by Dr. Fitzgerald Hill, 2004

"Oral Deposition Of Omon Fitzgerald Hill" in case of Jerry Lee Baldwin vs. the Board of Supervisors for the University of Louisiana System, the University of Louisiana at Lafayette and Nelson Schexnayder, 19th Judicial District, Parish of East Baton Rouge, State of Louisiana, Sept. 6, 2007

"Personal Services Contract Between San Jose State University Foundation And Richard Tomey" and "Offer Of Appointment Between San Jose State University And Dick Tomey," Jan. 4, 2005

"The Score," A Hiring Report Card For NCAA Division 1A and 1AA Football Head Coaching Positions by Dr. C. Keith Harrison, Arizona State 2004

"Strike Three: Umpires' Demand For Discrimination," Research Paper by Christopher A. Parsons (University of North Carolina), Johan Sulaeman (Southern Methodist University), Michael C. Yates (Auburn University) and Daniel S. Hamermesh (University of Texas) 2007.

"Superior Performance: Inferior Opportunities," by Dr. Fitzgerald Hill, presented to Councilman Alonzo Bates' Sports Forum at the Charles H. Wright Museum of African American History, Detroit Michigan, March 21, 2003

"Testimony Of Dr. Fitzgerald Hill For The U.S. Congressional Subcommittee On Commerce, Trade And Consumer Protection," February 26, 2007

"Vital Signs: Examining The Status Of African American Football Coaches at NCAA Division 1A Colleges And Universities," by Dr. Fitzgerald Hill, presented to the University of Kentucky African American Studies and Research Program's Race And Sport in 20th Century America Lecture Series, Feb. 24, 1999